Islam in a World of Nation-States

Islam in a World of Nation-States

JAMES P. PISCATORI

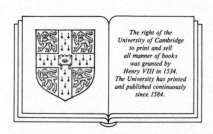

The right of the
University of Cambridge
to print and sell
all manner of books
was granted by
Henry VIII in 1534.
The University has printed
and published continuously
since 1584.

PUBLISHED IN ASSOCIATION WITH

The Royal Institute of International Affairs

Cambridge University Press

CAMBRIDGE

LONDON   NEW YORK   NEW ROCHELLE

MELBOURNE   SYDNEY

Published by the Press Syndicate of the University of Cambridge
The Pitt Building, Trumpington Street, Cambridge CB2 1RP
32 East 57th Street, New York, NY 10022, USA
10 Stamford Road, Oakleigh, Melbourne 3166, Australia

First published 1986

Printed in Great Britain at the University Press, Cambridge

British Library Cataloguing in Publication Data

Piscatori, James P.
Islam in a world of nation-states.
1. Islam—Political aspects
I. Title   II. Royal Institute of International Affairs
297′.1977   BP52

Library of Congress Cataloging-in-Publication Data

Piscatori, James P.
Islam in a world of nation-states.
"Published in association with the Royal Institute of
International Affairs."
Includes index.
1. Islam and state. 2. Islam—20th century.
I. Royal Institute of International Affairs.
II. Title.
JC49.P57 1986   322′.1′0917671   86–8275

ISBN 0 521 32985 X
ISBN 0 521 33867 0 (pbk.)

VN

Contents

Illustrations

All illustrations are reproduced by permission of the British Museum

Preface

This book grew out of a research project initiated by the Royal Institute of International Affairs, which was designed to look at the political implications of the Islamic revival. Two volumes connected with this project, dealing with the importance of Islam to the domestic political life and to the foreign policy of several countries, have already been published: *Islam in the Political Process* (Cambridge University Press, 1983) and *Islam in Foreign Policy* (Cambridge University Press, 1983). Larger questions were always present but only indirectly addressed in these studies: is there something about Islam which makes it incongruous with the idea of nationalism and with the institution of the nation-state? Are Muslims moving towards realization of the long-cherished goal of supranational unity? — n̄ʋ.

This volume answers the first question, invoking the traditional legal and political theory and relying principally on the historical experience and modern intellectual consensus of Muslims. The conclusion – that Islam and the nation-state are indeed compatible – will strike some as obvious and others as highly contentious, depending on whether one is outside the faith or a devout believer, but depending also on what one's view of the theory is. All, however, will sense that one side of a complex argument has been presented and that 'the other hand' must still be put forward. It is my intention to do that in a companion volume assessing the transnational character of Islam.

In the discussion to follow here, I have used a modest scheme of transliteration: I have indicated the 'ayn (') and the medial hamza (') only, but have omitted all other diacritical marks. To make an Arabic noun plural, I have simply added an 's' to the singular form. The common spelling of place names has been used, and in cases where a Muslim author has written in European languages, I have adopted his own spelling of his name. Dates throughout the text refer to the Christian, or so-called Common, Era; the reader will find that the dates of individual Muslims mentioned in the book are incorporated into the index. To assist the reader further, a glossary and general chronology of the Muslim world are appended.

That the book has been completed at all is due, in the first place, to the generosity of the Ford Foundation, which funded the project. I am also grateful to the Nuffield Foundation for its assistance. In addition, Adeed Dawisha gave me valuable support, and John L. Esposito and Moorhead Wright offered useful comments. Lynne Payne turned rough handwriting into a glistening typescript; and Pauline Wickham edited the manuscript with unfailing judgement.

I hope, finally, that I will not embarrass Albert Hourani and J.P. Bannerman by claiming them as the most intimate associates of this book: I am not at all sure any more where their ideas leave off and mine begin.

March 1986   J.P.P.

1 Interpreting Islam in the modern world

The general purpose of this book, and of the companion volume to follow, is to see what significance Islam has for contemporary international relations. This book will concentrate on whether the historically European institution of the nation-state is acceptable to Muslims today, and the companion volume will concentrate on the increasingly transnational dimensions of Islam today. Although these are important topics, very little work has been done on them.

Several books have appeared in the past several years which deal with the internal political roles of Islam, but there have been very few which examine the external dimension. Not many Western readers have access to the literature written in Arabic on the subject – either to the classical texts that elucidate what the *shari'a*, or Islamic law covering all aspects of human conduct, has to say about war, peace, and diplomacy,[1] or to the books of the last two decades which, in dealing with Islamic classical theory, are able to take cognizance of the modern discipline of international relations.[2] The classical theory has been explained to varying degrees in works written in European languages,[3] but it was not until Majid Khadduri's contributions, written in English, that it was systematically presented to a wide audience.[4] His work remains the principal exposition of this theory, although of course others have addressed the subject in English.[5] Of the studies that concentrate on the Islamic practice of international relations, the standard collection of essays is now twenty years old,[6] and other studies, while undoubtedly first-rate, are narrower in focus.[7]

Most of these books concentrate on the classical theory, and those that look at practice have little to say about the modern practice of international relations and its relationship to the theory. This book draws on many of these contributions but tries to cover for the reader the several ways in which Islam is relevant to world politics today. One has the immediate impression that modern practice has little to do with the doctrine, and, if this is so, we may well wonder what effect it has on reformulating the doctrine. I will argue that there is a modern doctrine which follows modern practice, and that this is as true of general questions as of international relations in particular.

Perhaps it is inopportune to try to do this when we are so close to the events of the Iranian revolution, which have done more than anything else recently to disturb the pattern of international relations and to arouse people's curiosity – and fear – of Islam. Yet, it is precisely because the issues have seemed so urgent and the images so powerful that it is useful to try to make sense of them now. There is no doubt that many people talk of Islam as posing a radical challenge to Western interests. This seems to be the case to them because they believe that Muslims have acquired a new political self-consciousness and activism. According to this view, this new activism will induce Muslims either to turn to the Soviet bloc in order to offset what they regard as Western economic and cultural neo-imperialism, or at the least to discriminate against Westerners in order to reaffirm an ancient hostility to Christians generally. Many people also draw the conclusion – from the media coverage of the harsh penalties of Islamic law and of the veiling of women – that Islam stands for a medieval legal and social order. This view in turn helps to suggest that, when it comes to international relations, Muslims are simply not at home in the modern state and in the modern politically and culturally diversified system of states, and therefore would like to see a revival of the early transnational community of believers as the primary political unit.

Leon Uris seems to have combined many of these assumptions of Muslim conduct in explaining why he wrote *The Haj*: 'My objective in the book was to warn the West and Western democracies that you can't keep your head in the sand about this situation any longer, that we have an enraged bull of a billion people on our planet, and tilted the wrong way they could open the second road to Armageddon.'[8] Because the way in which policymakers and others think of Islam is bound to be affected by common assumptions such as these,[9] it is the intention of this book, and of the one to follow, to question them. In doing so, I hope to provide an alternative way of looking at Islam as a factor in international relations and as a framework which gives Muslims the rationale, and in part at least the tools, for identifying and implementing state policy. This implies that there is another, more appropriate and practical, view of international and transnational Islam than is commonly held.

There is, however, no pretension to prove anything, and it is unavoidable that this will be a personal interpretation. The best that one can do when dealing with contentious and contemporary affairs is to persuade the reader that the weight of evidence seems to fall on one side rather than another. In trying to do so, though, I will make assumptions throughout the argument that ought to be clear from the outset. The most difficult concerns the meaning of Islam itself.

Definition and independent judgement

The only definite things one can say about the term 'Islam' are that it is protean and imprecise. Every Muslim can agree that the profession of faith, 'There is no God but God and Muhammad is His Prophet', is an article of faith and not susceptible to differing interpretations; but as regards the meaning of many other principles and ideas, and whether they are beyond question and change, there is little agreement. The believer says, 'Look to the Qur'an', but, like all fundamental documents, it is what the reader makes of it. Ask, 'Does it support polygamy or monogamy, socialism or capitalism, equality of women or inequality, birth control, parliamentary democracy?', and the answers hinge on what one hopes to find. Although scriptural interpretation is problematic in every religion, it is especially so in the case of Islam and for several reasons.

First, the Qur'an itself encourages some degree of interpretation by planting doubts about the immutability of the revelation. This must be seen as ironic, since generations of Muslim jurists have perpetuated the pious fiction that no further legislation is possible after the exhaustive and definitive legislation laid down in the Scriptures. In fact, however, the Qur'an invites questioning, and therefore interpretation, when it admits – with remarkable candour – that certain verses are 'obscure' or 'ambiguous', and that only God knows what they really mean (3:7). But this candour can hardly be reassuring to the believer earnestly trying to understand the verses, nor will he find comfort in the emphasis throughout the Qur'an that revelation can change with divine whim: 'If We willed, We could take away that which We have revealed to you' (17:86). This is more than merely an affirmation of God's absolute sovereignty, since it is clear that there were in fact systematic revisions in the Qur'an (2:106, 13:37, 16:101, 22:52). These revisions laid the basis for the medieval theory of 'abrogation', *nasikh wa'l-mansukh*, which gave doctrinal veneer to revision of revealed law, *and* implied that if the revelation to the Prophet had changed with changing circumstances, the law which flows from the revelation would also change – particularly since it is conceded that parts of the revelation are ambiguous.

Second, there is near universal agreement that, in interpreting and reinterpreting the Qur'an, custom based on the example of the Prophet (*sunna*) clarifies and supplements it, but the very pragmatism of the *sunna* makes justification of widely varying positions all that much easier. There are many instances of this pragmatism. When, in 628, the still pagan Meccans prevented him from making the Pilgrimage, the Prophet compromised with them and agreed to wait until the following year to enter the city. All the while he used the truce to gain strength for the final battle between them. In another instance, rather than smugly insisting he was in the right because he was God's Prophet, he agreed to resort to

3

arbitration to settle a dispute with the Bani Qurayza, a Jewish tribe. It is this undogmatic character that so attracted Carlyle:

I like Mahomet for his total freedom from cant . . . In a life-and-death war with Bedouins, cruel things could not fail; but neither are acts of mercy, of noble natural pity and generosity wanting. Mahomet makes no apology for the one, no boast of the other. They were each the free dictate of his heart; each called-for, there and then.[10]

The variability, and sometimes inconsistency, have bothered some Muslims, however, and have led such scholars as the Mu'tazila in the eighth century, Sayyid Ahmad Khan in the nineteenth century, or Ghulam Ahmad Parwez in this century to cast doubt on the authenticity of many of the specific 'traditions' of the Prophet (*hadiths*), which record his sayings and actions and in their totality constitute the *sunna*. But the critics have been a very small minority. The great majority of Muslims accept the authority of the *sunna* as a whole, and the view that there is nothing wrong with the Prophet having changed positions with the circumstances. Indeed, it is the mark of a prudent statesman to do so and it testifies, I believe, to the flexibility which runs through the heart of Islam. The Shi'a add the example of the Imams to that of the Prophet, and find pragmatism and flexibility here as well. For example, 'Ali, the Prophet's cousin and son-in-law, and his successors to the Shi'i Imamate, Husayn, Zayn al-'Abidin, and Muhammad al-Baqir, all demonstrated their willingness to defer to the prevailing authority when it was hostile to their views. Even when he became Caliph, 'Ali compromised with his bitter rival Mu'awiyya rather than fight to the end (I will refer to this again in Chapter 3). The fact remains, though, that the flexibility which is reflected in the practice of the Prophet and the Imams has, on the one hand, encouraged the general idea in Islamic jurisprudence that whatever is 'necessary' (*daruri*) and in 'the public interest' (*maslaha*) must be deemed to be Islamic, while, on the other, leaving it unresolved how that is to be decided and who is to do the deciding.

Third, the problem of who decides is immensely complicated by the fact that although the individual's membership of the community of believers is emphasized, the sense of a definitive spiritual authority over him is missing. The idea is well established in Islam that no mediator exists between God and man, and thus that there is no priestly caste endowed with esoteric wisdom or sacramental powers, although, it must be said, deference to the teaching of certain extraordinarily gifted individuals is an Islamic tradition. Yet, according to the Qur'an, in submitting to the supreme authority of God, the individual becomes God's *khalifa*, or vicegerent, on earth (2:30; 6:165); as such, he is endowed with intelligence, and his salvation is no other man's business. Legal scholarship builds on this idea with the concept of *ibaha*, whereby the individual's freedom of action outside the area of specific divine commands is acknowledged. As long as he believes that there is only one God and that His

Prophet was Muhammad and follows explicit scriptural injunctions, the individual really becomes the arbiter of his own faith.

Fourth, the *'ulama* (scholars of Islamic law) may be prepared to exercise their independent judgement (*ijtihad*) to determine what the Word means here and now, but (following the same principle of no intermediaries between God and man) no ecclesiastical authority exists to settle disputes among them. Islamic history testifies to the many differences that have gone unresolved. Not only has there been the division between the Sunni and Shi'i *'ulama*, but there have been several divisions within each broad group. The Sunnis divided into four major legal schools – Hanafis, Malikis, Shafi'is, and Hanbalis – whereas the Shi'a divided into Imamis, Isma'ilis, Zaydis, and their offshoots. It is true that from time to time in predominantly Sunni countries authoritative judgements are made on a group's orthodoxy, as when the Bhutto government in Pakistan declared the Ahmadis to be non-Muslims in 1973 and when President Zia confirmed this decision in 1984. But since these are political decisions, induced by political considerations, they tend to intensify rather than resolve the theological controversy. Similarly, an authoritative judgement on such contentious issues as the permissibility of birth control or a peace treaty with Israel, both of which the Egyptian *'ulama* were instructed to rule on, is really a matter of government fiat.

The Shi'a, by way of contrast, over many centuries have evolved provision for a hierarchy of authorities, with *ayatullahs* ('Signs of God') at the top. Even then some of these become grand *ayatullahs*, and, in a relatively recent innovation, one of them, by his learning and piety, may become the sole source of 'imitation' (*marja'-i taqlid-i a'la*), to whom both deference and tithes are due. But there is no obligation to acknowledge one person in this way, nor is it clear to what extent he must be obeyed if one is in fact chosen. In general, the relationship among those at the top has never been clear, as the tension between Ayatullahs Khumayni and Shari'at-madari suggests. Certainly the emergence of one of them, Khumayni, as the supreme political leader (*rahbar*) and 'the guardian of affairs' (*waliy-yi amr*)[11] has been a bone of theoretical, as well as practical contention, within Iran's Imami Shi'a community.[12]

Fifth, Islamic jurists long ago accepted that it was impossible to attain complete uniformity of interpretation, and in fact sanctioned the diversity that flows from the exercise of *ijtihad*. This is the idea of *ikhtilaf*, that there is a permissible diversity of doctrine in Islamic law. Taking their clue from the alleged saying of the Prophet, 'Difference of opinion among my community is a sign of the bounty of God', the jurists went even further, arguing that it is as natural as a tree of many branches or a garment of many threads.[13] However, they were merely putting a good face on the entrenched differences that arose in disparate parts of the Islamic empire and crystallized into the four orthodox schools of law. And, in doing this, they unintentionally provided a blanket justification that others could use to legitimate their divergent views.

Sixth, and last, the concept of *ijtihad* itself has been transformed in recent times, and this transformation has made it easier for Muslims to invoke it in defence of their interpretations of Islam. The classical theory held that only the *'ulama* could exercise it, and then only in strict accordance with rules of reasoning, principally those of analogical deduction (*qiyas*). Even then the result was seen as mere conjecture, and would become definite knowledge only when general agreement evolved as to its validity. I shall have more to say about the nature of such agreement below, but it should be noted here that it is usually assumed that one such general agreement arose among Sunni jurists at the beginning of the tenth century to the effect that further *ijtihad* would be confusing and harmful.[14] Consequently, its 'door' was to be firmly shut.

In fact, the door never was completely shut. The blame for the so-called closure is often assigned to al-Shafi'i, the great jurist of the late eighth and early ninth centuries, who was determined to resolve the dispute between the Hanafi and Maliki schools over whether, after the Qur'an, the independent judgement of learned officials constitutes a valid source of law. In his exposition of a systematic theory of the sources of law, he emphasized the need to follow the *hadiths* of the Prophet, and to observe precise rules for interpreting them. Although he stressed the *hadiths*, it is unfair to say that he gave them 'a higher authority' than the Qur'an, thereby imposing 'a strait-jacket' on Islam's development.[15] However, al-Shafi'i did in effect say that *ijtihad* was not a right but a privilege, even among the *'ulama*, and in this way set the stage for the general acceptance in the tenth century that the privilege could be exercised only by reference to the established orthodox opinions – that is, only within the confines of the club of the four orthodox schools of law. With the argument thus that *ijtihad* is a privilege, the door may have been pushed to, but it was never, either in theory or in practice, completely closed and locked.

In fact, Sunni jurists never altogether abandoned *ijtihad*. For example, the eleventh-century philosopher and jurist, al-Ghazzali, argued that *ijtihad* was permissible when based on sound scholarship,[16] and in the fourteenth century Ibn Taymiyya argued that to resolve disputes rulers should rely on the independently reasoned opinions of the *'ulama*, who, in turn, may follow the opinions of those they respect. Indeed, the Hanbalis generally claimed that the consensus limiting interpretations to the four legal schools was itself invalid, since only the consensus which prevailed at the time of the Prophet and his four immediate successors was definitive.[17] Hanafi jurists were always free to rely on *istihsan*, the preference for interpretations or rules in other schools of law that seemed more in line with considerations of equity, and Maliki jurists were always free to decide on the basis of *istislah*, a consideration of what was consistent with the public interest.

Yet, if in these ways the door of independent judgement was not completely closed, neither was it completely open. The term 'closing the door of *ijtihad*' (*insidad bab al-ijtihad*) seems not to have gained currency until the twelfth century,[18] but it must still be said that Muslims from the tenth century onwards increasingly came to accept that there should be serious limitations on interpretative licence. This was so, in the first instance, because they accepted the premise that the then four legal masters and their immediate disciples had exhausted the valid interpretative possibilities of the law; independent reasoning consisted of applying the precedents to different circumstances or of finding analogical relevance in the precedents for matters not specifically dealt with in the orthodox books.[19] Over time, particularly after the sixteenth century, the feeling grew that fewer and fewer people were qualified to exercise *ijtihad*. Therefore the exercise of even this qualified form of judgement inevitably surrendered to 'imitation' of what had gone before. Limited *ijtihad* gave way to *taqlid*, the idea that precedent must be faithfully followed or 'imitated'.

Contrary to common belief, the Imami Shi'a also circumscribed *ijtihad*. From the tenth to the thirteenth centuries the very word did not seem to appear in Shi'i writings; the emphasis instead was on *'aql*, or reasoning by syllogism (rather than analogical deduction (*qiyas*), as practised by the Sunnis). Before the eleventh century, the Akhbari school, with its hostility to *ijtihad* and emphasis on the traditions (*akhbar*) of the Imams, clearly prevailed. The situation soon began to change. In the eleventh century a special field of study for inferring rules from basic principles (*usul al-fiqh*) began to emerge, but it was only later, in the seventeenth century, that the idea of certain learned people having the ability to interpret and offer opinions became widely accepted, and the 'Usuli' school took definite shape. At this very moment, though, the Akhbari school reasserted its dominance and insisted that one's pre-eminent duty was to follow the traditions; any individual's judgement, by contrast, was bound to be fallible.[20]

A great sea-change, however, began to set in from the eighteenth century. In the case of the Shi'a, both the government's weakness and the *'ulama's* independence of the government in Iran encouraged the *'ulama* to assert their power. This led to the re-emergence of the Usuli school, now more self-conscious and rigorous than it had been earlier. It taught that it is the duty of every believer to follow a living *mujtahid* (one who exercises *ijtihad*), and soon it became the dominant school in the Imami Shi'ism prevailing in Iran. In the Sunni countries, the shock of Western imperialists easily defeating Muslim soldiers and the rude introduction to Western liberal ideas gave impetus to a view that had already emerged for local reasons with the reform movements of Muhammad Ibn 'Abd al-Wahhab in Arabia and Shah Wali Allah in India: Muslims had become weak because of passivity as well as impiety, and this passivity was encouraged by the very idea of imitation or *taqlid*. Ibn 'Abd al-Wahhab deliberately encouraged the use of *ijtihad* in order to unearth the first principles of Islam, which he felt had been lost, and Wali Allah did the same in order to put Islam and the changing Indian society in tandem. But both put the doctrine of *taqlid* in the dock of the court of Muslim opinion. The Ottoman reformers in the mid-nineteenth century indirectly contributed to the prosecution by criticizing the stagnation that had permeated Muslim life, and the Christian Arab nationalists also had an effect by articulating the European idea of the nation-state and thus, over time, prompting Muslim Arabs to consider alternative ideas to those which they believed Islam had generated.

The intellectual response that started in the late nineteenth century was overwhelming: Mortaza Ansari, Jamal al-Din al-Afghani, Muhammad 'Abduh, 'Abd al-Rahman al-Kawakibi, Muhammad Iqbal, Hasan al-Banna, Isma'il Mazhar, and virtually every major intellectual,[21] regardless of whether they were Sunni or Shi'i and of their place in the spectrum of thought, argued that the restriction on *ijtihad* had been disastrous and that its door must be thrown wide open. The eighteenth-century reformers had laid the groundwork by calling for *ijtihad* to restore the early legal sources, but from the late nineteenth century the call was intentionally for *ijtihad* to reinterpret the sources in line with modern circumstances.[22] This broader view of *ijtihad*, and harsher criticism of the deleterious effects of *taqlid*, are even more prevalent today.

Al-Sadiq al-Mahdi, a major Sudanese religious and political leader, for instance, says that, 'along with despotism, social injustice, and economic stagnation, the regime of *taqlid* is responsible for destroying the inner vitality and purposefulness of the Islamic *ummah* [community] and so preparing it for foreign domination'.[23] King Fahd of Saudi Arabia has likewise acknowledged 'the need to find Islamic solutions to the problems of the age' and has specifically endorsed the use of *ijtihad* to do this.[24] Implicit in most of these arguments is criticism of the traditional *'ulama* for having promoted their own interests over those of the community, and this criticism has helped to diminish their standing as guardians of the law. Al-Mahdi lashes out at the 'traditionalists' for reviving a self-perpetuating 'reign of *taqlid*' in reaction to Muslims who have become 'acculturationists', accommodating themselves to the Western way of life,[25] and even King Fahd has said: 'We notice that the divisions among Muslims have led the *'ulama* to refrain from confronting the new problems of life with unanimous opinions. Brothers, today you see many events and questions from which problems have accumulated . . .'[26]

It is not surprising, therefore, that the door is now far more open than ever it was, and this is what I mean by a major change occurring. The proponents of *ijtihad* have had one purpose in mind: to make Islam relevant to the demands of the modern world and, in this way, to defend it against the West. In doing so, they have been concerned less with procedure than with results. In consequence, it is not clear at all who can exercise *ijtihad*, when, or by what rules, even as important modifications of the law have taken place in its name.[27] We are left to conclude that this 'neo-*ijtihad*'[28] is more amorphous than the old one, but (and probably because of this) infinitely more permissive and available for use. In effect, what was seen as a privilege is now seen as a right.

All of these factors add up to an inescapable conclusion: that it is nearly impossible to say with authority at any one moment what Islam is and what it is not. This is the conclusion that the Munir Report, which looked into the anti-Ahmadi riots in Pakistan in 1953, came to when it asked the *'ulama* to define what a Muslim is, and found no agreement at all. Its inquiry was 'anything but satisfactory, and if considerable confusion exists in the minds of our *'ulama* on such a simple matter, one can easily imagine what the differences on more complicated matters will be'.[29] Although history does show that there is some doctrinal coherence – Sunnis *are* distinct from Shi'a, Hanbalis from Hanafis – and perhaps a cultural style that we can broadly describe as Islamic, in the beginning and end 'Islam' comes down to the individual heart and mind. The core of Islam, I believe, is hard but, despite what the jurists say, it is small. As one tradition of the Prophet has it, 'O Prophet of Allah, tell me something of Islam which I can ask of no one except you. He said: "Say, I believe in Allah; then be upright".'[30]

Here, then, is the core; apart from this, there is much uncertainty. Four of the five pillars of the faith have been subjected to dispute and different inter-pretations at one time or another. Some question whether prayer (*salah*) needs to be done five times a day, and whether men and women should be segregated. There is also some argument about whether the prayers need to be done collectively and publicly. The Iraqi government, for instance, does not allow Iranian prisoners-of-war to pray together or in public, and believes that the Qur'an does not require them to do so.[31] It is not clear whether *zakat*, or alms-giving, is obligatory and, if it is, whether it is for the individual to disburse or for central government to collect; and if it is to be collected by central government, what percentage of income should be collected and how often. Nor is it clear how it should be disbursed and for what purposes. Some, like the Iranians, believe that the *hajj*, or Pilgrimage, should become a political occasion rather than remaining simply an expression of faith. And there has been some contention that fasting (*sawm*) is cruel in societies in which starvation is widespread; or, as President Bourguiba of Tunisia argued, harmful to the running of a modern economy, the great obligation of our time; or unfair in northern countries such as Denmark, where there are many Muslim guest-workers and where observance of Ramadan is complicated by the long hours of daylight in the summer months.

Only the profession of faith in Allah and the Prophet (*shahada*) remains beyond question, and it is recognition of this, I think, which accounts for the realistic definition of what a Muslim is in the revised 1973 Pakistani constitution:

'Muslim' means a person who believes in the unity and oneness of Almighty Allah, in the absolute and unqualified finality of the Prophethood of Muhammad (peace be upon him), the last of the Prophets, and does not believe in, or recognize as, a Prophet or religious reformer, any person who claimed or claims to be a Prophet, in any sense of the word or any description whatsoever, after Muhammad (peace be upon him).[32]

Of course behind this definition lay the political motivation of excluding Ahmadis from the Islamic community, and thus of effectively making them second-class citizens in a country that was deliberately proclaiming itself an Islamic state.[33] But also present was the religious recognition that the very heart of Islam centres on the oneness of God and the finality and supremacy of Muhammad's prophecy. This recognition gives clear expression to what I have been arguing and doubtless to what offends many of the devout – that the highest common factor is not very high, and that there is nothing to stop Muslims from contesting and redefining everything else. It seems appropriate to say of Islam, as Pompidou said of Gaullism, that 'it is not doctrine but conduct'.[34] Islam is, as many observers have emphatically stated, what Muslims say it is; but it is even more emphatically what Muslims show by their actions they accept it to be. In practical terms, although not in theology, there are as many Islams as there are Muslims.

The objection will be raised that this approach does not explain which Muslims are to be canvassed for their views, or resolve the problem that what Muslims say may not be what they do. I in fact accept that what Muslims say and do differs from person to person, place to place, and time to time; and that what Muslims say that Islam is is not necessarily consistent with their conduct in the name of Islam. This variability is an irritating but a natural feature of every religion and ideology. The basic point, surely, is that Islam is not a monolith, having the same meaning for all and being everywhere the same; nor is it an unchanging and dogmatic faith, written in concrete.

Mu'ammar al-Qadhdhafi has the virtue sometimes of stating simple truths frankly: 'There is the Koran, and there are the Muslims; the Koran is one thing, and the Muslims are something else. Muslim beliefs, especially in this modern age, are not completely identical with what is stated in the Koran.'[35] Although he implies that we can all agree on what the Qur'an says, which I find doubtful, or that we should all agree on what he says the Qur'an says, he does make the larger point, with which I agree, that if we want to know about Islam today, we must think of it more as conduct than as theology and doctrine. This is the point Clifford Geertz made over fifteen years ago: 'It is a matter of discovering just what sorts of belief and practices support what sorts of faith under what sorts of conditions. Our problem, and it grows worse by the day, is not to define religion but to find it.'[36]

The importance of politics

If I were to leave it at this, I would give the impression that Islam is principally religious or ritual conduct and perhaps only secondarily political conduct. This impression of politics coming second to rituals is precisely what many contemporary writers actually endorse, even though they say they are simply reaffirming the conventional wisdom on the subject. According to this conventional wisdom, Islam is a comprehensive phenomenon, making no distinction between sacred and secular: all creation is suffused with the ineffable oneness of God. This inseparability of sacred and secular is not simply pantheism, it is argued, because nature is decidedly created and God uncreated. Yet, because God's dominion is absolute, it would be pointless to make distinctions between the earthly and the heavenly cities. The Augustinian view starts with the assumption that man's fall from grace caused the breach, and that only an explicit act of divine redemption can fill it. The Qur'anic view, however, is that man is God's vicegerent and that whatever failings he may have, they are no more a diminution of God's sovereignty than they are a cause for God's intervention. The world is set right simply because God is in His heaven; the sacred does not need to save the profane because they form one indivisible realm.

The indivisibility of religion and politics follows from this premise, it is generally felt. If Christ's separation of what is due to God and what due to Caesar accounts for the European medieval theory of the two swords – one spiritual, wielded by the Pope, the other temporal, wielded by the emperor – the Qur'anic emphasis on the oneness (*tawhid*) of all things principally accounts for the Islamic medieval view that Islam is indistinguishably and at the same time 'religion and state' (*din wa dawla*). Also accounting for this view is the historical example of Muhammad founding a political community originally at Medina based on religion. The 'Constitution of Medina', which dates from roughly 627 and which outlines the obligations of believers and non-believers in this new community, gives clear expression to the idea that Muhammad was both prophet and political leader. There is much to the idea that 'the Founder of Islam was his own Constantine'.[37]

It is not surprising, therefore, that Islam should be described as a tall tree with many branches and deep-spreading roots, covering not only political but all other aspects of life;[38] or as an indivisible whole consisting of political, economic, social, ritual, and moral segments.[39] 'Here was Islam,' E.M. Forster wrote of Dr Aziz's sentiments, 'his own country, more than a Faith, more than a battle-cry, more, much more . . . Islam, an attitude towards life both exquisite and durable, where his body and his thoughts found their home.'[40] This view of a whole of inseparable parts is still the conventional wisdom, despite the fact that another view has rivalled it for centuries. Ever since the eleventh century, and the

Turkish Seljuk dynasty in particular, the distinction between religious and political authority has been clearly recognized. Although they would not admit it, many modern writers have accepted the distinction: they have separated – and ranked – religion and politics. They have gone about this in two ways.

One way is to argue that religion has been distorted by its intimate connection with politics. This was the point of 'Ali 'Abd-al Raziq's notorious attack in the mid-1920s on the idea of the caliphate as a political institution. The Prophet had not sanctioned it, he said, nor were the results compatible with Islam. Indeed, Islam had been painted with the broad brush of political tyranny because of the way Arab tyrants had used the religious institution of the caliphate to validate monarchical rule.[41] Many people would also argue that much of the post-World War II literature on development and modernization has cast unfair aspersions on Islam by assuming that it gives rise to a pre-modern economic and political system, and by concluding that it is itself pre-modern or medieval. I will return to this particular body of literature in Chapter 6.

The second way in which modern writers have separated the supposedly inseparable is by arguing that politics has been distorted by the intimate connection with religion. This way is far more important than the first way for the point that I want to make. Many writers, particularly secularists, have argued that the fatalistic and authoritarian nature of Islam guarantees that the politics associated with it will be tyrannical or at best undemocratic. But many more writers, mostly committed Muslims, while also feeling that Islamic politics has been distorted, approach the subject from the opposite standpoint.[42] Unlike the secularists, these Muslims – despite differences between them which have led some to be labelled conservatives and others liberals – agree that the blame for the distortion deserves to be put on wicked, or at least selfish, politicians. Fazlur Rahman has put the case forcefully: 'The slogan, "in Islam religion and politics are inseparable" is employed to dupe the common man into accepting that, instead of politics or the state serving the long-range objectives of Islam, Islam should come to serve the immediate and myopic objectives of party politics.'[43]

In effect, then, these Muslim writers break down the inseparability thesis. But they do more. They rank the separate elements: in the language of the social sciences, Islamic values are thought to be the independent variable and politics the dependent variable in the relationship. The secularists think that the only way to avoid autocratic politics is to remove politics from the religious realm, whereas Muslims of the persuasion I have been describing think that politics, and especially politicians, must be made even more subject to religion. Yet to reach these different conclusions they both start with the same assumption: that in the natural Islamic condition, for good or evil, politics is dependent on Islam the religion, or, to put it another way, that Islamic values determine Islamic politics. Fazlur Rahman, whom many people call a 'modernist' or a liberal, is critical of both secular and conservative Muslims, but he too assumes that if only politics were dependent on Islamic values, we would be able to avoid much of the trouble:

Secularism is not the answer – quite the opposite. But the politics being waged most of the time in these [Muslim] countries is hardly less pernicious in its effects than secularism itself. For, *instead of setting themselves to genuinely interpret Islamic goals to be realized through political and government channels – which would subjugate politics to interpreted Islamic values . . .* – what happens most of the time is ruthless exploitation of Islam for party politics and group interests that subjects Islam not only to politics but to day-to-day politics; Islam thus becomes sheer demagoguery.[44]

The problem with this way of arguing is that it treats religion and politics as ideal categories and takes no real account of them as social phenomena. It thus fails to see that their conduct is often in conflict because their motivations are in conflict. If we set aside the logic of faith, there is no reason why truth should triumph over power. But, more to the point, it is very rarely possible when speaking of motivations to make such simple equations of religion and truth, and of politics and power. The history of every civilization shows that both religious and political institutions operating in society are contenders, and very often competitors, for people's loyalties and hence for power. In this sense both are political, but in the process the religious most often ends up being subject to, or used by, the explicitly political – quite contrary to what a great deal of contemporary Muslim opinion holds.

Islamic civilization is no exception to this tendency: the Sunni *'ulama* have had a long history of being in the pay, and therefore of reflecting the opinions, of the Caliph or Sultan. And it became generally recognized that the balance of power between Caliph and Sultan had shifted in favour of the latter. Indeed, as early as the twelfth century, Sultan Sanjar, although acknowledging that he had received his charge from the Caliph, affirmed that 'we received this by right and inheritance'.[45] Medieval political theory came to endorse the shift in power by arguing, rather like medieval Christian theory, that maintaining the political and social order was the highest duty of all authorities in this life.[46] Among the Shi'a, the endorsement came much earlier. In the eighth century the sixth Imam, Ja'far al-Sadiq, formally acknowledged the institutional division of the Imamate and caliphate until such time as God would give victory to the Imam. He thereby implicitly accepted the superior temporal power of the 'Caliph', by which he meant the political authority.

It is the opposite ranking, religion first and politics second, or a different assumption, religion determining politics, which we have seen in the literature, that troubles me. I will assume that politics has a life of its own and influences the evolution of values more often than this literature would have us believe; politics is more often independent of than dependent on religion. It is thus not enough to say that Islam is 'the religion of the Muslims'.[47] For my purposes, Islam is better seen as the political beliefs and conduct of Muslims, what they say as well as what they actually do. The view that makes politics separate from and independent of religion will no doubt strike people as strange, given the description of Islam by Muslims themselves, but it may help to dispel the all too frequent assumption one encounters in non-Muslim circles that *din wa dawla* spells political absolutism and always engenders the church militant. The view that Islam is more usefully thought of as conduct than doctrine will also no doubt bother many people, but it does avoid the unrealistic assumption that beliefs exist separately from the people who hold them, or ideas from those who think them.

But this puts the case too starkly. It seems, for example, to exclude the possibility of the independent existence of ideas. Naturally, I acknowledge that certain thoughts transcend time and place, and that these thoughts have definite meanings. Yet, at the same time, it must be said that ideas are rarely so remote from human aspiration that they fail to motivate conduct. And when they do motivate conduct, the ideas inevitably undergo some change and are affected or qualified by what people make of them or do to them. Indeed, it is perhaps only to be expected that people possess ideas even as they are possessed by them, that they change ideas even as they are changed by them. This possession of an idea that sets one marching, and the making over of it in the process, is what I mean when I say that there are as many Islams as there are Muslims.

I seem also to deny that any general conception of Islam exists apart from the core, the profession of the faith. Goethe's line comes to mind: 'If Islam means submitting to God, we all live and die in Islam.'[48] The truth, of course, is that several ideas grow out of the *shahada* which all Muslims everywhere would accept: that Islam rejects all forms of animism and pantheism; that God is all-powerful but not paternal and thus could not engender a son; that God is merciful and that His most wondrous mercy is the Qur'an itself; that Muhammad was a man, as Christ was a man; that Muhammad's life was exemplary and is inspirational; that the revelation transmitted to Muhammad is the final and universal revelation, confirming earlier revelations but explicitly applying to all men, not just one nation or people, and giving them their last warning.

Several political ideas grow out of the *shahada* and also seem unexceptionable: that all mankind constitutes one spiritual community but that there is also a temporal community of believers which may or may not coincide with the universal community; that God does not directly govern the community of believers but that its government is based on His revealed law (it is not a theocracy but a nomocracy);[49] that governmental edicts and legislation must not contradict the revealed law; that obedience is owed to the guardians of the law – in the first instance, the Prophet himself and, later, his successors to temporal power, though not to prophetic power; and that the actions of the governors themselves must be judged by the standards of the revealed law. These ideas mark off the Islamic political field, but we can also see that it is a broad field in which many questions – such as who decides on the succession to the Prophet, what form of regime (monarchy or democracy, for example) is sanctioned, and exactly when political revolt is permissible – are left unanswered. In truth, this broad field is really a battleground where many other ideas, such as the permissibility of birth control or the prohibition on interest-taking, must contend.

Looking for consensus

This suggestion of a contest of ideas raises another objection to what I have said. If Islam varies with the individual believer, how can one say that there is an Islamic position on any topic, and determine what it is? Subject to the qualifications already made, this can be done, I believe, by reference to the prevailing consensus or general agreement I alluded to earlier. This is the notion of *ijma'*, which is naturally and intimately linked with the notion of *ijtihad*: *ijma'* is the collective result of individual minds employing independent judgement, and *ijtihad* itself is often prompted only when there is a consensus on an issue. There is a chicken-and-egg quality to the relationship, but what is certain is that there is no incompatibility between the two. The problem, rather, has to do with the nature of agreement. Although a reassuring saying of the Prophet holds, 'My community will never agree on error', jurists have disagreed considerably on what constitutes agreement, or, more to the point, how much agreement and whose agreement are necessary.

It is clear, however, that over the centuries a gradual loosening of the idea has occurred. Malik ibn Anas, founder of one of the orthodox law schools, had argued that *ijma'* is limited for all time to the agreement of the Medinan jurists. He took this restrictive view because he was contending with the Iraqi jurists, who, he thought, were too easily deviating from the *sunna*, Al-Shafi'i, wanting to limit the growing number of traditions that seemed to be appearing, defined *ijma'* as the unanimous agreement of the Islamic community as a whole. Even his own followers, however, found that this standard virtually prohibited any agreement, and they tried to modify it. Al-Ghazzali, for example, argued that unanimity is required only for the fundamentals of the faith, whereas the details are better left to the general – and vaguely defined – agreement of the *'ulama*. Some went on to say that the agreement of scholars in one generation is all that is required.[50] More recently, others have argued that *ijma'* exists even if there are objections, so long as the majority are in agreement; or, if only a few scholars agree, so long as there are no objections.[51] It is readily clear that there has been a great deal of disagreement on what constitutes agreement.

However, there seems to be a widespread acceptance today – indeed a consensus – that *ijma'* varies according to the circumstances of the times and that it may be said to exist when, roughly speaking, most religious authorities and intellectuals are in agreement. The most obvious thing about this statement is its imprecision. Indeed, everything can be queried: how much agreement, whose agreement, when and where?

As regards the last question, whether *ijma'* varies from place to place, there are differing views. The Caliph 'Umar, in the seventh century, is believed to have encouraged the believers to follow their local consensus,[52] but he meant consensus on the specific application of the law and not on the broad understanding of principles. In the modern period, Muhammad Iqbal spoke of entrusting *ijma'* to one legislative assembly,[53] whereas Kemal Faruki has suggested that national legislatures throughout the Islamic community be entitled to work out their own *ijma'*.[54] Both are possible, but the kinds of issues that I shall be discussing in this book and in the companion volume – nationalism, pan-Islam, etc. – are universal questions, and thus the consensus that I will look for is that of the general community of Muslims across the world.

The broader and political nature of these questions, moreover, might seem to suggest that *ijma'* is not the appropriate concept here at all. Coulson suggests that *ijma'* has always had the broader meaning of 'the collective expression of a common religious conviction' as to the fundamentals of the faith.[55] But I think there has also been an analogous notion of political consensus in Islamic history. For example, a well-established consensus among Sunnis holds that candidates for the caliphate must have sufficient knowledge of the Qur'an to be able to exercise *ijtihad*, be of sound mind and body, and probably (though there is some disagreement here) be of the Quraysh family, the family of the Prophet. Among the Shi'a, the consensus is that governance rightly belongs in the hands of the Imams who can trace their descent directly from the Prophet through his daughter Fatima and son-in-law 'Ali. Sunni consensus endorses the reality of superior power to that of the Caliph and argues that there is a religious obligation to obey the Sultan. Shi'i consensus endorses the practice of 'caution' (*taqiyya*), whereby Shi'a may deny or obscure their beliefs in order to survive in a society where the public expression of these beliefs would lead to persecution or death. Both Sunnis and Shi'a agree, though for different reasons, that the *'ulama* are people to be consulted about the affairs of state because of their specialized knowledge of the law. They both have also agreed that non-Muslims who are resident in the Islamic community (*dhimmis*) are allowed clearly defined concessions conditional upon their meeting certain clearly defined duties. More recently, since roughly the end of the nineteenth century, Sunnis and Shi'a have agreed that Islam stands for democracy, limitations upon the powers of the governors, and an obligation of those who govern to provide the people with a system of social welfare.

This political sense of *ijma'* has tended to merge in the past century or so with the more technical – and usual – sense of the term. It has given rise to the view that not all *ijma'* needs to be retrospective, as the classical jurists claimed, and that it is possible to speak of consensus existing without the benefit of a later generation's *ijtihad*. Even the supposedly arch-conservative Hanbali jurists of Saudi Arabia accept that there is an *ijma'* 'in every age', and imply that this is recognizable in every age.[56] King Fahd endorsed the idea of contemporary *ijma'* when he launched the Saudi-backed Council of Islamic Jurisprudence: 'The situation [today] is serious, and the responsibility before God is greater than the *ijtihad* of any one person on new events; so *ijtihad* must be supported by the *'ulama* in concert (*qabul al-'ulama*) after thorough research in an examination of old and new jurisprudence.'[57] This is also the assumption which underlies the view of such so-called liberals as A.K. Brohi that *ijma'* is 'the process of making a by-law' in order 'to carry on the movement for the propagation of Islam'.[58] As far as the 'when' goes, therefore, I shall be emphasizing the present but also dealing with the past.

The related matters of how much agreement and whose agreement are the real problem. They troubled the imagination of the classical jurists, as I have indicated, but have also troubled modern thinkers. Faruki has taken the matter of 'how much' furthest, suggesting that *ijma'* may be said to exist when a preponderant majority of legislators – he suggests 75 per cent – are in agreement.[59] Since, however, no formal legislative body exists by general mandate of the community, it is impossible to think of *ijma'* in terms of votes cast and ballot results. I doubt that a concrete answer to this problem can be found, and thus one is thrown back to thinking in almost mystical terms: no one can say how much consensus is required for consensus to exist beyond the instinctive belief, conditioned by our age, that it should involve a 'majority' or 'most'. And the determination of when that majority exists must be left to the observer's appreciation of the *Zeitgeist*. It is hardly a satisfactory methodology and is not to be excused by the fact that the methodology of the social sciences is generally rough and unsatisfactory. But the alternative is to abandon the effort to analyse the concept in a present-day context, which strikes me as isolating and blinkered.

The matter of who decides is irritatingly unresolved too. Just as the *'ulama* no longer exclusively control *ijtihad*, they are no longer the sole arbiters of *ijma'*. Iqbal thought that it was essential to involve informed laymen in order 'to stir into activity the dormant spirit of life in our legal system',[60] and, even though his proposed legislature has not materialized, 'laymen' have indeed become important in determining consensus. One reason why this is so is the diminution in prestige of the Sunni *'ulama*. As I mentioned earlier, there has been a definite opinion in the past century that part of the cause, if not the main cause, of Islam's decline was the *'ulama*'s insistence on closing the door of independent judgement. More recently, both secularists and religious activists have added to the chorus of criticism. The secularists put emphasis on the *'ulama* encouraging a servile attitude among the people and see them concerned, like Talmudic scholars, 'to juggle syllogistic lore'[61] and as irrelevant to the building of a modern society.

It is sometimes hard to distinguish among the religious activists, but there do appear to be two different emphases. Those who put the greatest emphasis on the need to change Islamic interpretations to keep up with the times tend to argue that the *'ulama* have turned into a tradition-bound priestly class.[62] Those who put the greatest emphasis on the need to return to the basics of the faith argue that the *'ulama* have succumbed to the power of the modern state or have come to ape the ways of thinking of the Western imperialists, and thus are hardly interested in, or barely understand, the Qur'an and *sunna*.[63] All the critics overlap in seeing the *'ulama* as committed primarily to protecting their own narrow interests and, in doing so, as misleading the believers.

Another reason why the *'ulama* are no longer accepted as the sole guardians of *ijma'* is that the change in educational outlook which has taken place has affected the way Muslims look on religious authority. On the one hand, recognition has been growing in the past quarter of a century that students of Islamic law need to have a grounding in Western approaches to law as well as in the humanities, and that students in the *madrasas*, Islamic schools, need to study the sciences and humanities in addition to the more traditional Islamic subjects. For example, the Islamic University in Islamabad in its four-year LL B degree course, which is designed to produce *qadis* (judges) and *muftis* (specialists empowered to deliver legal opinions), requires students to take courses in non-Islamic law (covering contracts, torts, conveyancing, etc.), 'Pakistani studies', and English; and law students at the International Islamic University in Malaysia are similarly required to study common and comparative law and English, in addition to the usual Islamic legal subjects.[64] With regard to the *madrasas*, the process has perhaps been taken the furthest in Indonesia, where 70 per cent of the curriculum is now devoted to non-religious subjects.[65] As regards state schools, on the other hand, there has been, at least in the past few years, an increasing emphasis on the Islamization of curricula. This Islamization has not occurred everywhere, but Islamic subjects now occupy a greater part of the curricula of Egyptian, Sudanese, Pakistani, Turkish, and Malaysian schools than was the case even five years ago.

The effect of the first trend has been to legitimate what once were called 'secular' subjects and, by implication, those who are expert in them. The World Conference on Muslim Education, which was held in Mecca in 1977, contributed greatly to this process by endorsing a philosophy of integrated education. The rationale was that the Islamic idea of oneness naturally extends to education, but the recommendations of the Conference must be seen as an implicit criticism of the narrow and inward-looking nature of Islamic education in the past. Henceforth educational planning was to be based on the twofold classification of 'perennial' knowledge, derived from the Qur'an and *sunna*, and 'acquired' knowledge, that which was 'susceptible of quantitative and qualitative growth and multiplication, limited variations and cross-cultural borrowings as long as consistency with the Sharia as the source of values is maintained'.[66] The effect of the second trend has been to give experts in secular subjects a claim to some insight into religious matters.[67] Hasan al-Turabi, leader of the Muslim Brotherhood in the Sudan and former Attorney-General, gives this claim a ringing endorsement when he says, 'Because all knowledge is divine and religious, a chemist, an engineer, an economist, or a jurist are all ulama. So the ulama in this broad sense, whether they are social or natural scientists, public opinion leaders, or philosophers, should enlighten society.'[68]

The broadening of who is relevant to consensus-making matches the position of those writers, such as Kemal Faruki, who believe this development is only natural, since *ijma'* was always the prerogative of the community as a whole and not that of just the *'ulama*.[69] It also matches the historical situation that learned men who were not recognized as *'ulama* exercised important influences, even in Iran, whose official Shi'ism has maintained the position that no *ijma'* is valid without the participation of the Imam, or infallible leader of the Shi'i community. In fact, however, this uncompromising position was softened by the belief that during the Imam's absence (*ghayba*), which began in 874 and is still continuing, the most learned of the religious scholars are entitled to exercise independent judgement and to endorse the consensus of the time.

The position was also softened by the fact that, from the mid-nineteenth century, learned lay intellectuals, *raushanfikran*, have come to have important followings and to affect the way in which discourse on religious and political issues is formed. Ahmad Kasravi was one such person in the early part of this century, and more recently 'Ali Shariati became so important an advocate of Islamic revolution that even Ayatullah Khumayni, who has emphasized the religious and political paramountcy of the *'ulama*, [70] has tolerated the honour which many of the young give to this critic of the *'ulama*.[71] In general, it must be said, though, that the *'ulama* throughout the Islamic world have reacted bitterly to the idea that laymen can exercise *ijtihad* and participate in consensus-making, and have denounced such participation as tantamount 'to distorting the religion of God and the worst type of heresy'.[72] Yet, for all the reasons that I have given, this view must be seen as going against the current.

In sum, an unmistakable broadening of the concept of *ijma'* has taken place in recent centuries, to the point at which neo-*ijma'* has emerged along with neo-*ijtihad*. It differs from the old concept by the wider range of issues that it covers, its immediacy, and the greater number of people who have something to say about it. But the traditional distinction between three types of consensus is still relevant. The first is consensus of speech (*ijma' al-qawl*); the second, consensus of action (*ijma' al-fi'l*); and the third, which has been less used than the others, consensus of silence, implying assent (*ijma' al-sukut*).

I shall be dealing mainly with the first two: that is, with the pattern of what Muslim thinkers say and write on a subject ('speech') and with the pattern of what Muslims do with regard to it ('action'). Statesmen and political leaders obviously dominate the consensus of action, but very often they also have prominent influence in shaping the consensus of speech, or the intellectual consensus of the times, as was the case with Egypt's 'Abd al-Nasir and Indonesia's Sukarno. This, of course, is not a new situation. What is new, however, is the ability of national leaders, with the extensive apparatus of state and modern communications at their disposal, to mould opinion and to engage in political education, particularly of the young. For this moulding of opinion to be effective, the national leaders have often to engage deliberately in Islamic symbolism and rhetoric, which in turn helps to shape or colour the consensus of the time.

The recognition of the importance that national leaders have, however, compounds the elitist bias of *ijma'*. Perhaps this bias should not be a cause for concern, given that the early jurists conceived of *ijma'* as a privilege and denied the existence of any such thing as consensus of the masses (*ijma' al-'awamm*). But we are dealing with neo-*ijma'*, which is broader and more open. Even so, it is hard to take this mass opinion into account because it is hard to gauge opinion in undemocratic societies. This problem is unavoidable. But a more telling criticism can be made. It is that Western observers inevitably pay attention to the 'modernists', who are more congenial, more like us Westerners, rather than to the 'fundamentalists' or 'traditionalists', who represent a great deal of mass opinion. To tune into those who speak and write in familiar ways is to concentrate on the articulate and the powerful, and this is to see Islamic consensus as something neat, reasoned, and oriented towards the *status quo*, while making light of the contradictions, spontaneous emotionalism, and revolutionary sentiments that also often appear.[73] I will try to give some attention to this other section of opinion, thereby acknowledging that consensus is very rough on the surface and constantly shifting below. But it will be clear that I see a close connection, owing to political education and cooptation, between what the elites believe and the masses believe, and do not think there is always a wide gap between them. Moreover, it will be clear that distinctions between 'modernists' and 'fundamentalists', or whatever terms one chooses to use, are not always obvious to me, and consequently I will try to avoid such labels.

One final matter needs comment. The criticism that there is a bias in Western scholarship towards the published text rather than the people fits in well with Edward Said's now-celebrated attack on what he regards as Orientalism. Said argues that the outside observer of Islam is engaging, unwittingly as often as not, in a political exercise which tends to become a form of imperialism. The information that these Orientalists hit upon may help in devising actual programmes of pacification, as was often the case in the nineteenth century, but even today, when scholars claim that they are independent of their governments, their scholarship becomes a form of invasion that cannot fail to produce the unspoken assumption, 'we are superior to you'. This inevitably happens, according to Said, because the Orientalist reduces the humanity of those whom he studies by categorizing them, distilling the essence of their heritage, and abstracting trends, thereby turning people into manageable concepts and stereotypes.[74]

There is a powerful argument here, and indeed an uncomfortable margin of truth to the charge that Orientalism has been imperialism by other means. The relationship between Orientalist and government has had little to do with enlightenment for its own sake and much to do with improving the efficiency of colonial policy. It can be argued that the scholar has some moral responsibility for the effects that his work produces, but Said's criticism goes further than this. He suggests that the effects of the Orientalists' work are bound to be bad, and he leaves one with the impression that only Orientals can study the Orient, or Muslims Islam. Following this criticism to its logical conclusion, therefore, would put a full stop to much cross-cultural scholarship, which would clearly be unwise. Said's implied way of avoiding the problem, moreover, would be dangerous. The Orientalist, he says, may go on with his work if his politics is correct: that is, not 'artificially neutral'[75] when it comes to the evil influence deriving from multinational corporations, American power, or Zionism. However, in saying this, Said comes uncomfortably close to the Orientalist ideologies that he denounces with but another well-intentioned, though distorting, ideology.

Although I do not know whether anyone can be neutral, I at least start with the assumption that to be 'artificially neutral' is no bad thing. It also seems to me that having made solemn acknowledgement of the political snags, the researcher can try to minimize the serious problem of simplifying and stereotyping the life of a people by concentrating on specific issues within specific times and locations. Yet, in the end, I suspect that a considerable amount of simplifying and stereotyping has to be done if any discernible patterns are to emerge, in this book, about Islam and the nation-state, and about Islam and transnational relations in the companion volume to follow.

2 The nature of the Islamic revival

There is no denying that a significant body of Muslim opinion is critical of contemporary international relations. I have a vivid memory of listening to a small group of African and Asian Muslim students in Karachi who bitterly denounced the institution of the nation-state, and also their own governments for being tools of the imperialists in failing to encourage Islamic unity. All the while, their elders, keeping silent, squirmed uncomfortably in their seats. In a sense, these students gave voice to an important strand of thinking in the modern period that completely rejects the very ideas of nationalism and the nation-state and, in some people's opinion, represents the voice of the current revival. In this chapter, I shall examine what the revival means and look at the general effects that it has produced.

The Muslim view of Islam's decline

Much of the disappointment, even bitterness, which some Muslims express about the nation-state, reflects their view that reality has diverged from what they perceive the ideal to be, that the practice bears no relationship to the theory. There is certainly nothing uniquely Islamic about this divergence: practice rarely conforms to what is thought of as the theory. But the divergence tends to become greater and the disappointment more acute in times of rapid change. That is what is happening now, and in part it explains the much-vaunted Islamic revival: the feeling among many Muslims that Muslim practice has been faulty and that major changes are necessary.

Muslims themselves are certainly conscious that history has brought them to an unhappy state. They differ a great deal in analysing the causes, but they all seem to agree that Islam has been in decline. There are, roughly speaking, three schools of thought on the subject.

The first holds that the cause of the decline is the deviation of the believers from the true path. This school has its antecedents, most directly, in the thinking of such people as Muhammad ibn 'Abd al-Wahhab who, in the mid-eighteenth century, believed that because of their ignorance or indolence Muslims failed to follow the precepts of the religion. The school today includes such distinguished figures as the Pakistani jurist Javed Iqbal, son of the great philosopher and poet Muhammad Iqbal. He suggests that as a result of perverting the essence of Islam, Muslims became captive to 'autocratic sultanates', 'sterile mulla-ism', and 'decadent Sufism'. Because of the lust for power, both political and clerical, and the attractions of mystical aloofness, Muslims fell victim to an unproductive and basically irrelevant Islam.[1]

The second school of thought holds that the reason for the decline lies with Islam itself. The proponents of this view would not be surprised at what Mr Justice Iqbal has to say, but they would maintain that the problems which he points to are part of the very nature of Islam and are not merely the result of distortions by the believers. Most people who feel this way shy away from direct criticisms of Islam, and speak instead of the absence of any analytical tradition and scientific methodology in Arab Islamic society, never quite making it clear whether they see the fault as lying with Arab civilization or Islamic civilization. Isma'il Mazhar, for instance, made the point that traditional beliefs imprisoned the minds of modern believers and therefore that an opening – presumably onto a secular vista – was required.[2] Qustantin Zurayq, a Christian writer long associated with the American University of Beirut, came to a similar conclusion in examining the meaning of the defeats of 1948 and 1967. He said that the Israelis were victorious because their social order is predicated on a modern ideology that encourages the growth of industrialization and values rational inquiry. Arabs must follow suit, separating religion from politics and adopting modern, liberal ideas.[3] Several Muslim writers have accepted this line of reasoning and argued for restricting the public role of Islam.[4]

The third school of thought puts the blame for Islam's decline on the West and, more particularly, on Westernized Muslims for the ease with which unworthy and harmful innovations (*bida'*) have come into practice. The Egyptian Muslim Brother Sayyid Qutb is the best exponent of the argument, claiming that Islam declined when Muslims coveted the mechanical energy of the West without realizing that spiritual emptiness would follow. The West, to put it simply, is an attractive though false model and, in so far as Muslims follow it, they deviate from 'the straight path' (*al-sirat al-mustaqim*).[5] Reacting against the heavy involvement of Americans in Iran during the Shah's period, the Iranian revolutionaries, religious as well as secular, have taken the argument further by talking about the West poisoning their society. The West thus becomes a pestilence that kills the very heart of Islamic society: 'Westoxification' (*gharbzadegi*), not simply Westernization, is now the cause of the decline.[6] Muslim student activists throughout the world have enthusiastically taken up this theme and have unrelentingly attacked fellow Muslims for helping to spread the poison, or, to change the metaphor, becoming the 'carcass merchants of Western culture'. To be Westernized in order to be 'progressive' is to be 'enslaved'.[7]

Background to the revival

Whatever the causes of decline may have been, there is a widespread assumption among both Muslims and non-Muslims that Islam is experiencing a 'revival', or 'resurgence', or 'reaffirmation'. It needs to be said, first, that these are convenient and understandable shorthand expressions. Any one term is as acceptable as any of the others (I will use 'revival'), so long as it is understood that all of them would be misleading if their use implied that Muslims have only recently rediscovered their faith and dusted off the Qur'an. The truth, of course, is that Islam has been a constant component of the believers' lives. In addition, the idea of revival would be misleading if it implied that the more pronounced zeal and visibility of Muslims today are novel. This view would ignore that throughout Islamic history many activists have shattered the calm and have thought of themselves as purifiers or 'renewers' (*mujaddids*) of Islam. Indeed, there have been many other times when an observer could say, as Lady Duff Gordon did in the 1860s, that 'a great change is taking place among the Ulema, that Islam is ceasing to be a mere party flag'.[8] One thinks of the agitation surrounding the Hashimiyya in the eighth century; the Carmathians in the tenth; the Fatimids in the tenth and eleventh centuries; the Naqshbandiyya, particularly Ahmad Sirhindi, in the late sixteenth and early seventeenth centuries; Ibn 'Abd al-Wahhab of Arabia in the eighteenth; Uthman dan Fodio of western Africa in the early nineteenth; the followers of al-Afghani, 'Abduh, and Rida, often referred to as the Salafiyya, in the later nineteenth century; and the Muslim Brotherhood in this century.

Moreover, any one of the various terms for the revival would be misleading if it were taken to imply that a uniform process is at work, or that Muslims share one vision of the future. As was indicated in Chapter 1, Muslims differ a great deal on important questions – on account of cultural differences, the teachings of various legal schools, the influence of particular leaders, the ethnic mix, and the degree of exposure to Western or secular ideas. Nevertheless, despite the differences, there is no doubt that a new dynamism has appeared since the late 1960s. Muslims have come to feel that the disparity between what Islam ordains and what people do is intolerable, or to feel that they must reaffirm that Islam is important to their social and political lives. Often they have come to feel both.

John Voll has usefully argued that there are four ways to approach the explanation of the current revival: (1) to emphasize the strengths of Muslim society, especially the oil wealth; (2) to emphasize the weaknesses of Islam in handling modernization; (3) to emphasize particular and changing circumstances rather than general patterns; and (4) to emphasize historical continuity and to see evolving development, not fits and starts.[9] Each of these approaches makes a great deal of sense, and some of them have been followed by Muslims themselves in analysing what is happening today. But they give a part of the picture, and probably no one of them would be sufficient by itself to give the whole picture.

Let us look, for instance, at the approach which emphasizes the strengths of Muslim society. Considerable attention has been given to the connection of the oil price revolution and the Islamic revival.[10] One exponent of this view gives principal credit for the revival of the late 1970s to the oil boom of the mid-1970s. The boom is said to be the cause of the revival because the new wealth gave rise to independent centres of power, notably Saudi Arabia and Libya; because it set in motion the process whereby a charismatic leader, Khumayni, came to dominate the Muslim stage; and because it gave Muslims an opportune infusion of vitality.[11] Other writers put primary emphasis on the self-confidence of Muslims: oil has brought about this new assertiveness, and this accounts in large part for the 'international successes of Islam' – institution-building and conferences – which in turn are largely responsible for the revival within individual countries.[12]

These are, nevertheless, really two arguments, which are not equally convincing. First, there is the argument that oil wealth has generated a revolutionary social process, and, second, that oil wealth has provided the means for revolutionary activity. The first deals with underlying causes and is thus different in scope from the second, which deals with the capability to do things. I will return to the first argument later, but the second argument is troubling mainly because it underestimates the importance of other factors.

Indeed, one may well wonder whether this way of arguing, centring on having the resources to act, does not put the cart before the horse. Certainly it is the case that would-be revolutionaries remain unhappy schemers but not doers if they lack the means to act. Ends *are* linked to means. However, the availability of the means (oil) does not in itself account for the pursuit of the ends (revival) in the first place. In fact, to argue otherwise is to flirt with the fallacy in logic, *post hoc, ergo propter hoc:* 'after the oil revolution, therefore because of it'. Moreover, this view of the genesis of the revival reduces everything to the material dimension and, in essence, simplistically makes the spiritual dimension dependent on the material dimension. As I have argued throughout, religion is probably more often dependent on politics than politics is dependent on religion, but spiritual yearnings are something else. They are not as institutionalized as religion, or as capable of manipulation. Finally, this view gives to the revival a greater uniformity than in fact it possesses; it paints a picture of greater cohesion than is deserved.

Did oil give rise to the revival, or did the revival assure that the oil wealth would be spent in a particular way? The question may strike some as useless, or indeed as irrelevant, as the chicken-and-egg paradox, but it does serve to highlight the basic question: would there have been a revival in the 1970s without the oil revolution? The answer must almost certainly be yes. There have been other revivals in previous centuries without the benefit of oil. And, in our century as well, although the possession of vast amounts of capital may have accelerated the process, and perhaps also helped to coordinate Muslim activities, the revival had begun well before the oil revolution of the 1970s.

Reasons for the revival

In looking for an explanation of the revival, therefore, we must take a somewhat longer view. Four broad reasons come into sight.

First, the defeat of Egypt, Syria, and Jordan in the 1967 war with Israel shattered the morale not only of the Arabs, who lost in a head-to-head fight with the enemy, but also of most Muslims, who lost the holy city of Jerusalem. This was not just a defeat or a loss; it was *al-nakba*, '*the* disaster' – the culmination of a long series of setbacks and humiliations which stretched back in modern times to the first militarily unsuccessful encounters that the Ottoman Muslims had with the Europeans. These defeats had given rise to a sense of inferiority, which at first was based on an appreciation of technological, though not theological, inadequacy. But now, in the mid-twentieth century, the loss of sacred territory led many Muslims to conclude either one of two things – either that Islam was an inferior religion, or that they were inadequate believers who had not lived up to the ideals of Islam and therefore deserved their fate.

Most Muslims seem to have concluded that they – or at least their governments – had gone astray, although by and large they did not work out the implication of their failure: that the other side, the enemy, had done something right. This inability or unwillingness to grasp the nettle was the despair of many intellectuals, but, probably because of its simplicity, the popular conclusion concentrated the emotions: Muslims needed to be better Muslims, and their governments more Islamic, if God was to spare them further calamity, or if they were ever to have a chance of recapturing Jerusalem. At the very least the Israeli occupation outraged them, and in the common outrage Muslims everywhere found a stronger identification with each other than had existed previously in the modern era. Some Arab Muslims, in particular, came to see a certain hollowness in Nasirism, the ideology that had seemed the panacea for the Arabs' problems, and were prompted to search for an ideology and programme that could be both coherent and effective. Even before the war, some had come to regard 'Abd al-Nasir as an impious and incompetent tyrant, and as such a greater enemy than the Israelis.[13] But, when it came, the catastrophe of 1967 forced many others to reconsider basic principles and to look for an Islamic ideology.

It is all the more ironic, then, that in 1985, less than twenty years after the 1967 war, many Muslim – mainly Shi'i – activists in Lebanon came to see the Palestinians as an obstacle to their own Islamic revolution. They reached this conclusion as a consequence of disputes, over power and territorial control in Lebanon, and these disputes, along with the generally heightened awareness of Islam since the Iranian revolution, led them to de-emphasize the Palestinian struggle *per se* while putting more stress on liberating Jerusalem, the third holiest city of Islam. For whatever reason, then – the defeat of the Arabs by Israel or the conflict between Palestinians and Shi'i groups in Lebanon – a new sense of Islamic commitment has emerged out of the general Arab–Israeli imbroglio.

Second, the process of development has been a contributing factor. It has stimulated the revival in two main ways: (*a*) it has often strained the social and political fabric, thereby leading people to turn to traditional symbols and rites as a way of comforting and orienting themselves; and (*b*) it has provided the means of speedy communication and easy dissemination of both domestic and international information.

(*a*) The most important dimension to the first point is the unsettling and unrelieved exodus of people from the countryside to the cities. For example, between 1960 and 1975 the rate of increase in the urban population exceeded the growth of the industrial labour force in Egypt by 2 per cent, Iran by 3 per cent, Iraq by 8 per cent, Jordan by 18 per cent, Kuwait by 14 per cent, Lebanon by 3 per cent, Morocco by 10 per cent, Saudi Arabia by 11 per cent, Syria by 3 per cent, and South Yemen by 13 per cent.[14] More recent data would undoubtedly show this trend continuing. Most rural migrants quickly become the urban poor, victims of their own hope, swallowed by the very process which they believed would liberate them. Unscrupulous contractors exploit the members of this seemingly inexhaustible labour pool in order to build as cheaply as possible the new buildings that dot the urban landscape, and government is often unwilling or unable to protect them and to give them basic shelter. In countries such as India and Nigeria, they are also subjected to ethnic or racial discrimination and made to feel that they do not belong and that they probably never will. Many of their children are likely to be forgotten, escaping the educational net and remaining largely unprotected against serious disease.

I must not leave the simplistic impression that these rural migrants have the same destiny or produce the same effect everywhere that they settle. These obviously differ with the culture, the state of the economy, and the size of the city. With regard to the last point, for example, migrants are able to spread rural attitudes more widely in small provincial towns than in the large cities, and not simply because of the difference in size. As Şerif Mardin shows in the case of Turkey, the provincial towns provide fertile ground for Islamic sentiment because the petty-bourgeois merchants and the small-scale farmers feel exploited by the large capitalists and alienated from their Europeanized culture.[15] But there does seem to be a general connection between the sense of not belonging and the turn to religion. In places where Sufi *tariqas*, or brotherhoods, are present, such as Morocco or Senegal, the mystical assimilation of a local saint's grace (*baraka*) is a powerful antidote to the joylessness of everyday life. In some societies, such as Iran, where well-established religious institutions provide some degree of financial assistance, or at least cushion the move from the countryside, migrants naturally come into close contact with the religious officials. In Lebanon the Shi'a who have migrated from the south or the Beqaa Valley to Beirut do not seem to lose their sectarian identification. If anything, they become more aware of it. In the city and suburbs, as outsiders needing the patronage of families to which they do not belong, they feel that they have incurred dishonour and lowered the status that they had in the countryside. In such an alien environment, the political point of reference is no longer family, as it was in the village, but sect.[16] In other societies, such as Nigeria, where extreme economic imbalance and a climate of religious tension prevail, the migrants become natural recruits of millenarian movements. The official report on the Kano disturbances in December 1980, in which the followers of the self-proclaimed prophet known as Maitatsine wreaked horrendous devastation, explained this phenomenon well:

We have earlier made mention of his [Maitatsine's] application for a piece of land to erect temporary structures. His intention, we believe, was to provide accommodation for these men coming from the rural areas since he knew very well that the first problem they would face on arrival at Kano was accommodation . . . These fanatics who have been brought up in extreme poverty, generally had a grudge against privileged people in the society, whose alleged ostentatious way of living often annoyed them. Because of the very wide gap between the rich and the poor in our society and coupled with the teaching of Muhammad Marwa [Maitatsine], they were more than prepared to rise against the society at the slightest opportunity. After all they did not have much to lose . . . They did not own more than the clothes they wore. They had nothing to fall back to.[17]

In every case, the migration from the countryside has helped to spread rural attitudes in the cities, particularly a pronounced emphasis on Islamic tradition. It has thus given impetus to the urban Islamic revival.

The effects are less dramatic among the middle classes, but many of these, too, are unhappy with the process of development. As sophisticated education has become increasingly available, technicians, lawyers, engineers, and teachers have become the new 'productive' middle class in place of the old bazaaris and landowners. These latter resent the loss of status and influence and are suspicious of the Western advisers, suddenly indiscreetly visible, who are purportedly exemplars of a different lifestyle and set of values, and are supposed to show the local people the way to a more efficient and prosperous future. The former, the members of the 'new' middle class, are impatient with the old ideology and anxious to better their position socially and politically.

Poverty and deprivation affect the attitudes of the rural migrants and, equally true, greater wealth and an improved social position affect the attitudes of the middle classes. It is precisely because the middle classes are better off that they are dissatisfied; their appetite has been whetted and they want more. This is particularly true of the lower middle class. According to Saad Eddin Ibrahim's profile of Egyptian Islamic militants, over 70 per cent were from modest, not poor, backgrounds and were first-generation city-dwellers.[18] Nazih Ayubi shows further that there is a difference in social background between those who attend al-Azhar and those who attend the secular universities, and that it is this latter, upwardly mobile and largely non-peasant, group that yields more of the new activists than we might have guessed. In fact, there is nothing new in this pattern: for example, of the 1,950 members of the main assembly of the Egyptian Muslim Brotherhood (al-Ikhwan al-Muslimun) in 1953, only 22 were not of the educated urban middle classes.[19]

For many urban Muslims, however, the sense of not belonging, of being neither fully modern nor suitably traditional, has been the price of success. A 1971 study of middle-class Egyptians indicated that a high proportion did not feel integrated into society and in fact regarded their relations with other people in terms of hostility and even conflict.[20] Religion may not hold the answer for these people, but they are automatically attracted to it because the religious instinct runs deep and because such secular ideologies as Nasirism and Ba'thism have seemed so obviously wanting – both materially and spiritually. Most members of the middle classes will express their religious feeling through the state-controlled religious establishment and will oppose a radical challenge to it.[21] Yet some will turn to more radical alternatives as they sense that the religious establishment is indistinguishable from a regime whose policies appear to close doors to them, even as they open doors to foreign political and business elites. (President al-Sadat's economic policy of attracting outside investment was called *infitah*, or 'opening'.) These Muslims will take to radical and often violent activity as they shout 'Allahu Akhbar!' ('God is most great!'), but they have something in common with those others who feel at sea. Islam, not clearly defined but keenly felt, is their mooring. The metaphor is different in a short story by the Egyptian writer Alifa Rifaat, but the point is the same: for the middle-class woman trying to come to terms with her new sexual assertiveness, 'the five daily prayers were like punctuation marks that divided up and gave meaning to her life'.[22]

(*b*) The other way in which the process of development has stimulated a sense of renewal is by advancing the dissemination of information throughout the developing world. Despite the static plight of the sub-proletariat or *lumpenproletariat*,[23] there have been substantial improvements in literacy among the rest of the population; moreover, radios have become a common possession. As a result, people are now more in touch with what is going on in the rest of the world, and are anxious to formulate Islamic positions on current political, economic, and social issues – or, in other words, to think of the world's problems in Islamic terms. At the same time, Muslims come to know how dissatisfaction and protest against injustices can be and have been, in other places, framed by reference to Islam.

The fast and efficient distribution within Iran of Ayatullah Khumayni's sermons, delivered in exile and recorded on cassettes – 'revolution-by-cassette' – demonstrates further how modern information technology can help people focus their discontent and build their identity around one set of ideas, even though the exponent of those ideas is far removed. To put it the other way around, it shows how religious leaders can use popular feelings by appealing to traditional values, even when they are not physically present: this projection is the powerful extension of the mosque sermon (*khutba*). Khumayni provides the most celebrated example, but there are others. Cassettes of the sermons of Shaykh 'Abd al-Hamid Kishk, an Egyptian *'alim*, are played throughout the Middle East. Young people are particularly attracted by them, as young people throughout Malaysia are attracted by recordings of the *khutbas* of Haji Hadi Awang, who, from his base in rural Trengganu, rails – impartially – against infidels and healf-hearted Muslims alike. Because of the emphasis on community, the importance of the mosque as a central meeting-place, the gathering together of Muslims from all over the world during the Pilgrimage, and the respect given to such official interpreters as the *'ulama*, Islam constitutes a vigorous communication system of its own and is what Marshal Lyautey called 'a sounding board'.[24] Modern technology has dramatically enhanced this capability.

The third general reason for the present revival, in addition to the intellectual and spiritual malaise since the 1967 war and the effects of the development process, is that Muslim societies have been caught up in the universal crisis of modernity. Most Muslims, like virtually everyone else in the developed and developing world, are feeling ill at ease with a way of life that places less and less emphasis on loyalties to the family and seems to find religious institutions increasingly irrelevant. In the past century a discernible shift towards the individual has taken place within societies – i.e., towards lessening the individual's dependence on the extended family (even in such socially conservative Gulf shaykhdoms as Qatar),[25] weakening parental authority, liberating women, and questioning the authority of the clergy. No direct causal relationship exists of course, but this period has also seen an alarming increase in divorce, alcohol and drug addiction, nerve disorders, and crime. It is not surprising, therefore, that 'dropping-out', or 'evaporation' (*johatsu*) as the Japanese say, has come to seem attractive to many. At the very least, modernism has led to a diminution of belief: 'After the dizzying history of the last fifty years, the world has grown strange, and people floated.'[26] Iranian writers, for example, are now beginning to talk about modernity, not modernization, as the problem, and the notion that something is missing in one's life seems to have generated a time of 'secular discontents',[27] leading many to wonder whether the age has lost its way and to ask, 'What is it, after all, to be modern?'

Modernity gives rise to a basic search for identity, in which many people accept that knowing oneself comes through associating with the crowd rather than seeking to rise above it. This search is in fact an individual act of self-discovery, but because of Islam's intense association of the individual believer with the whole community of believers, it seems as if it is an act of self-abnegation. Muslims in a sense are looking for what Daniel Bell called 'new rites of incorporation', which link today's deracinated individual to a community and a history.[28] And yet, in another sense, this is wrong: they are looking, rather, for *old* rites of incorporation that appear to be new even as they are familiar. Religion, precisely because in the past it answered questions on life and death and provided its followers with moral links to each other, becomes the means by which individuals hope to answer the new question of what it is to be modern, and, in so doing, to gain perhaps a reassuring, common world-view. In this respect, born-again Christians and veiled-again Muslims are responding to the same broad phenomenon.

Islam supplies a particularly powerful rite of incorporation because it puts great emphasis on the idea of community and on the Prophet's time as the model for the organization of society. Prior to the revelation that Muhammad received, the people of the Arabian peninsula had worshipped several gods and organized themselves according to tribal, blood ties. But it was the radical innovation of Islam to insist that each person is to be subservient to the one true God and to look upon every other person as brother. This community is based on the bonds of morality, not blood or tribal custom or expediency, and involves the acceptance of responsibilities towards God and men. Although the *umma* incorporates all the believers, it will eventually become universal and include all mankind. In the meantime, Muslims are to follow the example of the Prophet and, in the case of the Sunnis, his four immediate successors, 'the rightly guided Caliphs', or, in the case of the Shi'a, the Imams. It is this perception of fraternity, and of a glorious past, that gives all Muslims – Sunnis and Shi'a – a powerful sense of belonging.

Finally, the fourth general reason for the revival is that the conditions of political development in these societies have tended to heighten the importance of Islam as a political ideology. Because most of these societies are poor in institutions and dominated by unelected rulers, it is natural for those in power to look for a way of legitimating themselves. Legitimation may perhaps be too grand a word to convey what I mean: rulers seek evidence of approval from the ruled or, at least, evidence of acquiescence or the absence of outright opposition. Several monarchies are especially adept at using Islamic symbols for this purpose: the Moroccan king makes much of his traditional title, Commander of the Faithful (*amir al-mu'minin*); the Saudi king finds a naturally sympathetic response when he speaks of his role as protector of Mecca and Medina; and the Jordanian king is careful to emphasize his descent from the Prophet. Monarchs probably always need reassurance, but the need in the case of these leaders has certainly become greater and more definite since the unleashing by the Iranian revolution of a violent ideological storm whose avowed purpose has been to overcome all the remaining shahs of the Muslim world. The fact that development schemes seem to be losing momentum or running into trouble has further contributed to the uneasy climate.

This defensiveness on the part of the existing leaders has been apparent not only in the traditional monarchies, but also in the republics, where such leaders as al-Sadat and Mubarak of Egypt and al-Numayri of the Sudan have faced considerable opposition to their rule and have found it expedient to put Islam to their service. Al-Sadat, for example, found it useful – although it was extremely controversial – to have a *fatwa* from al-Azhar supporting his peace treaty with Israel; Mubarak has created an official Islamic publication, *al-Liwa al-Islami* (*The Islamic Standard*), to rival the popular and often censorious Muslim Brotherhood publication *al-Da'wa* (*The Call*); and al-Numayri courted Sufi leaders and made concessions to the Muslim Brothers, such as the introduction of Islamic law. In Malaysia as well, the government, although keenly aware of the multi-ethnic composition of the population, has increasingly affirmed its Islamic credentials, and the ruling party, the United Malays' National Organization (UMNO), has claimed that it is the largest Islamic party in the country.

In all these countries governments have been able to use Islam with such ease because, as an ideology, it is vague in content yet highly charged: people instinctively respond to it as a general symbol but also as a guide to their loyalties. Its vocabulary, too, is thoroughly familiar to everyone, thereby guaranteeing that the government's message cannot be missed. Napoleon recognized the value – and ease – of using Islamic symbolism at the time of his invasion of Egypt in 1798. His proclamation to the people of Egypt began with the standard Muslim invocation of 'God, the Merciful, the Compassionate' (*bismallah*), and went on to say: 'I worship God (may He be exalted) far more than the Mamlukes do, and respect His Prophet and Glorious Quran . . . [T]he French also are sincere Muslims.'[29]

Governments have also been able to use Islam to their own ends because it lends itself readily to nationalization: or, to express it differently, they have been able to make it part of the bureaucracy. Even the Malaysian federal government, which is sensitive to states' rights, pre-eminently including the right to regulate religion, has moved to bureaucratize Islam. It has not only created such coordinating bodies as the National Council for Islamic Affairs, the National Fatwa Council, and the Religious Affairs Division of the Prime Minister's office, but has also taken over a number of religious schools in the states. In effect, then, governments have recognized the power of Islam and sought to harness it to their own ends.

But just as Islam can be used to legitimate, so can it be used to express opposition. And there are signs that this use has been increasing too. The increase has come about partly as a result of the Shah's overthrow, but also because in many countries in which there are no regular outlets for political expression Islam has been found to be an effective and relatively safe way of making a political stand. Governments have been hesitant to suppress groups speaking in the name of Islam because of the need to appear orthodox themselves, in order either to forestall domestic opposition or to attract aid from Muslim 'patrons' such as Saudi Arabia. As a result, many Muslim groups have been relatively free to criticize their governments, albeit in a circumspect way. The Muslim Brotherhood has been doing this in Jordan, where it has been tolerated as long as it remains a loyal opposition; this pattern was also true of the Brotherhood in the Sudan for most of the al-Numayri regime. Furthermore, it has happened in Algeria and Tunisia, where Muslim groups have acted as a kind of pressure group that tries to influence policies rather than to replace the regime.

In regimes so repressive that they brook no dissent and regard Muslim criticism of any sort as a threat to their survival, the 'Islamic alternative' almost invariably has become more radical. It has become a kind of party, whose aim is to replace the regime, rather than a pressure group. This radicalization of a political alternative of course happens in any repressive society, as it did in Poland, where Solidarity may be thought of as the opposition party. It even happens in societies perceived by only a small minority to be repressive, such as West Germany, which is totalitarian in the eyes of the Baader-Meinhoff gang. My point is not to demonstrate the uniqueness of Muslim societies but merely to indicate that in the Muslim case, too, ostensibly ideological – or religious – groups may become politically radicalized in certain circumstances.

Islam might acquire an even more contentious political centrality, a revolutionary character, if social and economic conditions were dire. This would be the case if there were a marked division between the haves and have-nots, or, to use the terminology at once Qur'anic and secular of the Iranian revolution, between the 'oppressors' (*mustakbarun*) (16:22–3) and the 'oppressed' (*mustad'afun*) (4:97). The rural poor and new urban immigrants would constitute the 'oppressed' (or the 'disinherited', as is said in Lebanon),[30] and the large landowners and urban middle-class professionals would constitute the 'oppressors'. In this situation, as was the case in Iran, politics would become increasingly polarized and vicious as all were caught up in a double revolution of expectations: peasants expecting the good life in the dazzling capitals; professionals and intellectuals expecting greater influence, status, and political participation. Both sides would be destined for disappointment, and would inevitably see each other as obstacles. The professionals and intellectuals would come to regard the urban immigrants as a drain on scarce resources; and, more importantly, given the role played by street politics in the increasingly city-dominated developing countries, the 'disinherited' would come to regard members of the new professional middle class as new oppressors, who used Islam as a tactic to gain mass support but who really cared only about advancing their own narrow self-interest. Moreover, those who said they wanted to make Islam relevant to the conditions of the modern world would be seen as having sold out to, or at least compromised with, the Westernized, secularizing leadership. It is in this way that 'modernist' groups, such as the Masyumi party in Indonesia, lose ground to more 'traditionalist' ones, such as the Nahdatul Ulama.

In effect, then, a revolution of *falling* expectations would take place, particularly among the rural poor and urban immigrants. Seeing a prosperous future recede on the horizon, they would naturally cling to the only comfort of the present, the pillar of traditional faith, and, in doing so, would give political expression to the frustration and indignities of living on the margin of the society. It is a phenomenon that Soviet writers have come to regard as inevitable: 'It is natural for them, therefore, to express their socio-political aspirations and protest against colonial and imperialist oppression in religious form.'[31]

Interpreting the revival

The impression that I have left, though, is too stark. There is really nothing inevitable about revolutionary activism among the dispossessed; 'the wretched of the earth' rarely have enough energy left over from the struggle of daily life to mount revolutions. As Farhad Kazemi points out, the Iranian situation was an exception to the general pattern that had been seen in Iran previously and elsewhere, which shows the rural poor to be by and large content with their meagre lot in the cities and politically passive.[32] But there does appear to be a great deal of truth in the point that they turn to religion, even if they do not take to arms. It is hard to generalize further, since the real reasons for political activism will be found in the specific conditions of the various countries.

For example, one cannot explain the importance of Muslim groups in Egypt without explaining the roots of the Muslim Brotherhood in Egyptian soil and the more or less constant struggle between the Brothers and those in power, particularly the Nasirists. In the case of Syria, one would need to refer to the hegemony of the Ba'th Party and the peculiarly hegemonic role that al-Asad's 'Alawi companions play within the party. Opposition to the dominance of the party and to the 'Alawis is the common point of a diffuse opposition that has taken on a quasi-religious guise. With respect to Tunisia, one would have to explain how its Mediterranean culture and the heavy hand of Bourguiba's secularism since independence have restricted the role of Islam. In the case of Nigeria, one would seek to explain the growth of Sufism by reference to the persistence of tribal and regional identities, the growth of Christian proselytizing, and the importance of the traditional *al-majiri* system of Qur'anic education, whereby itinerant teachers disseminate ideas to the young. As regards China, one would have to point not only to the liberalization that issued from the post-Mao change of leadership but to the way in which such ethnic groups as the Uighurs and Kazakhs look to Islam for solidarity against the Han people.[33]

This point – that Islamic politics are not monolithic – is fundamental, but it should not obscure the fact that the current revival is part of broader historical developments. According to one view, it must be seen as part of the revolutionary wave which began with the French Revolution but which has increasingly taken on Marxist form.[34] There is something to this interpretation: one can readily detect evidence in the rhetoric of Iran's revolutionary leaders of what one writer calls 'third worldism' – that is, the belief that the West has controlled and exploited the developing world.[35] Khumayni himself has taken what originally may have been the Marxist theme of attacking imperialism and attached to it the religiously symbolic theme of satanism: America, the arch imperialist, is the Great Satan. One can also see the ease, and utility, of blending Islamic and Marxist categories in the writing of the lay intellectual prophet of the revolution, 'Ali Shariati. Indeed, it is not an exaggeration to say that many of Khumayni's unpalatable ideas became acceptable, or at least that their unpalatability was reduced, by their association with Shariati and his ideas in the popular mind. Shariati reformulated the main Islamic argument against the Shah by explicitly associating political and social revolution – the commitment to overthrowing tyrants and unjust systems – with Shi'i heroism. In the Arab world, Ahmad Ben Bella, first president of Algeria, has recently linked a new Islamic consciousness with 'anti-imperialism'.[36]

Yet it is one thing to say that Islamic revivalists borrow Marxist language and another to imply, as Elie Kedourie does, that they are advocating a variation on the Communist revolution in which the promise of 'a Californian horn of plenty, a Swedish heaven of sexual liberation',[37] spurs on the radical Muslim in much the same way as the idea of a classless society spurs on the unhappy proletarian. The reference of course is to the fabled luxuries of paradise that are promised to those who die in a just war. However, even this allusion to a kind of eschatological materialism cannot hide the fact that the Muslim activist wants to create a new *spiritual* order, and that thus in the end his revolution is fundamentally different from that of the Marxist.[38] But I must concede that, though the aims differ, both are ideologies that seek to create political orders, and in this sense they are similar.

There is another general view, held by many Muslims as well as non-Muslims, that the revival must be seen as part of a long historical process that began in the eighteenth century with the direct experience of European imperialism. For example, one writer has argued that the present revival is the third stage in a movement whose first stage was the defensive assertion that Islam is modern and can compete with Europe, and whose second stage was the Muslim elite's wholesale adoption of Western ways. The present stage, unsurprisingly, is a reaction to the preceding one.[39] Whereas most Muslims may not be so analytical, they would endorse this general view. The messianic tradition cuts deeply into Islamic history, but, even when the dramatic appearance of the Mahdi is missing, Muslims understand that the community occasionally needs to undergo renewal (*tajdid*).

This kind of interpretation has obvious merit, since it does what history does: it provides context and *gravitas*. It helps to explain why the present revival is as it is, and it makes the revival seem more than merely superficial. Historical perspective is especially important when it comes, for example, to understanding that 'development' was an upper-class phenomenon until recently, which entailed the elite's adoption of certain characteristics from the West and its material as well as spiritual estrangement from society long before the contemporary period. However, the historical perspective can be taken too far: it might underplay the importance of unexpected and radical events such as the oil revolution of the mid-1970s; and it can be misleading if it makes the revival seem less vibrant or less passionate than it is. There is a danger of forgetting that what Anthony Wallace calls 'revitalization movements' occur because individuals feel themselves to be under severe stress and are dissatisfied with the prevailing social order and identity.[40] It is true, to a large extent, that the revival is the sum of individual unhappiness.

But, to an even larger extent, the revival is the sum of individual contentment. I asked people throughout the Muslim world why they had become more devout than they had previously been. No one mentioned the social, economic, or political dislocations that I have dwelt on, and no one framed an answer in terms of emotional or psychological distress. More often than not, whether an Indonesian woman activist, a Malaysian politician, an Egyptian journalist, a Pakistani engineer, or a Jordanian lawyer, they shrugged and said simply that it had happened almost imperceptibly. If they mentioned any specific influence, it was the example of so many other people like themselves who had obviously become more religious. I imagine that less educated and less urbanized Muslims would have been no better able to explain what had happened.

Their inability to point to the factors that I have mentioned does not mean, of course, that these factors had no place. Clearly, I think that they did. But it does suggest that to many Muslims, the social, economic, and political factors were unimportant or irrelevant; in any event, they say, they would have felt the need to be more devout. There is thus a certain artlessness, almost ingenuousness, in their view of the revival. And this must remind us that, when all is considered, we are dealing with people's hopes and beliefs. These hopes and beliefs may become powerful currents that carry people along – almost, but not entirely, in spite of the social, economic, and political currents.

Conclusion

Several general points emerge from the preceding discussion. First, something that we can call a revival has clearly occurred. Muslims in all parts of the world have become more devout, concerned not only with the faithful observance of ritual but also with the social, economic, and political application of Islamic values. It makes little difference that Islam means many different things to different people. What counts is that all these people believe that Islam, not a secular ideology, increasingly shapes their attitudes and directs their actions.

Second, although revivalist sentiments run broad and deep and are unquestionably genuine, their catalyst is the variety of discontents associated with the development process. Migration from the country to the cities, high inflation, inadequate housing, Western economic penetration, and other factors have brought many people to the point of frustration, even confusion. In this frame of mind, they have taken a fresh look at what they are and want to be, and at what kind of future Islam promises them.

Third, partly because of these discontents and partly because of the example of the Iranian revolution, many Muslims have attempted to make Islam politically relevant. No doubt some Muslims use Islam to achieve their own narrow ambitions, but many others lay blame for the inadequacies of their life at the door of government.

Fourth, no real coordination of activity exists among the revivalists. The appeal to Islamic values, the sense of deprivation and deracination, and the inspiration drawn from the Iranian example are common elements, but the form that the revival takes and the effect that it produces vary according to circumstance and place.

However, the emotional nature of the revival has captured most attention in the West and generated negative, undifferentiated images. 'Militant Islam'[41] has become a favourite epithet, although its use is by no means new. In 1853 Palmerston had written that the Ottomans were not 'reawakening the dormant fanaticism of the Musulman race'. But what sympathy there was in this comment was prompted by specific Russian designs on the Ottoman empire at the time, and not by an unusually enlightened attitude towards the Muslim world.[42] Indeed, in the second half of the nineteenth century, Islam was invariably seen as fanatical. Some Europeans thought that Islam was interfering with the nationalist aspirations of the Christian peoples of the empire. Carlyle, for example, argued in 1877 that 'the unspeakable Turk should be immediately struck out of the question' and Bulgaria 'left to honest European guidance'.[43] Other Europeans – especially in the quarter-century from 1880, when a nationalist movement was stirring in Egypt and Mahdism appeared in the Sudan – thought that Islam was fanatical because it promoted the nationalist aspirations of Muslim peoples.[44]

The general condemnation of Islamic fanaticism for being at once anti-nationalist and pro-nationalist had as its common assumption that Islam was not acting in the interest of the European powers. Whether it was the Ottoman attempt to thwart Christian nationalists or the Muslim attempt to gain independence from the West, Islam was fanatical because it ran counter to imperial interests. But it was the converse formulation that became the standard explanation of Muslim conduct: Islam was hostile to the West because it was fanatical. As might be expected from dealing with such a crude stereotype of Islam, however, the differences among Muslims were obscured. Consequently, Muslims came to be seen as a uniformly emotional and sometimes illogical race that moved as one body and spoke with one voice.

In the twentieth century, many Westerners have continued to think in this way and to assume, implicitly or explicitly, that Islam's emotional militancy belies the idea that Muslims can have differing political or national interests. In 1934, with the agitations in India on his mind, Lord Strabolgi prophesied in the British parliament: 'There will be attempts made, the beginnings are visible now, to make a Mahomedan political bloc, not friendly to the British Raj, not friendly to the British empire, from, at any rate, Cairo to Delhi. This is the kind of unity we may end in seeing if we are not extraordinarily careful.'[45] The revival dating from the late 1960s, and particularly the tumultuous upheaval of the Iranian revolution, have given new life to such views, even among generally level-headed observers of international relations. Raymond Aron, for example, warned of the Islamic 'revolutionary wave', generated by 'the fanaticism of the prophet and the violence of the people', which the Ayatullah Khumayni has unleashed.[46] Cyrus Vance has explained that a major reason why, as Secretary of State, he opposed any rescue mission to obtain the release of the American hostages in Iran in 1980 was fear that it would precipitate an 'Islamic–Western war': 'Khomeini and his followers, with a Shi'ite affinity for martyrdom, actually might welcome American military action as a way of uniting the Moslem world against the West.'[47]

The idea that Muslims have variable and often conflicting national interests is absent in these statements, and thus many Westerners seem to assume that national divisions are somehow antithetical to Islam's real nature. This view has perhaps been intensified by the current revival, but in order to assess it we need to explore the relationship between Islam and national pluralism in the longer historical record.

3   The theory and practice of territorial pluralism

Throughout Islamic history there has been tension between political conform-ists and nonconformists, a tension that is as relevant to the study of Islamic international relations as it is to that of Islam's role within individual societies. This tension is not, of course, a unique phenomenon, but it appears to have been more acute in a civilization that has an exceptionally clear normative vision and that prides itself on literal obedience to God's Word. One could call the two types realists and idealists, but because these terms have come to connote in the literature of political science the proponents and the opponents of *realpolitik*, with their different assumptions on the nature of the state, power, war, and political morality, I prefer to use the terms conformists and nonconformists.

My reference is to Muslims who are in agreement, or not, with the prevailing political order.[1] There is no intention to create a typology of Muslim thinkers, as others have, according to their views on a whole range of contentious issues, such as the proper sources of the law, the relevance of the original community of believers, acceptable innovations, *ijtihad*, change, Western ideas, or the role of religion itself in public life.[2] Rather, my focus is narrower and on one question: how do Muslims react to the prevailing political reality? That is, how do they react to the prevailing power structure and its ideology? Conformists, obviously, accommodate themselves – and often, in the process, what they and others see as Islam's meaning – to the political reality; nonconformists do not, since they hope to change the political structure in the direction of what they think Islam is. Or, to put it another way: conformists go along with the West and the nation-state, whereas nonconformists, who have much in common with some Islamic revivalists, reject the nation-state.

It is not surprising that these two types have appeared in Islamic history. Conformism may be said to be encouraged by the very word *islam*, if it is taken, as it usually is, to mean 'submission' to an almighty God; and by the many Qur'anic injunctions to 'obey God, the Prophet, and those in authority among you' (4:59).[3] Moreover, a kind of passive resignation is endorsed when the

Qur'an emphasizes otherworldliness in asking, 'What is the life of this world but play and amusement?' (6:32). Nonconformism also finds encouragement in the Qur'an, but it suggests that the life of this world is deadly serious – and too important for passivity: 'Not as a jest did We create heaven, the earth, and all that is in between' (21:16). It goes on to say that men must combat evil with good (13:22, 41:34) and do justice (16:90). Consistent with this emphasis on changing the world for the good is a different interpretation of the word *islam*. According to the proponents of this view, because the word derives from the fourth, causative, stem form, a more accurate rendering than 'submission' is 'committing oneself' to God's will.[4] Such activism, moreover, may mean that obedience to established authority is not always called for. A *hadith* of the Prophet explains that 'when [a Muslim] is required to do that which is sinful, there is no obligation to hear or obey'.[5]

But despite these rationalizations we must be careful not to think of conformists and nonconformists as fixed philosophical categories. Whether one is a conformist or not depends, of course, on the changing nature of the political reality. For example, the followers of 'Ali, the Prophet's blood relative, believed that only direct members of his family should govern the community. Consequently, they were nonconformists when Abu Bakr, 'Umar, and Uthman were the first three Caliphs; conformists when 'Ali finally became the fourth Caliph; but nonconformists again when the Umayyads became Caliph after 'Ali's murder. More recently, the Jama'at-i-Islami movement of Mawlana Mawdudi in Pakistan was nonconformist until the present government of Zia ul-Haq initiated an Islamization programme, which the Jama'at has largely accepted. Even when one is happy to conform generally to the political reality, there may be nonconformism on specific issues. For example, the usually compliant *'ulama* of Indonesia, who have accepted the secular national ideology, the Pancasila, reacted very strongly against the government's attempt to implement a new marriage law that would have departed significantly from Islamic family law.[6]

What is even more complex is that conformity to a prevailing political norm does not always mean conformity to the *form* which the norm has taken elsewhere. For example, there is no question that democracy has become a dominant political idea of our time, and that most Muslims are conformists in the sense of accepting that it is good and believing that Islam is intrinsically democratic.[7] But many Muslims reject it in the particular form of a multi-party parliamentary democracy, proposing instead, as the Gulf Muslim governments do, the tribal custom of *shura*, or consultation, as the appropriate democratic form.

This complexity is found in the way Muslims have responded to the prevailing international political reality of our time – the territorial state, or, simply, the nation-state.[8] Although I will argue that most Muslims must be seen as conformists, there are variations in their acceptance of the idea of the state; and in particular it is by no means certain that, in conforming, they mean to accept the Western form of the state. Yet, if one were to follow the conclusion of many Western scholars, it would appear that most Muslims have not been conformists at all but rather have rejected the state.

Because these Western writers have had considerable influence on the way we think about Islam and international relations, it is worth summarizing their views. Although there are variations in emphasis and they would not see themselves as constituting a school, they generally put forward three arguments:

(1) The concepts of modern international relations, particularly the concept of the nation-state, have no equivalents in traditional Islamic political theory. Bernard Lewis says that 'foreign policy is a European concept' and is 'alien and new in the world of Islam'.[9] This is so because Islam emphasizes the division of the world into *dar al-islam*, or the realm of Islam or peace, and *dar al-harb*, or the realm of war. The aim of the Islamic world is to expand at the expense of the non-Islamic *dar al-harb*, and Muslims are encouraged to resort to holy war (*jihad*) to do this. Elie Kedourie says that the idea of 'the lively multiplicity of political authorities' is not endemic to a civilization where 'loyalty to Islam . . . ought to constitute the sole political bond'.[10] Adda Bozeman says that Islam is inimical to the 'core idea of the state', and this has been specifically true of the Middle East, where 'communities of believers, or freely floating sects unconfined by spatial bounds', have been the norm.[11] Her reference is to the idea of the *umma*, the community which joins together all Muslims everywhere and which eventually, Muslims hope, will be truly universal.

(2) This intellectual legacy weighs heavily on the minds of modern Muslims and prevents them from conforming to the prevailing concepts of international relations. Lewis makes an exception of Turkey and Persia, which have a long history of sovereign existence, but he argues that the Arab Muslim states today seem able to think of the West only in terms of a monolithic *dar al-harb*: 'the West is a source of all evil' and 'Arab policies are still at the mercy of a model of ethnic and communal collectivism which treats the West as a collective enemy'.[12] Kedourie says that the modern nation-state cannot really emerge among Muslims, since their own political tradition of 'passivity and resignation' is as 'impracticable' now as it has always been.[13] Bozeman says that 'the imported secular public law simply cannot be expected to displace the native religious law, just as the Occidental idea of the state cannot win over that of the consensus of believers'.[14] Rudolph Peters believes that the traditional ideas have such a hold on Muslim intellectuals that any of their 'sweeping assertions about Islam recognising the equality of all mankind and the reciprocality in inter-state relations, amount to no more than gratuitous and non-committal slogans'.[15]

CHECKMATE!
Such Diplomatic Dodges he taught him to employ,
Until the Slyboots Sultan was beaten by our Boy.

Punch, 30 September 1882

Something of this attitude underlay the nineteenth-century Orientalist view, as seen on this page, that the Sultan was inevitably insincere and even duplicitous in international negotiations.

(3) It is almost inevitable that, in so far as Islam is a factor in international relations, it will work to the disadvantage of the West. Lewis, writing in the mid-1960s, thought that the Arabs' perception of the West as evil gave the advantage at that time to the Soviets.[16] Writing more recently, Bozeman argues that 'the West now pays a heavy price' for failing to understand that the Arab Muslim states do not operate as Western states do, and therefore that they will not resolve their dispute with Israel in the same manner as disputes among Western states are settled. Moreover, Islam has a strong potential for undermining the efforts of such a modernizing reformer as the Shah of Iran, and thus for destabilizing a regime upon which the West might depend.[17] Finally, J.B. Kelly suggests that

there is an 'enduring and deep-seated resentment' of the Christian West and a 'contempt for Western civilization' among Arab Muslims, and that this 'has dangerous implications for both the Arabs and the West'. In particular, this animosity translates into a welcome *entrée* for the Soviets: 'the animosity borne by the Muslim Arab world for the Christian West is of such intensity that it was bound sooner or later to cause the Arab maxim of the "the enemy of my enemy is my friend" to operate to embrace the West's most powerful and malevolent foe.' Moreover, the oil price rises of 1973 'amount to nothing less than a bold attempt to lay the Christian West under tribute to the Muslim East'.[18]

These are strong views, but they are understandable, perhaps, for two reasons. First, much of the classical and medieval theory supports the view that Islam is pre-eminently concerned with the creation of a universal community and is intolerant of those who are not Muslims. Indeed, the Qur'an and *hadiths* have many references to the need and the desirability of fighting the unbelievers, often to the bitter end. This is the idea of *jihad*, which is particularly emphasized in the case of the polytheists (*mushrikun*). For example, the Qur'an urges the believers to fight them 'wherever you find them' until they repent or are eliminated (9:5), and a *hadith* records the Prophet as saying, 'I am ordered to fight [the polytheists] until they say, "There is no God but Allah".'[19] 'People of the book' (*ahl al-kitab*), other monotheists such as Jews and Christians, are also to be fought until they pay a special tax and are 'subdued' or 'humbled' (9:29). Generally, the *hadiths* tell us that 'whoever fights to make Allah's Word superior fights in God's cause', and that even a single journey for this purpose is 'better than the world and all that is in it'.[20] It is this expansionist zeal which accounts for the medieval, 'Abbasid elaboration of a bifurcated world – the *dar al-islam* and *dar al-harb* that Lewis discusses. Moreover, within the realm of Islam, the non-Muslims who pay the tax – what Kelly colourfully calls 'tribute' – in exchange for protection are to suffer certain disadvantages and are not to be treated equally with the Muslim citizens. For example, they are not allowed to display their religious symbols openly or to carry arms.[21] This discrimination is, of course, entirely consistent with the Muslim view of Islam as the last and most perfect of the revelations, but is understandably detested by non-Muslims.

The imperative to advance the Islamic community also accounts for the sharp hostility directed against those who profess to be Muslims but are not deemed to be sincere or loyal. The Qur'an puts Muslim 'hypocrites' (*munafiqun*) in the same category as unbelievers (*kuffar*): their 'abode is hell and destiny evil', and true Muslims are to treat them mercilessly (9:73, 47:4). The believers must fully conform, unlike the Bedouin of the desert, who only outwardly submitted (48:16). Moreover, no distinction is to be made among believers except in piety, and any deviation in the practice of the faith becomes an affront to the sacred values of the community and thus merits certain and swift punishment. This punishment is accomplished by means of a form of collective security, whereby all the upright believers fight the perpetrators of dissension (49:9) and apostasy (2:214, 4:90–1) 'until there is no more rebellion (*fitna*)' (2:193). An incalculably strong motivation to fight in this cause – against the polytheist, the non-Muslim monotheist, or the Muslim rebel – is the promise of paradise for those who die in battle in God's service. The Qur'an and *hadiths* are clear that they become martyrs, not really dying but remaining 'alive with their Lord' (3:169) and gaining automatic admission to paradise.[22]

Second, the views of Western scholars derive further support from a well-established and strong tradition among Muslim intellectuals that Islam rejects the very ideas of nationalism and the nation-state. Ameer 'Ali, for instance, put political and territorial pluralism in a negative light by arguing that it came about because of the individual and class greed of the Umayyads.[23] Abu'l-'Ala Mawdudi stressed that in an ideological sense the Islamic state is 'universal and all-embracing'; 'its sphere of activity is coextensive with the whole of human life'.[24]

Although these sentiments are keenly felt by an important group of Muslims today and help to explain why Western scholars would hold the view of an uncompromising, crusading Islam, it would be wrong, I think, to conclude that most Muslims today are nonconformists in the specific sense of rejecting the reality of the nation-state. There are three reasons why I think that this conclusion is wrong:

(1) The classical and medieval theory is not as simple and clear-cut as the views summarized above. On the contrary, it provides a basis for the conformist view, in addition to the nonconformist view.

(2) The practice of Muslims over time indicates an overwhelming acceptance of the reality of territorial pluralism, and today the 'consensus of action' (*ijma' al-fi'l*) is firmly on the side of the state.

(3) Over time authoritative Muslim writers have come to elaborate a new 'consensus of speech' (*ijma' al-qawl*), which argues that the territorial state is a natural and even worthy institution.

The first two points will be discussed in this chapter, and Chapter 4 will be devoted to the third.

Classical and medieval theory

I do not propose to go into great detail on the classical and medieval theory; as I indicated in Chapter 1, a well-developed literature can be found on this, to which the reader should refer. But I do want to make clear that there are two sides of the Islamic theoretical coin. We may take it that a basic urge of all Muslims is to recapture the unity they feel has been lost, 'to arrive where we started and know the place for the first time'.[25] However, there are two kinds of unity – the 'one community' of all mankind (2:213) and the unified community of the believers (3:103). The two do not necessarily contradict each other, for Muslim unity, according to believers, will serve as the prototype of universal unity, and eventually 'Allah will bring all of us together' (42:15). But what is important here is the implicit recognition of the actual *non*-universality of the Islamic community, and thus of ideological and political – and perhaps even territorial – divisions.

This subtle allusion is developed in several ways. First, the Qur'an seems to sanction the idea of such divisions. It says that God divided men into nations and tribes for a purpose – *li-ta'arafu*, to come to 'know each other' (49:13) – and that the divisions of language and colour 'are signs for those who know' (*li'l-'alimin*) (30:22). Moreover, in one injunction to obey God and His Prophet (4:59), it adds, in the plural, 'and those in authority among you' (*wa ulu'l-amr minkum*). At another point, it says knowingly, 'If God had so willed, He would have made them one community' (*umma wahida*) (42:8).

Second, the Qur'an and *hadiths* elaborate a view that is distinctly at odds with the one which focuses on the *jihad* as an instrument of Islamic militancy and expansionism. This alternative view is of a tolerant, non-violent Islam that accommodates itself to the reality of divisions and non-Muslim centres of power. According to this line of reasoning, there is to be no compulsion when it comes to religion (2:256), for what matters is the quality, not the extent, of the faith. Believers will find paradise if they 'perform the required prayers, fast during Ramadan, do what is lawful, avoid what is unlawful, and do nothing further'.[26] It is certainly important for Muslims to commit their wealth and very lives (61:11) to 'strive' ceaselessly against falsehood,[27] but actual combat constitutes the lesser form of 'striving' (*jihad*, literally) and is to be avoided if at all possible. Indeed, the Prophet is reported as saying that whereas 'war (*al-harb*) is deception', [28] the greater *jihad* is working for the good and against evil. Rather than relying primarily on the sword, the Muslim is to use his heart, tongue, and hands for the good of his own soul (29:6) and to build the just society.[29]

Of course fighting is enjoined in the cause of righteousness, but primarily for self-defence: 'Fight in the cause of God those who fight you, but do not be aggressive, for God does not love aggressors' (*al-mu'atadin*) (2:190). There is an obligation, however, to fight in order to protect the *dhimmis* (non-Muslim subjects of an Islamic state), whose rights generally should be upheld and who should not be overtaxed.[30] Although, as I mentioned earlier, *jihad* can take the form of holy war against polytheists, unbelievers, and Muslim hypocrites and rebels, Muslims are encouraged to end the fighting if the enemy has the momentary advantage[31] or withdraws from active hostilities (4:90). They may even conclude a treaty with the enemy, which takes precedence over any obligation to their fellow Muslims: 'If they [Muslims] ask you for help in the matter of religion, it is your duty to help them, except against a people with whom you have a treaty (*mithaq*)' (8:72). And, as the Prophet did, they are to tolerate foreign delegations.[32]

Third, this pragmatic spirit which concedes the reality of pluralism was reflected in the 'Abbasid elaboration of the early division of the world into *dar al-islam* and *dar al-harb*. Although it is often thought that this bifurcation is a testament to an Islamic arrogance, showing universalist pretensions,[33] it can also be seen as recognition of territoriality as an inescapable fact to which the law must bend. It builds on *hadiths* which require that the non-Muslim warrior (*al-harbi*) must have a kind of *laissez-passer* (*aman*) before he is allowed entry into the Islamic realm and that he must be killed if he does not have one.[34] Thus, according to most writers of the Hanafi school, the spoils of war need to be taken to *dar al-islam* in order to be legitimately divided; the manumission of a slave by a Muslim in the non-Muslim world has no validity; and Islamic law has no authority even over those who commit murder in *dar al-harb*, a land beyond the pale.[35]

The Malikis similarly emphasize the territorial aspect of the law: the *imam*, or leader, is to divide the spoils of war in *dar al-harb*; enemy merchants are to have their goods taxed at the rate of one-tenth of their worth when they enter *dar al-islam*; and there is 'great merit' for Muslims serving in the frontier guard (*ribat*), protecting the realm from surprise attack or sporadic incursion.[36] The Shafi'is carry the recognition of territoriality further by arguing that there can be a third area, *dar al-sulh*, or *dar al-'ahd*, in which non-Muslim states have agreed to pay tax or give up some of their territorial rights to the Muslim community.[37] They are in effect the international equivalent of the *dhimmis*.

Fourth and last, these recognitions that the reality of territorial divisions qualifies the ideal of Islamic universality set the stage for the medieval thinkers who accepted that there is pluralism within *dar al-islam* as well as between it and *dar al-harb*. They did this by casting a critical eye on the supposed unity of the Islamic community around the caliphate and finding it fictitious. For example, al-Mawardi elaborated the qualifications of the Caliph and made it seem that only one Caliph could rule and that he was the prime political authority. But al-Ghazzali argued that the Caliph has less power than al-Mawardi would have us believe. He also suggested that al-Mawardi, the great theoretician of the caliphate, did not adequately explain how the Caliph owes his very position to the real centres of power.[38] Ibn Taymiyya went further in stressing that, because of Islam's essential religious unity, it need not have only one political regime,[39] and Ibn Khaldun endorsed the idea by arguing that the factual rise and decline of political units is entirely natural and, by implication, in accord with Islam. Group feeling and religious devotion are neither intrinsically nor practically incompatible. In fact, they reinforce each other and help the political units to grow bigger. Ultimately, however, these various 'states' are destined to come and go according to the whim of history, the laws of social logic, and the will of Allah.[40] Although the caliphate provided the façade of unity, then, large cracks were discoverable and were made to seem perfectly normal.

For these reasons, it may be said that the theory supports a view at odds with that presented by many Western scholars and even by some Muslims. This alternative view is conformist because it holds that Islam endorses pluralism and encourages what we would call today a kind of peaceful coexistence between the Islamic community and the non-Islamic one. Indeed, the scriptures imply, and the legal texts make explicit, that Muslims must accommodate themselves to the fact, and even to the idea, of territorial sovereignty.

Consensus of action

The second reason why I think that Muslims today are able to accept the premises of the modern state system is that historical Islam – that is, Muslim statesmen acting in history – has proved to be more flexible than many might have thought possible. Bernard Lewis, for instance, thinks that Muslims showed little interest or ingenuity in dealing with the European powers until relatively late. According to him, Muslims had no particular interest in European scholarship in the sciences, philosophy, and literature until the late fourteenth century; he gives them little credit for transmitting Greek scholarship to medieval Europe, for, he says, most of the translations were done by non-Muslims, and at any rate 'the translation movement from the Greek came to an end in the tenth century'. Moreover, whereas Cambridge had a chair in Arabic by 1633 and Western studies of Middle Eastern languages and culture were well-developed by the time of the imperialist invasions at the end of the eighteenth century, 'it was not until well into the nineteenth century that we find any attempt to produce grammars and dictionaries of Western languages for Middle Eastern users'. Lewis also points out that the Muslim rulers' lack of interest in diplomatic relations with Westerners was shown in their reliance, particularly in the seventeenth century, on Westerners to represent them in European courts; Shah 'Abbas, for example, used Sir Anthony Sherley and his brother for this purpose.[41]

One can take exception, however, to the case that Lewis makes. For example, he seems to underestimate the genuine Islamic interest in Hellenism and the impact of such Muslim scholars as the twelfth-century writer Ibn Rushd (or Averroës), who translated, and wrote commentaries on, Plato's *Republic* and most of Aristotle's works ('books of learning from Byzantium/Written in gold upon a purple stain'[42]). In addition, Western travellers of the seventeenth century, such as Pietro della Valle and Olearius, came across Muslims in Persia who were studying Latin and German. More important, as one critic points out, Lewis's argument that Islam was a civilization without curiosity leaves the impression that it was uniquely so, particularly since he compares it with the Europe of the Renaissance. But if Islam was centred on itself and inward-looking for centuries, it was no different from Chinese and Hindu civilizations in certain periods – or from Christendom before the Renaissance, for that matter. In comparison, indeed, Islam seems to have been rather 'more open, notwithstanding its arrogance and conservatism'.[43]

MUSLIM RELATIONS WITH NON-MUSLIM STATES

But whether or not there was civilizational indifference, and whether or not this was due to an Islamic sense of superiority, it is clear that Muslim rulers found no difficulty at all in having formal diplomatic dealings with non-Muslims when it was necessary to do so. These relations occurred even in the Prophet's time. When he was unable to prevail over the Jews of Medina and the Christians of Aqaba and Najran, he concluded formal treaties with them. Moreover, he concluded the Hudaybiyya treaty, which brought a truce in 628 between the believers in Medina and the polytheists of Mecca when the former needed more time to gain strength against the latter; and he sent envoys to the Byzantine, Egyptian, Persian, and Ethiopian rulers (although these had the definite purpose in mind of inducing their conversion to Islam).

There are other early examples. The fifth Caliph of the Umayyads, 'Abd al-Malik, concluded a truce with the Byzantine ruler and even paid tribute to him in the interest of securing one flank in order to be able to turn against Muslim rebels on the other flank. His son, al-Walid, sought and received aid from the Byzantines in decorating the Prophet's Mosque in Medina and the Great Mosque in Damascus. We also know that trade regularly occurred between the Umayyads and the Byzantines.[44]

The 'Abbasids rather more routinely concluded treaties with foreigners, for a number of reasons – in particular (since the time of the Caliph Harun al-Rashid in the late eighth and early ninth centuries) in order to ransom their prisoners of war. They also regularly and lavishly received foreign envoys in Baghdad as representatives of fellow sovereigns. Around the year 800, for example, Caliph Harun received an ambassador from Charlemagne and sent one in return to Aix-la-Chapelle.

During the Crusades, too, there were several formal treaties with Christian princes, such as the one in 1192 between Saladin and the English king Richard I facilitating Christian pilgrimage to the Holy Land. Al-Malik al-Kamil, the fourth Ayyubid governor, agreed in 1227 to return Jerusalem to Christian control in order to avoid having his Muslim enemies make common cause with the invading German emperor Frederick II. For this, rather than earning eternal opprobrium, he is generally valued as a prudent and skilful statesman.

The Ottoman experience

The history of the Ottoman empire provides many examples of Muslim statesmen coming to terms with their position in the world. The most important Ottoman example is the treaty of alliance between Sulayman the Magnificent and Francis I of France in 1535. The Sultan, having failed to take Vienna a few years earlier, appreciated the need to divide his Christian opposition. The resulting treaty is remarkable for its flexible approach and shows how far he was willing to go: he recognized Francis as his equal; 'valid and sure peace' was to prevail between them for their lifetimes, and not merely for the ten years which many Muslim jurists prescribed as the maximum length of a treaty between Muslims and non-Muslims; French citizens in the Ottoman empire did not have to pay the tax required of *dhimmis*, and they were to be tried in their own courts for disputes among themselves; they were not to be made to become 'Turks' (i.e., Muslims); and other Christian rulers, including the Pope, were invited to receive similar benefits by adhering to the treaty.[45] In fact they did not do so, but Queen Elizabeth of England took advantage of this precedent and, with an eye on the Spanish threat, was able to secure what was essentially a commercial treaty with the Ottomans in 1580.

Formal capitulations were granted to France in 1569 and England in 1601. Eager to share in the commercial benefits which these privileges conferred on the two powers, the Dutch Republic dispatched an envoy, Cornelius Haga, to negotiate similar terms. Caught at first between the parsimony that his government imposed on him and the munificence that custom at the imperial court required, he succeeded eventually with the help of well-placed officials at court. In the agreement of 1612, the young Sultan Ahmad I made a number of concessions on the status of Dutch citizens resident in the empire: no tribute or tax would be exacted; the Islamic law of inheritance would not be applied to their estates; disputes among them would be settled exclusively by the Dutch authorities; and they could become Muslims only of their 'own free will' and not be made to convert. In further deference to European sensibilities, Dutch diplomats could produce wine for their own use.[46]

By the end of the seventeenth century two events ensured that the Ottomans would accept – or be forced to accept – the diversity of European politics. The Treaty of Westphalia (1648), which marked the end of the Thirty Years War among the major European powers, and the Muslims' failure, for the second time, to capture Vienna (1683) symbolize these developments. The first event gave formal expression to the definitive replacement of medieval Christendom by independent and secular nation-states, and the second meant that the

Ottomans lacked the power to push forward the frontiers of the Islamic empire against these states. A series of treaties now recorded the undeniable fact that the Muslims had met their match. The Treaty of Carlowitz in 1699 marked the clear defeat of the Ottomans at the hands of the Austrians and even provided for the cession of lands to the victor. The Ottomans ceded further lands to the Austrians in the Treaty of Passarovitz of 1718 (but they received some back, and the treaty must be seen as a territorial draw); and a 1739 treaty with the Russians pledged 'perpetual, constant, and inviolate peace . . . on land and sea'.[47]

The Ottomans made another kind of concession in the revision of Sulayman's treaty with France in 1740 and in the Treaty of Küçuk Kaynarca of 1774 with Russia. In the earlier capitulations, the Sultan had agreed that non-Muslim Europeans who were temporarily resident in the empire were not to be considered as *dhimmis*.[48] This was a deviation from the traditional view on the subject, but an even greater change occurred when it was accepted that the fate of Christians who were born into and lifelong residents of the empire might be of concern to the European powers. Although in 1649 the French king had unilaterally proclaimed his right to protect the Maronites of Lebanon, the Sultan now made some recognition that in limited circumstances non-Muslim rulers had a legitimate interest in the internal governance of *dar al-islam* itself.

The recognition, or concession, was never as considerable as the Christian powers said that it was, and hence Russia's claim to protect all Greek Orthodox subjects, a cause of the Crimean war, must be seen as a dubious interpretation of the treaty. Yet the Ottomans did agree to provisions that deviated from the traditional theory of the treatment of *dhimmis* and thereby conceded that non-Muslim powers had an interest in how the Ottomans treated their own Christian *dhimmis* (that is, Ottoman, not foreign, subjects). Beyond generally pledging 'to protect constantly the Christian religion', they agreed that, in territories being returned to them, 'the Christian religion shall not be exposed to the least oppression any more than its churches, and that no obstacle shall be opposed to the erection or repair of them; and also that the officiating ministers shall neither be oppressed nor insulted'. They went even further and agreed to a change with regard to some of their own Muslim subjects. Although Islamic law clearly prescribed death for apostasy, they agreed not to punish those Muslims who, as prisoners of war in Russia, voluntarily converted to Christianity.[49]

A movement away from the traditional theory which allowed no infidel interference in the affairs of *dar al-islam* was clearly under way, and concessions on the internal governance of the empire only increased as Ottoman rulers became acutely aware of the empire's weaknesses in the face of both Western and other Muslim powers. This general recognition largely accounts for the Tanzimat period, which occupied more than a third of the nineteenth century and saw a number of reforms designed to make the empire conform to the ideas of liberal – and efficient – government. Many of the leaders genuinely believed that a reordering was needed and that the Western model was attractive, but they were also well aware of the close connection between domestic reform and outside interference. At times they wanted to attract this interference. For example, in 1839 the Sultan, having recently suffered a major military defeat at the hands of his nominal vassal in Egypt, Muhammad 'Ali, hoped to convince the European powers that he was worthy of support. To this end he issued a decree known as the Hatt-i Sherif of Gülhane, which made a number of administrative reforms and announced, significantly, that 'these imperial concessions are extended to all our subjects, of whatever religion or sect they may be'.[50]

More often, however, in demonstrating their commitment to reorganizing their affairs, and particularly to treating their Christian subjects as equals, the Ottoman reformers hoped to ward off European interference. For there could be no doubt in their minds that the Europeans would intervene. In 1842 the Ottomans had no choice but to acquiesce in a virtual *démarche* on Lebanon. They were trying to reassert their control over the province, but the tension between the Maronite and Druze communities alarmed the great powers and prompted a plan for autonomy for the two communities. Although the Ottomans officially exchanged 'communications and observations' with the Europeans, it was clear to them that the future of their Lebanese subjects lay in the Europeans' hands. As the Ottoman Foreign Minister gingerly put it, 'the Sublime Porte in the search for a solution of so delicate a matter of domestic jurisdiction prefers to conform itself to their [European] wishes rather than oppose them'.[51]

Two years later, the Sultan again demonstrated his willingness to accommodate European sentiment. In 1844 he carried to a logical conclusion the Treaty of Küçuk Kaynarca (which seventy years earlier had accepted the conversion of Muslim prisoners of war in Russia) and unambiguously committed himself not to apply the death penalty to any Muslim who left Islam and converted. For a Muslim ruler to make concessions on the treatment of non-Muslims was one thing, but for him to make concessions on his dealings with fellow Muslims was decidedly another. There was more appeasing to be done, however. On the eve of the Congress of Paris after the Crimean war, for example, the Sultan tried again to prevent the Europeans from directly moving to arrange his domestic affairs. Although the British and French had sided with him against the Russians, who had pretended they were acting to protect the Greek Orthodox community, the support was dictated purely by balance-of-power considerations and certainly did not imply that the British and French were uninterested in how the Ottomans treated their *dhimmis*. In an imperial edict, or *firman*, in February 1856, the Sultan undertook to convince them of his good faith by vigorously reaffirming the rights conferred in 1839. He guaranteed that no discrimination in employment, taxation, or legal status would arise between his Muslim and non-Muslim subjects; that mixed tribunals would adjudicate disputes between them; and, generally, that no obstacles would be put in the way of practising any religion.

This approach was successful in securing the commitment of the great powers in the Treaty of Paris not to intervene in the relations of the Sultan with his subjects, but it did not succeed in actually preventing them from intervening. This the European powers decisively did in 1860 in Lebanon because of inter-community fighting and massacres, and because it appeared that the Druze were getting the upper hand over the Maronites. The following year, by agreement of the Sultan and the great powers, the Règlement Organique was promulgated, by which Mount Lebanon received a Christian governor and became virtually autonomous. In February 1867 France, with the backing of Britain and Austria, forced the Sultan to make further reforms, and it was under this shadow that he visited Europe, the first such peacetime visit by any Ottoman Sultan. The reforms on law and education that were to follow in the next few years led to the promulgation of the first written constitution in Islamic history. With the pattern of European intervention firmly imprinted on his consciousness, the Grand Vizier Midhat saw in the promulgation of a liberal constitution in 1876 a way to persuade European diplomats, then gathering in Istanbul to devise a reform programme, that the Ottomans could devise an effective programme themselves. It was also seen as a way to win support in the likely war with Russia, which in fact occurred the following year. Thus the constitution curtailed the power of the Sultan and reiterated that all citizens, regardless of religion, were equal before the law. With the unfavourable realities on his mind, the Sultan was obviously prepared to concede much to the infidels of *dar al-harb*.

The gambit did not work, though, and the Treaty of San Stefano, which ended the Russian–Ottoman war of 1877–8, merely left the empire further weakened. At the Congress of Berlin (which replaced San Stefano) the Sublime Porte had to make major territorial concessions and to acknowledge once again that it intended equality for all its citizens regardless of religion. Moreover, it accepted that the European powers were the protectors of 'ecclesiastics, pilgrims, and monks of all nationalities' in the empire, and of their property, and that it could not change the *status quo* in the Holy Land. A further price had been the abandonment of Cyprus in order to secure British participation in the congress. In return, the Sublime Porte secured what appeared to be a general British commitment to the defence of the empire against further Russian encroachments. Disraeli, the British Prime Minister, of course had no intention of giving such protection, although he did want to stop Russian moves towards Egypt.

Disraeli was able to exploit the Ottomans' conviction that they would need to make unprecedented offers to the British in order to obtain the protection they so greatly needed. In a letter to the Ambassador in Istanbul in November 1877, Disraeli revealed how far the Sublime Porte might be willing to go:

I ought to tell you . . . that six months ago, the present Grand Vizier was in communication with an Englishman at Constantinople, one Bright, since dead, with the view of raising a large sum from England by the sale of Turkish possessions; all this on a large scale – the *suzeraineté* of Egypt for example, or Crete . . .[52]

Although this did not come to pass, an indicator of Ottoman desperation in the face of the harsh settlement which Russia had imposed at San Stefano was the compromise of Islamic principles to apply in British Cyprus: a *shari'a* court ('Mehkéméi Shéri') was to take 'exclusive cognizance of religious matters, *and of no others*, concerning the Mussulman population'; and a Muslim official had to work with a British official to administer the property and funds of Islamic schools, mosques, and cemeteries.[53]

The Persian experience

Further evidence of Muslim conformity to territorial pluralism may be found in the history of the Persian empire. The Persians also quickly understood the superior power of the West and conformed to the idea of diplomatic relations with Western states. Although most of the Ottoman and Persian concessions were made under Western threat, this was not true of a royal decree granting capitulatory privileges to Europeans which Shah 'Abbas issued in 1600. Because its purpose was to attract a military alliance with European powers, it was immoderately generous:

Our absolute commaundement, will, and pleasure, is, that our cuntries and dominions shall be, from this day, open to all Christian people, and to their religion: and in such sort, that none of ours, of any condition, shall presume to giue them any euil word . . . Neyther shall our religious men, of whatsoeuer sort they [i.e., merchants] be, dare disturb them, or speake in matters of their faith. Neyther shall any of our justices haue power ouer their persons or goodes, for any cause or act whatsoeuer.[54]

That he was serious was confirmed by a royal decree of 1623 pertaining to the Dutch, whereby a Dutchman committing any crime was exempt from Persian justice, even if he 'should be found in the company of a woman', and by capitulations given to the French in 1708.[55]

The first formal alliance with a European power did not come until 1801, when Fath 'Ali Shah, seeking support for his territorial claims to Afghanistan, concluded a treaty with Britain. Britain had looked upon this treaty as a way of forestalling French designs on India, but it was to be disappointed very shortly thereafter when, in 1807, the Shah reversed alliances and concluded a treaty of alliance with France. According to its terms, Persia would break diplomatic relations with Britain in return for a permanent alliance of the two countries and for the more concrete reward of French support of the Persian claim to Georgia and a French undertaking to reorganize the Persian military along European lines.

It was to little effect, however, and in 1813, in the Treaty of Gulistan, Persia concluded its nine-year war with Russia by conceding ownership of Georgia and making other territorial concessions, including the exclusive right to use the Caspian Sea. Provision was also made for regular diplomatic contacts between the two countries and for commercial agents to reside in various cities. These concessions to Russia clearly increased Persia's vulnerability, and may have been responsible for yet another *renversement d'alliance*, this time in favour of Britain. In 1814, only seven years after the alliance with France, the Persian government pledged 'a daily increase of friendship which shall last for ever between the two most serene kings [of Persia and Britain], their heirs, successors, their subjects, and their respective kingdoms, dominions, provinces, and countries'. Britain promised not to interfere in internal Persian matters or to entertain any designs on its territory and, more positively, to send troops from India to help if a European power were to attack Persia. Persia promised not to allow any European power to transit its territory towards India.

The British were primarily concerned with French intentions in the area, and the Persians were worried about Russian territorial designs. There was also joint concern over Afghanistan. The British feared that if Persian power were to extend there, as it had during the period of Nadir Shah (1736–47), then Russia's influence and intrigue could not be far away, particularly since the Treaty of Gulistan allowed Russian consuls to operate throughout the Shah's dominions – a right not granted to the British. In the resulting 1814 treaty, there was a British concession of sorts to help in the Gulf: 'Should His Persian Majesty require assistance from the English Government in the Persian Gulf, they shall, if convenient and practicable, assist him with ships of war and troops.'[56] But much more important for our purposes was that Persia positively committed itself to fighting against its Muslim neighbour in the event of British–Afghan conflict. Relations with the infidel power were thus now valued for the advantage that they would give in inter-Muslim relations.

War between Persia and Russia went on, however, from 1826 to 1828. At its conclusion, in the Treaty of Turkmanchay, Persia made more territorial concessions and gave Russian citizens extraterritorial privileges. To assuage aggrieved Persian sentiment, Russia encouraged the Shah's designs on Afghanistan, but this encouragement only alarmed the British, who forced Nasir al-Din to pledge not to attack Herat. He went further and pledged himself to renounce any claim to sovereignty that would arise, in the manner of traditional caliphal practice, from having his name imprinted on coins or mentioned in the mosque sermon on Fridays. The Persians nevertheless occupied Herat in

October 1856, prompted by the Russians. It was to be a short occupation, however, for the British, having occupied part of Persian territory by way of response, forced the Persians' hand. They induced the Persians to abandon their claims and even to refer differences between them and their Afghan co-religionists to British mediation – a remarkable concession to an infidel power. The Persians also agreed to admit resident British consuls and generally to treat British subjects in Persia in line with most-favoured-nation provisions.

Persian–American relations were less contentious, but they demonstrate again the developing pattern of regular diplomatic contacts with non-Muslim states. Probably with Russian encouragement, the Persians sought a commercial treaty with the United States in the hope of securing aid for the development of the Persian navy. The resulting agreement of 1856 closely resembled the Persian–French agreement of the year before and was not in general as badly balanced as the agreements with Russia and Britain. The major lack of reciprocity was in the capitulatory privileges accorded to American citizens in Persia: disputes between them on Persian soil were to be resolved by reference to American law, whereas disputes between Persians on American soil were to be resolved not by reference to Persian law, but also by reference to American law. As Shah 'Abbas's decree showed as early as 1600, the Persians hoped once again that there would be utility in a freely granted concession to a more powerful state.

The experience elsewhere

As further evidence of the Muslim acceptance of pluralism and of peace with the infidels, one can cite examples from the relations between Western states and Muslim states on the periphery of these two great Islamic empires. There are many such instances, but I will refer to only a few. For example, Henry III of Castile sent envoys to the Central Asian ruler Timur (often known as Tamerlane), and they were present at the decisive battle of Ankara in 1402 when Timur defeated his Ottoman rival, Bayazid I. Timur treated the European envoys with respect and is reported to have greeted them with the expansive exclamation: 'Behold! here are the ambassadors sent by my son, the king of Spain, who is the greatest king of the Franks, and lives at the end of the world. These Franks are truly a great people, and I will give my benediction to the king of Spain, my son.'[57] Timur dispatched an ambassador of his own to this newly discovered 'son' at Castile, and charged him with delivering a flattering letter as well as the gift of jewels and of two Christian women who had been prisoners of Bayazid.

In North Africa the garrison of Algiers, nominally under Ottoman sovereignty, concluded a Treaty of Peace and Commerce with France in 1628, which established that they were 'true and good friends'.[58] In 1609 and 1610, the

During his campaigns in Asia Minor, Timur (Tamerlane; 1336–1405) received envoys from his fellow Muslim, the Sultan of Egypt (who accepted his authority), and from the non-Muslim Byzantine emperor, John VIII. Once Georgia had become his vassal state, he returned to the court at Samarkand and received there many other envoys.

This miniature depicts the arrival of ambassadors of Henry III of Castile (1379–1406) in 1403–4. The delegation is led by Ruy Gonzalez de Clavijo (d. 1412), who wrote a valuable account of court life at Samarkand, particularly the marriages of Timur's grandsons. The Europeans are here depicted in English-style costumes of the time of George III. B.M. Or. 158, folio 322b: *Malfuzat-i Timuri*, Mughal, early nineteenth century.

Moroccan king Mawlay Zaydan sent envoys to the Hague with the aim of securing a comprehensive trade agreement with the Dutch Republic. He hoped, no doubt, thereby to win political support for an attack across the Straits of Gibraltar on the Spanish. In the event, his entreaties resulted in a limited agreement whereby the Dutch provided armaments in return for access for their men-of-war to Moroccan ports. His successor, Sultan al-Walid, concluded a treaty, in 1631, with Louis XIII of France, principally to secure his promise not to assist rebels against the Sharif' authority. Such was also the purpose behind his ultimately unsuccessful letter to Charles I of England inviting a treaty.[59] Although the treaty of 1631 and a subsequent one in 1635 were temporary, the treaty of 1682 between Morocco and France declared that the future would be peaceful between the two. Morocco concluded a treaty with Britain in 1721 whereby 'the English may now, and always hereafter, be well used and respected by our Subjects'. In the event of a dispute between two British subjects in Morocco, the British consul was to adjudicate and 'do with them as he pleases', whereas in the event of a dispute between two Moroccans in British territory, it was to be settled by a tribunal of one Christian and one Muslim in accordance with British law.[60]

In the early nineteenth century, the European powers, particularly Britain, became increasingly alarmed over piracy in the Persian Gulf. The Bombay Marine took action against the pirates on several occasions, and after a number of unsuccessful attempts to impose order, the British government induced the *shaykhs* of trucial Oman and of Bahrain to sign a General Treaty in 1820. In undertaking not to engage in piracy, the Arabs bound themselves not only to peace with Britain but, more important, to rearrange their external affairs in accordance with British wishes. They were to align themselves with the British against the remaining piratical Arabs, but in the interests of peace and civilization they were not to be over-zealous:

The putting men to death after they have given up their arms is an act of piracy and not of acknowledged war; and if any tribe shall put to death any persons, either Mohammadans or others, after they have given up their arms, such tribe shall be held to have broken the peace; and the friendly Arabs shall act against them in conjunction with the British, and God willing, the war against them shall not cease until the surrender of those who performed the act and of those who ordered it.[61]

The trucial Arabs also committed themselves not to transport slaves. Although the Qur'an says that the manumission of slaves is a sign of virtue (90:12–13; also, 4:92, 58:3), the holding of and trafficking in slaves were tolerated, if not often encouraged, in Islamic history. The treaty thus imposed a change of longstanding Muslim practice.

It must be said, though, that the main European interests in the Middle East and North Africa were commerce and imperial rivalry. With the French in

راه نبود کرد زچهار دروازه که بچهار طرف آن مربع که نشته بودند و میان آن
فضائی بزرگ بود و درمیان فضا که نی طلبه سخنه مقدار لچرب و خیمه بزرگ
و نیز خطائی دربش لصنب کرده و ماندشاه نشینی دهانها دربشته و تالار ی
ازچوب و سایبان هابرافرخته چنانکه دران لچرب اپث بنیاتقط و زرزیر
و نیزه بزرگ صندل احی نهاده بوده و ازچرب و ازچپ دربست دکرصندلیها
و بمیان کجائی بچپ نشسته و امرای خطائی بطرف راست قرار کرفته

Shahrukh Mirza (1347–1447; r. 1405–47) was the fourth son of Timur and succeeded to the control of his Central Asian empire, including Persia and Turkistan. Shahrukh was considered a very devout Muslim, and even thought to have worked miracles. But his relations with fellow Muslim princes were sometimes strained and rarely cordial. His letters to the Ottoman Sultan, Muhammad I (r. 1413–21), reveal a certain arrogance, for example. But he was curious about, and respectful to, the Chinese, with whom he exchanged ambassadors. We know that Tibet sent an envoy to his court in 1421, and that he dispatched 'Abd al-Razzaq al-Samarqandi (1413–82), a noted historian, to China in order to maintain friendly and peaceful relations with the non-Muslim rulers there.

This miniature depicts a feast given by a Chinese dignitary in honour of the envoys sent to China by Shahrukh in 1421. B.M. Or. 12995, folio 80a: 'Aja'ib al-buldan, passages from Rawzat al-safa, Qajar, 1280 A.H./1863–4.

Algeria (1830) and the British entrenched in the Gulf and Aden (1839), the Arabs were in no position to resist European pressure for extraterritorial privileges. Capitulations became the standard practice: between Britain and Morocco in 1856, Britain and Tunis in 1863, and Italy and Tunis in 1868, for example. The Sultan of Muscat and Oman appreciated the value of granting these privileges to the United States, and in 1832 invited it to conclude such a treaty, which would also declare permanent peace between them. With this treaty, and similar ones with France in 1844 and the Netherlands in 1877, the Sultan was able for a period to escape the widening net of British protection in the Gulf.

The net was wide indeed. In 1835 Britain imposed a maritime truce during the pearling season on the warring coastal shaykhdoms of the Gulf and extended the hitherto temporary arrangements temporally and spatially in the 1853 Treaty of Maritime Truce in Perpetuity. Britain was able to extend its influence to the Wahhabi interior of Arabia when in 1866 it secured an agreement from the Saudi *amir*, 'Abdullah ibn Faysal, not to attack British-protected territories, including Muscat, except to collect *zakat* from the tribes, as 'has been customary of old'.[62] By mid-century, then, Christian Britain had achieved a position of predominant influence on inter-Arab, inter-Muslim, relations.

The policy of the Indian Muslim rulers towards, first, the Mongols and, then, the Hindu rulers of what is modern India demonstrates further the basic point that I have been making: that the Muslim prince was perfectly capable of grasping, and practising, the principle of territoriality with regard to non-Muslims. Iltutmish, the Sultan of Delhi from 1211 to 1236, concluded what was effectively a non-aggression pact with the Mongols, whereby he agreed not to give quarter to any Mongol enemy and they agreed to recognize and uphold the territorial integrity of his lands. Even when Baghdad, the imperial and caliphal centre, fell to the Mongols in 1258, the Sultan took no action and, indeed, gave a lavish reception to Mongol envoys a mere two years later. The policy apparently paid off, for Hulagu, the Mongol chief, is reported to have warned his men against encroaching on the Sultan's territory: 'If the hoof of your horse enters the dominion of Sultan Nasir-u'd-din, all the four legs of the horse shall be cut off.'[63] Later, although the Muslim Mughal emperors attempted to expand their realm at the expense of the non-Muslim Deccans, the impulse that operated was *territorial* expansionism, not *Islamic* expansionism. Moreover, the emperor Akbar showed his sensitivity to the nascent idea of 'India' rather than to the well-established idea of the *umma*, and this prompted his policy of *sulh kul* ('peace for all'), whereby Hindu and even Christian practices were accommodated and inter-community harmony in general promoted. This is far from the image that many writers give us of what Islam would allow.

In Southeast Asia, too, one can point to examples of Muslim rulers entering into regular diplomatic relations with non-Muslim powers. In 1287, for example, the Sultan of Pasai, in northern Sumatra, sent ambassadors to China; he also recognized the need to placate closer non-Muslim states, and gave non-Muslim Javanese a privileged position within his sultanate. With the direct intervention and competition of the European powers in the general area from the seventeenth century, a number of treaties followed. The Dutch, via the Dutch East India Company, came virtually to control parts of present Indonesia: west Sumatra (1663), Makasar (1667), Mataram (1677), and Bantam (1684). These treaties must be seen as the result of the badly unbalanced relationship between the Europeans and non-Europeans, but we must not lose sight of the desire of the local Muslim rulers to benefit from trading privileges with the non-Muslim outsider *and* to enlist Dutch assistance against local enemies. For example, Sultan Amangkurat of Mataram hoped by his alliance with the Dutch to keep his internal, religiously inspired opposition at bay and his vassals in line.[64]

In Sulu, the still-disputed southern region of modern-day Philippines, Sultan Muhammad Alimuddin showed his pragmatism time and again during his troubled reign. Recognizing the need to accommodate himself to the growing presence of Spain, the major European power in the area, he initiated efforts to conclude a treaty of peace with it. It had rebuffed such an overture in 1725, but finally in 1737 Alimuddin succeeded in obtaining what he wanted – a pledge of permanent peace and the commitment of Spanish aid if he was attacked, though not if attacked by a European power. In the event, the danger, as he probably foresaw, came from within (owing mainly to his openness to Jesuit activity in his realm); but what followed was a succession of treaties between Muslim claimants to power and Christian trading and political rivals. In return for trading privileges, the man who deposed Alimuddin enlisted the help of the British in 1761, through the agency of the East India Company; and, in 1763, with the growing strength of the British entering everyone's political consciousness, Alimuddin himself concluded a treaty with the Company. He received this pledge: 'If the King of Xolo [Sulu] should be attacked the English shall assist him with such Force as the situation of their affairs will admit.' His lack of sensitivity to preserving Muslim territory was shown the following year, once back on his throne, when he *sold* territory under his control to the British and reportedly made clear that 'what was sold was irredeemable'.[65]

In what is now Malaysia, Sultan Muhammad Jiwa of Kedah, facing opposition from his courtiers and their allies in Selangor, also tried to enlist British support, again by means of the East India Company, but nothing came of the negotiations because of the Company's unwillingness to antagonize the rulers in Selangor.[66] And in 1819 the Sultan of Aceh, a region of modern Indonesia, concluded an agreement with Sir Stamford Raffles which, while conferring trading privileges on the British, was designed primarily to secure their recognition that he, rather than his rival from Penang, was the rightful ruler of Aceh. The Sultan was moved to give the British the right to decide which foreigners could reside in his realm: he agreed to exclude other Europeans and Americans, and even to exclude British subjects to whom the British resident agent objected.[67]

General historical patterns

Three points emerge from this review of Muslim relations with non-Muslim powers, especially the Western powers:

(1) If they did not exactly concede that the Western states were their equals, the Muslim states did regularly enter into territorial agreements with them and concluded peace, even 'peace in perpetuity', with them. Thus Muslim practice, particularly from the sixteenth century, put a full stop to the earlier debate among Muslim jurists as to the valid length of a peace treaty between Muslims and non-Muslims. Building on the example of the Hudaybiyya treaty which the Prophet himself concluded with the Meccans, most jurists, at least of the Hanafi and Shafi'i schools, had argued that such an agreement with non-believers could not last more than ten years.[68] The overwhelming weight of practice clearly pushed this view to the side.

(2) Muslims went further and virtually conceded that outsiders, contrary to the classical and medieval legal theory, had the right to interfere in the internal affairs of the Islamic homeland. This modification of the traditional approach to *dhimmis*, and of the unquestionable and complete jurisdiction of the *shari'a*, is an indicator of the extent to which territorial pluralism had moved to the front of the Muslims' political consciousness.

(3) Most of these modifications were a reaction to superior Western power, but sometimes they were a deliberate act of policy aimed at enlisting Western help against challenges from other Muslim entities. This pattern was true, for example, of the Ottomans, who were concerned about the successes of Muhammad 'Ali; the Persians, who were worried about the Ottomans; and many of the Southeast Asian rulers, who were worried about each other. Even the idea of the *umma*, then, did not prevail over the practice of regular international relations with non-Muslim states.

INTER-MUSLIM RELATIONS

As the last point makes clear, if Islamic history shows that Muslims came to terms with the reality of contending, if not superior, centres of power in the non-Muslim world, it also indicates that they accepted the reality of separate power centres within the Islamic *umma*. An early example is the dispute between 'Ali, the Prophet's son-in-law and the fourth Caliph, and Mu'awiyya, the governor of Syria and later the first Umayyad Caliph. Mu'awiyya called for arbitration as a way of resolving the bitter struggle over the legitimate succession to the caliphate, and 'Ali, unwisely as it turns out, agreed. The text of the arbitration agreement is remarkable for the way it makes the men equal: 'Ali, the Caliph, is described as representing 'the people of Kufa and their followers of the believers and Muslims', and Mu'awiyya, the rebel, is described as representing 'al-Sham [Syria] and their followers of the believers and Muslims'.[69] It is as if Pope Gregory had agreed to have his differences with Henry IV settled by arbitration at Canossa.

Later Islamic history confirms this tendency of the Muslim sovereign to concede that other, nominally subject, rulers had more power. This was the case at the 'Abbasid court itself when first the Barmaks and then the Buwayhids, with the connivance of the army, took charge. But more noteworthy is the centre's loss of control over the outlying provinces: for example, Spain under the Umayyads, Tunisia under the Aghlabids, and Egypt and Syria under the Tulunids, the Fatimids, the Ayyubids, and the Mamluks. In many cases, the Caliph's gift of a title-deed (*tasjil*) or land grant (*iqta'*) to the regional rulers gave a certain legitimacy to his loss of control,[70] but there was no disguising the fragmentation of the *umma*. To cite one example of how far territoriality had become entrenched within the *umma*, the Mamluk ruler of Egypt, Qalwun, in 1288 authorized Egyptian traders to carry passports with them on their visits to the Yemen and India to give to any merchant desiring to travel to Egypt. The idea of the unity of the empire remained only in the Caliph's name being mentioned in the Friday sermon and appearing on the coinage, as well as in occasional tribute being paid by the local dynasts.

The Ottoman experience

The Ottomans were unable to force the submission of the Persian Shi'a, but in 1590 the two rivals concluded a treaty whereby the Persians agreed to stop the cursing of the first three Caliphs, whom the Shi'a did not accept, and to cede large amounts of territory to the Ottomans. It was a religious and territorial compromise which Shah 'Abbas felt that he had to make if he was to prevent the Uzbeks from moving in on his empire from the east. The two came to a *modus vivendi* in 1639, ambitiously designed to last 'till the day of resurrection';[71] and it did last, remarkably, for more than eighty years. Significantly, the treaty laid down a frontier between the two states of the *umma* which remained the undisputed frontier for two hundred years.

The Ottomans, however, did not give up their attempts to encroach on Persia's territory, and in particular, in the 1720s, tried to take over the northwestern provinces. The general who was to become Nadir Shah brilliantly recovered the territory and later, in 1743, went on to inflict a major defeat on the Ottomans at Erivan. But internal revolts forced him into a truce, and shortly thereafter, in a treaty of 1746, the two antagonists agreed to exchange ambassadors every three years. This formalizing of what we would call today the interstate relationship between them must be set beside a remarkable statement in an appendix to the treaty, which seems to suggest movement towards unifying the Islamic community: 'The Persian people, having totally abandoned the unseemly innovations introduced in the time of the Safavis and having embraced the religion of the Sunnis, shall mention the Orthodox Caliphs, of blessed memory, with respect and veneration.' But this concession had more to do with the personal ambitions of Nadir Shah, who, in attempting to force the Ja'fari sect on his people and to get it recognized as the fifth Sunni school, hoped to become Caliph. His reputed embracing of Sunni Islam, along with his tyrannical ways, prompted his assassination before the treaty was ratified. However, in any event, the appendix itself went on to endorse the idea of territorial division between the two states by requiring each to deny refuge to citizens fleeing from the other's jurisdiction and to extradite any who did cross the border.[72]

The treaty of Erzerum (1823) reaffirmed the substance of this arrangement, minus the Persian deference to the orthodox Caliphs, and committed both not to interfere in each other's domestic affairs and to the idea that 'henceforward the Sword of Enmity shall be sheathed'.[73] The interstate relationship was even further formalized in 1847, when the boundary was reaffirmed, and in 1878 at the Congress of Berlin, when the Ottomans, weakened by war with the Russians, were impelled to cede territory to the Persians.

This pattern of external pressure on the Ottoman empire had a precedent in 1840, when Britain, Russia, Austria, and Prussia, against the wishes of France, induced the Sublime Porte to make territorial concessions to Muhammad 'Ali in Syria as well as in Egypt where he was established. The idea was to buy him off, inducing him to withdraw from Arabia, Crete, and other eastern parts, and thus to put an end to his formidable challenge to the integrity of the empire. Even the inclusion of deferential provisions to the superior sovereignty of the Sultan, such as collecting taxes and maintaining the army in his name, could not mask the concession to pluralism within the empire. Indeed, in the very next year, when British and Austrian troops defeated Muhammad 'Ali (who had not accepted the offer made to him), the Sultan conceded – for the greater good of stability – that this rebel was to be governor of the Sudan as well as of Egypt, and that in Egypt he and his heirs were to be governors as of right without need of formal investiture in the imperial capital.

The idea that Egypt was a separate state gained further currency in Ottoman circles when, in 1882, Britain invaded the territory in order to safeguard its financial investments and to secure the defence of the Suez Canal. As it turned out, the Sublime Porte did not ratify the Anglo–Ottoman convention of 1887 because of French and Russian opposition to the vague terms for the withdrawal

The Ottoman Sultan Bayazid I (ca. 1360–1403) extended the empire's territory in Anatolia and Asia and brought his realm into Europe as far as Athens and the Peloponnese. He was preparing to lay siege to Constantinople when the victories of the Central Asian Muslim prince Timur turned his attention eastward. In a devastating battle near Ankara in 1402, Bayazid lost almost all of his Janissaries to Timur's troops and was himself taken prisoner.

This miniature depicts Bayazid being brought before Timur after the battle of Ankara. It is now generally believed that Timur treated Bayazid with consideration, not imprisoning him in an iron cage as legend holds; it is even thought that there was distress in Timur's court when Bayazid died there in 1403. But despite this, the territorial rivalry between the two Muslim rulers had been intense. B.M. Or. 1359, folio 413a: *Zafar-namah*, Shiraz/Safavid, 959 A.H./1552.

of British forces. But what is more noteworthy for our purposes is that the Ottoman negotiators accepted, however unwillingly, the separate identity of Egypt – even though still ostensibly subordinate to Ottoman suzerainty – and recognized, at least tacitly, an equal role in Egyptian affairs for Britain. Thus, 'Egypt shall enjoy the advantages of territorial immunity', and, in the event of needing to intervene, 'the Ottoman troops as well as the British troops will be withdrawn from Egypt as soon as the causes requiring this intervention shall have ceased'.[74]

Although these examples suggest that the Ottomans had no real choice in the matter, it must be noted that they were always rather half-hearted in their attempts to use religious authority to bolster their political authority over other Muslims, and gave considerable freedom to such local rulers as the Mamluks in Egypt. In the early days of the empire, the Sultan was content to think of himself as *primus inter pares* and the greatest *ghazi* (warrior), and not as Caliph. When the Sultan's role as Caliph came to be emphasized, as in the Treaty of Küçuk Kaynarca in 1774, there was at the same time the recognition that religious privilege did not necessarily mean political privilege: 'As to the ceremonies of religion, as the Tartars profess the same faith as the Mahometans, they shall regulate themselves, with respect to His Highness, in his capacity of Grand Caliph of Mahometanism, according to the precepts prescribed to them by their law, without compromising, nevertheless, the stability of their political and civil liberty.'[75] This acceptance of a *de facto* division of religious and secular influence made it easy for the Ottomans to concede Muslim territorial pluralism when the Western great powers agitated for this in the nineteenth century; it was a point they had already conceded.

Indeed, the stress on the coincidence of the sultanate and caliphate had less to do with affirming the Ottomans' supremacy over other Muslims than with impressing the non-Muslim powers. Abdülhamid I, for example, made a show of his caliphal mantle in the late eighteenth century in order to try to secure the same right of patronage over co-religionists abroad as Empress Catherine had recently demanded at Küçuk Kaynarca. The late Ottoman treaties confirm that, apart from having his name mentioned in the public prayers as Caliph, the Sultan abandoned any pretence of wielding religious authority over the *umma*. He left this authority to the local *'ulama* (although these were nominally appointed from the imperial centre by the paramount member of the court *'ulama*, the *shaykh al-islam*).[76] The caliphate counted for little, therefore, and whatever universalist pretensions there were gave way to pluralist fact.

The experience elsewhere

This was also the situation with the Shahs. In addition to the agreements made with the arch-rival Ottomans, they entered into a territorial arrangement with

This miniature depicts Kamal al-Din Sadr (Husayn), envoy of Sultan Husayn Mirza (1438–1506) of Herat, at the court of Shah Isma'il (1487–1524) of Persia. Isma'il, who in 1504 had extended his realm as far eastward as Herat, is being congratulated on his conquests. In sending the ambassador, Sultan Mirza made a virtue out of necessity and grudgingly acknowledged Isma'il's conquests. At the same time he implied that there was a boundary to be upheld between his own territory and that of his fellow Muslim prince. B.M. Or. 3248, folio 110b: untitled history of Shah Isma'il, Isfahan/Safavid, ca 1650.

the Sultan of Muscat in 1856 and agreed to lease the port of Bandar 'Abbas and the islands of Qishm and Hormuz for a fixed annual rent. The Persians had designs on Afghanistan, but, as I mentioned earlier, Britain soon saw to it that these ambitions were curtailed. A treaty of 1856 obligated the Persians to resort to the good offices of the British in the event of differences with the Afghans, and this is exactly what they did in 1872 when they disagreed over title to Sistan and over division of the waters of the Helmand river. The two countries again called on a British arbitrator in 1902 after the course of the river shifted and thereby invalidated the earlier arbitral award.

Further afield, there were regular diplomatic relations, too, between the Muslim principalities of Southeast Asia: for example, between Chirebon, Damak, and Japara on the northern coast of Java. The Sultan of Aceh, 'Ala al-Din Ri'yat Shah al-Qahhar, who reigned between 1537 and 1568, sent envoys to the Ottoman Sultan several times in the hope of obtaining assistance against the Portuguese.

The relations of Mughal emperors with other Muslim rulers also illustrate how religious affinity really took second place to dynastic and imperial interests. The great diplomatic game of the region and the time brought the Sunni Mughals into broad alliance with the Shi'i Persians: both, though for different reasons, wanted to destroy the power of the Uzbekhs of Transoxiana and to take their territory. But since the Sunni Ottomans supported the Uzbekhs in their desire to contain Persian ambitions, conflict arose between the Sunni Mughals and the Sunni Ottomans. The distance between them precluded outright hostility, but even diplomatic exchanges were rare: for example, only two exchanges took place during the rule of Shah Jahan (1628–58) and only one Ottoman envoy travelled to the court of his son, Aurangzeb (1658–1707). But there were more regular Mughal contacts with other Muslim rulers. Akbar, for instance, sent envoys regularly to local princes, such as, in 1577, to the prince of Ahmadnagar and, in 1579, to the princes of Bijapur and Golconda, in order mainly to guarantee they would not create difficulties for him.

Naturally, the relations between Transoxiana and the Mughal empire were more troubled, and from time to time religion did surface as a bone of contention between them. Yet this really was a secondary matter and merely provided an excuse for the breaking of relations. The Uzbekh ruler 'Abdullah Khan, for example, said in 1586 that he had interrupted relations with Akbar because of his heresy, a charge which Akbar refuted by promising to do battle against the infidel Portuguese, who 'have lifted up the head of turbulence and have stretched out the hand of oppression upon the pilgrims to the holy places'.[77] The real attraction, and inherent problem, of their relationship was territorial ambition: 'Abdullah said the Persian Shah was heretical, yet he also wanted to partition Persia with Akbar; Akbar remembered his alliance with the Persians and emphasized that the Shah was related to the Prophet, yet nonetheless he wanted Qandahar. Because of common territorial designs, then, a treaty of alliance was concluded, also setting the boundary between the Uzbekh and Mughal realms. But nothing came of it. Akbar's greater interest lay, as he knew, in alliance with the Persians, with whom relations were correct but never cordial and always founded on expediency. The point is that these Muslim rulers regarded diplomatic relations with fellow Muslims both as normal and as a tool for self-aggrandizement rather than confraternity. This, indeed, was the message that Fakhr-i-Mudabbir left in his review of the diplomat's role in *Adab al-harb*: 'When he is asked about [his own] king, territory, retainers and subjects, he should speak in such a way as to place them in a superior position to all others.'[78]

THE TWENTIETH CENTURY

The present century has witnessed the emergence of independent states throughout the earlier colonized world, including the areas in which Muslims are found in significant numbers. If one is searching for the root causes of this emergence, there is no need to look much beyond the obvious pattern of internal Muslim weakness and external pressure and intervention, particularly in the case of the Ottoman empire, which the preceding pages have documented. The weakness of Muslims invited a European interregnum, which in turn fostered the growth of indigenous nationalisms. We can date the entrenched presence of Westerners roughly from Napoleon's invasion of Egypt in 1798, and certainly from the French control of Algeria in 1830, the British control of Aden in 1839, and the spread of French Catholic and American Protestant missionaries throughout the Middle East by mid-nineteenth century.

In the case of the Ottoman empire, internal weakness and external pressure probably reached their peak in the aftermath of the Young Turk revolution and the overthrow of Sultan Abdülhamid II. These events put both the non-Turkish imperial citizens and the European powers on notice that the time was ripe to make greater demands. In June 1913 Christian and Muslim Arabs met in Paris to demand decentralization of power and recognition of Arabic as an official language, and in the following month the British succeeded in obtaining the Sublime Porte's agreement to the virtual independence of Kuwait and the real independence of Bahrain, as well as its acknowledgement of general British hegemony in the Persian Gulf region. Filling the void created by the disintegration of the empire was the aim of the British and French during World War I, when, even as they were entreating Sharif Husayn of Mecca to declare an Arab revolt against the Turks in return for Arab independence, they were planning to divide the Middle East into spheres of influence. This is the well-known story of the Sharif–McMahon correspondence, leading to the 'Arab Revolt' of June 1916 and the secret Anglo–French agreement of a few months before, which ostensibly undercut the British pledge but whose gist may have been known by the Sharif at the time of his declaration of the revolt.

In any event, Husayn's appeal was limited mainly because Arabs outside the Hijaz, or western Arabia, looked upon it as a dynastic move. This was also the time of reaffirmation of the imperium – for example, the British absorption of Qatar in November 1916 into the network of treaty relations which asserted British predominance in the area. But despite this and the failure of the pan-Arab revolt, there was undeniable movement towards the emergence of local nationalisms. Some Arabs would have preferred a form of broad Arab nationalism, a Greater Syria, for example, uniting Arabs from several regions into a single whole, but instead the mandate system divided them into units called Trans-Jordan, Syria, Lebanon, and Iraq and through these pushed them into a system of nation–states.

The progress was not always smooth: the Shi'i *'ulama* in Iraq, for instance, instigated a tribal revolt against the British by issuing a *fatwa* (religious–legal opinion), which declared: 'It is not licit for a Muslim to choose a non-Muslim to govern Muslims.'[79] Yet the emerging national elites – composed of some aristocratic elements, but predominantly of the upper bourgeoisie – saw more clearly than the religious elements that there was much to gain from the mandatory arrangement. They would get protection for themselves against internal enemies and at the same time international recognition, thereby solidifying their power in two ways. The elites in the nearby non-mandatory countries also recognized the urgent need to secure international approbation, if for no other reason than to keep the British and French at safe distance. Reza Khan, later to become the first Pahlavi Shah, had recently come to power by military coup when, in 1921, he obtained from the new government of the Soviet Union, itself anxious for international recognition, a renunciation of all past claims to Iranian territory. Also in 1921 Mustafa Kemal Atatürk, in the process of consolidating his power and presiding over the emergence of a Turkish nation-state from the ashes of the Ottoman empire, concluded a treaty with the Soviet Union that disposed of territorial problems between them and committed them both to resisting an imposed settlement of World War I. Imam Yahya of the Yemen saw an opportunity to thwart any move by Britain to extend its influence over his domain by concluding a treaty with Mussolini's government in 1926, whereby Italy, for its own imperial interests, became the first European country to recognize 'the full and absolute independence of the Yemen and its Sovereignty'. [80]

The Al Saud in the 1920s were another example of an elite, which like the Yemeni elite, was traditionally and tribally based, but which sought international acceptance as a way of strengthening its position both at home and abroad. 'Abd al-'Aziz, who was to become Saudi Arabia's first king, was especially alive to the need to secure British recognition in particular, since his base of support within Arabia was narrow and he faced significant opponents in the region in the shape of the family of the British-backed Hashimites. He was so eager to get this recognition that, in 1915, in return for a formal treaty with Britain, he reluctantly agreed to restrict his foreign relations to dealings with the British alone, or with others through and with the approval of the British government. He also agreed not to give oil and other concessions without British approval. In 1925 he sought a revision of the treaty which would reflect his recent victory over the Hashimites in the Hijaz and which would make him seem more independent of the British. This appearance of independence was important, since now that he controlled the holy cities of Mecca and Medina he could not risk being seen as a subordinate of an infidel power in the eyes of his own conservative followers, or in the eyes of Muslims throughout the Muslim world, upon whom his treasury would depend for regular revenues. Most of the cards, however, remained in British hands, as one might expect, and ʿAbd al-ʿAziz had to abandon some of his aspirations.

The resulting treaty of 1927 highlights three points of general significance to the argument at hand, despite obvious differences in the composition of elites from case to case:

(1) The local elite sought great-power recognition primarily of 'the complete and absolute independence of [its] dominions'. ʿAbd al-ʿAziz eventually sought similar recognition from several great powers, including the Soviet Union and Nazi Germany.

(2) In securing this recognition, the elite had not only to recognize in its turn the validity of 'peace and friendship' with infidel powers but also to do much more – to concede to them a certain amount of power over the disposition of its own government. For example, although he would not be moved to abolish slavery altogether, ʿAbd al-ʿAziz did agree to allow the British consul in Jidda to continue the practice of manumitting slaves and 'to co-operate by all the means at his disposal with His Britannic Majesty in the suppression of the slave trade'.[81]

(3) The elite accepted that its relations with the Muslim elites of neighbouring territories were to be based on European norms of interstate conduct and were of international concern, and not on the idea that they were all brothers in one community whose relations were of no concern to non-Muslims. There is no doubt that the rhetoric of brotherhood was often voiced, and we know that ʿAbd al-ʿAziz in particular expressed objection to the public admission that an outside power could affect his relations with fellow Arabs.[82] In the end, however, he and other Muslim rulers demonstrated time and again their implied acceptance of the interstate model by trying to extend their own territory at the expense of their 'brethren'. ʿAbd al-ʿAziz, for example, tried, unsuccessfully it turned out, to wrest Aqaba and Maʿan from Trans-Jordan in the negotiations leading up to the

treaty of 1927, and in the mid-1930s he similarly tried to extend his domain as much as he could at the expense of Kuwait, Qatar, the Trucial Shaykhdoms, and above all the Yemen, with which he went to war.

In practice – despite the theory – Muslim–Western relations and inter-Muslim relations came to be measured by the yardstick of territorial sovereignty, while the yardstick of the *umma*, based on not conceding anything to the infidels and on keeping the relations of Muslims a family affair, seems no longer to have been applied. This is not to say that anyone believed these relations to be on an equal footing, and in fact one can argue that it was precisely because the Muslim elites clearly knew they were in an inferior position to the Western imperialists that they so quickly and effectively accepted the interstate model. It was not simply because it was imposed on them, though there is of course much to this argument: it had more to do with their learning early on that, to protect their own prestige and power, they had to play the international game. Playing this game meant first of all securing recognition from the great powers.

This whole-hearted commitment to national pluralism is demonstrated, above all, by the value that the Muslim elites attached to the League of Nations. Britain was keen to have Iraq and Egypt admitted as a form of international approbation of its new relationship with them, so keen in fact that it asked for an unprecedented special session to admit Egypt, lest any delay in placating Egyptian sovereign sensibilities endanger the 1936 treaty regulating the British military presence in the Suez Canal zone. For their part, the governments of Egypt, Iraq, Afghanistan, and Turkey were equally eager to gain admission, and to join Persia, a founding member of the League, in order to certify that they had arrived as full members of the exclusive international club. The League Covenant did not formally acknowledge the equality of members, but it did bestow equal voting rights on all members in the Assembly.

Though not exactly equal, they were at least less unequal than they had been formerly, and this new status began to work to their advantage, since the great powers now became reluctant to appear heavy-handed. In the dispute over the Anglo-Persian Oil Company in 1932–3, for example, the Persian government eventually secured a more favourable financial arrangement than had previously prevailed, and in the dispute between France and Turkey in 1936–8 over Alexandretta, then in the French mandate of Syria, Turkey eventually secured full possession of the province.

Of supreme importance to the Muslim states, as it was to every other state, was the principle whereby the League Covenant sanctified the territorial and political independence of every member. Turkey, Persia, and Iraq were particularly concerned to see that the essentials of the Covenant, pre-eminently this one, should remain unchanged. Persia and Iraq had good cause to be worried about this principle because they were involved in an ancient territorial dispute.

Even though the Iraqi government was not happy about the League's intervention on behalf of the Assyrians in Iraq in 1932, it appealed to the League's Council to take up the problem of control over the Shatt al-'Arab, the strategic waterway formed by the confluence of the Tigris and Euphrates rivers. There were pressing regional security reasons why the two countries came to an agreement in 1937, but the use of the League's machinery made the significant political point that both governments wanted to establish – that the dispute was international, just like disputes between Muslim and Western states or between Western states themselves. Each of the disputants had territorial claims and national interests, and neither expected that these would automatically coincide or be easily reconciled.

Once committed to the international game, then, there was no backing out: national divisions among Muslims were the logical consequence of the insistence on the independence and integrity of one's own territory. In inter-Muslim relations, the norm roughly from the 1930s to today has been to acknowledge the spiritual and cultural unity of faith while insisting on preserving the reality of territorial divisions. In 1936 Saudi Arabia and Iraq, for example, referred almost in the same breath to 'the ties of the Islamic faith and of racial unity which unite them' and to the desire 'of safeguarding the integrity of their territories'; and in 1938 Iraq and Persia were desirous both 'of strengthening bonds of brotherly friendship and good understanding' and 'of settling definitively the question of their frontier between their two States'.[83]

Every multilateral agreement up to the present makes perfectly clear that the form of association contracted must not be seen as a derogation or qualification of the individual sovereignties of the contracting parties. The Sa'dabad Pact (1937) among Afghanistan, Iran, Iraq, and Turkey insisted that each refrain from interfering in the internal affairs of the others and respect the inviolability of common frontiers. The Arab League Pact (1945), although 'desirous of strengthening the close relations and numerous ties which link the Arab states', is committed to preserving the independence and sovereignty of its members and requires that 'each member state shall respect the systems of government established in the other member states and regard them as exclusive concerns of those states'.[84] The now-defunct Baghdad Pact (1955, later CENTO) among Turkey, Iraq, Pakistan, and Iran insisted that they each not interfere in the other's internal affairs, and the Charter of the Organization of the Islamic Conference (1972), which has members from across the broad Muslim world, insists on the same point. It goes on to spell out in unambiguous terms that the organization is based on the principles of 'respect of the sovereignty, independence and territorial integrity of each member State' and of 'abstention from the threat of use of force against the territorial integrity, national unity or political independence of any member State'. By now these are commonplace commitments, even when those states that voice them also say they are 'convinced that their common belief constitutes a strong factor of rapprochement and solidarity between Islamic peoples'.[85]

The lessons of historical experience

The general point I wish to make is simple: far from recoiling at the thought of a pluralist world order, Muslim statesmen have readily conformed to it. In many cases they have been making a virtue out of necessity, but I have also shown how at other times they have made concessions to bolster their own positions, especially against Muslim rivals. In any case, what count are the rationale and the effect.

There is good reason, as I have argued, for suggesting that, in finding territorial divisions acceptable, Muslims can find justification in part in the early thinking of the community. They can also find justification in the practical conduct of early Muslims. There is a view that Islam had to struggle against the fact that it had no ingrained territorial idea because early converts were nomads and because Islam quickly became an urban phenomenon – both indicating the absence of attachment to the land. This argument, however, ignores the fact that some land was cultivatable, and that where this was so, an inherent sense of territorial divisions prevailed: this territory belongs to Ahmed and that territory to 'Abdullah. When the land could not be cultivated and nomadism or semi-nomadism resulted, one can point to the tribal pattern of keeping to set zones, or *diras*, to show that there was indeed a concept of territoriality which Muslims inherited and accepted. Some of these zones were distinct and separate, and some were accepted as held in common; but present always was a clear understanding of what belonged to whom and where 'borders' lay. If it was not a concept of territorial sovereignty, then at least it was a concept of territorial exclusivity.[86]

But even if this were not the case, and even if Muslims were forced to accept reality because of their weakness, we would not be able to dismiss the historical evidence as irrelevant. On the contrary, first, it constitutes what jurisprudents called the consensus of action (*ijma' al-fi'l*). It is the record of what Muslims have done, and this record is at least as reliable an indicator of what Islam is as what Muslims say it is.

Second, dogma interacts with ritual, the past with the present, to define one's faith. There is a complex dynamic by which practice that has evolved modifies theory, and the believer's perception of theory begins to change accordingly. Past conduct has a way of structuring what people expect and even what they value. But the present, with its powerful immediacy, has a way of structuring the past and making it seem familiar. As one writer has put it, 'The past influences a people's perceptions of the present; but the present provides an ever changing environment that constantly expands the limits of the human intellectual and perceptual horizon. This in turn modifies a people's memory of its past.'[87]

In this case, the historical pattern of territorial pluralism that I have described cannot fail to leave its mental impact on the believer and affect his view of Islam's compatibility with territorial pluralism. This overwhelmingly conformist pattern need not go on of course, and Muslims, finding the concessions to the infidels distasteful and no longer tolerable, may come to reject conformism. But the omnipresence of national pluralism today will provide a strong incentive to viewing the past, both practice and theory, simply as earlier versions of the present national pluralism. I will turn to this dynamic in Chapter 4. But, given that this pluralism is tantamount to an international law of nature now, we may well wonder whether there is any doubt that Muslims will go on for the foreseeable future much as they have in the past – contriving to regard what Cromer called 'the ceaseless jar of petty international rivalries'[88] as entirely unexceptional, and the nation-state as a normal feature of the Muslim experience.

4   The modern intellectual consensus on the nation-state

In addition to the theory and the historical experience described in Chapter 3, there is, as noted, a third reason why Muslims today are able to accept the premises of the international system. It is that an intellectual consensus has developed which sees the nation-state as part of the nature of things and perhaps even as inherently Islamic. This is the 'consensus of speech' (*ijma' al-qawl*), which jurisprudents have discussed, but which I take to involve a broader range of people than the traditionally recognized *'ulama*. It includes political leaders and the well-educated, predominantly young, professionals who constitute the elite. This consensus is so strong, however, and the elite's impact on shaping opinion so great, that in fact most citizens seem to share in it.

It is not surprising that the intellectuals hold this view on the nation-state, since they have benefited from, or laboured under (depending on one's point of view), the experience of Western-inspired nationalism. Alien ideas began to penetrate the Muslim world almost from the beginning of the Islamic era, but Western liberal ideas came to permeate its political heartland, the Middle East, in the early nineteenth century. These Western ideas became both pronounced and more widespread throughout the nineteenth century as the European powers competed with one another for influence in the Middle East, Asia, and Africa.

The intrusion set in motion a process of intellectual ferment in which succeeding generations of Muslim thinkers have sought to come to terms with the obvious technological and military superiority of the West – without abandoning the idea that Islam remains at the centre of the believer's life. It has not been a simple search: some have wanted primarily to avoid a blind return to the past and have accepted the need for change; others have wanted primarily to purify Islam of the innovations and deviations which the Westerners and, worse, Westernized Muslims introduced; others have come to see too many contradictions between Islam and the demands of modern politics and have opted for the restriction of Islam to the individual's private life; and still others have held a variety of opinions in between.

The roots of the consensus

However many schools of thought there are when it comes to answering the general question of how to be modern and Islamic at the same time, the situation is simpler when it comes to the basic question of international relations: is the nation-state acceptable to Muslims? It seems to me that those who answer that it is acceptable constitute the majority.

The nationalist intellectual current came into being, and then prevailed, in the Middle East (which experienced nationalism earlier than other Muslim lands), as a result of the deterioration of the Ottoman empire. The obvious weaknesses of the empire led many Arabs as well as Turks to look for an alternative, less grand form of political organization. The growing Western presence in the region as the Ottomans became weaker introduced the idea of the ethnically based and powerful nation-state as just such an alternative. The European model began to seem attractive, especially to the upper middle-class. Since many of these were non-Muslims, mainly Christians, they had much to gain in status and influence by espousing the secularist, nationalist ideas of the imperial rulers. Many of the Sunni *'ulama* also saw benefits in cooperating with the colonial establishment. This very same Western immediacy, however, in such socially and economically stratified societies as Egypt, Syria, or India, moved the lower bourgeoisie, the landed aristocracy, and some of the *'ulama*, all traditionally oriented and suspicious of the cultural affectations and political pretensions of the upper middle-class, to look to an even grander notion than that of the Ottoman empire. This they found in pan-Islam.

Ironically, the rise of pan-Islamic sentiments helped to establish the credentials of particularized nationalisms. In validating the idea of a territorial separation between 'us' and 'them', pan-Islam paved the way in particular for the idea of the 'the Arab nation'. It became an intermediary, in territorial terms, between the larger Islamic community (*umma*) and the smaller nation (*watan*). If one could accept the possibility of the intermediate notion of Arab nationalism, *qawmiyya*, then, one might ask, why were further divisions and more localized loyalties less possible? In effect, *qawmiyya* led inevitably to *wataniyya*, or what we think of when we speak of nationalism today.

Quite apart from the power of logic, pragmatic necessity exercised its own force on the thinking of Muslim intellectuals. Time and again we discover them seemingly contradicting themselves, advocating on one hand the unity of all Muslims and on the other the unity of a particular and far less inclusive territory. But, as Nikki Keddie points out with regard to Jamal al-Din al-Afghani, such contradictions are to be explained by pragmatism, the need to accept that there could be no real Islamic unity without reform and no reform without independence from the infidels. This meant that although pan-Islam was the ultimate goal, the more proximate and important one was to rid Muslims of Western colonialism. If there is irony in the idea of pan-Islam leading to the idea of nationalism, there is further irony in al-Afghani, the advocate of pan-Islam, arguing that religious unity was less important than national unity. Yet this was precisely what he argued, taking exception to what he thought was Sir Sayyid Ahmad Khan's intolerable toadying to the British of the Raj.

Al-Afghani thought that Sayyid Ahmad's endorsement of English as a unifying factor in multicultural India conceded too much and that more reliance needed to be made on local languages, particularly Urdu. Only in this way could the Indians understand modern sciences, acquire them, and thus emerge from the dark shadow of the British. Without seeming unduly concerned about the improbability of attaining linguistic unity in India, he concluded: 'There is no doubt that the unity of language is more durable for survival and permanence in this world than unity of religion since it does not change in a short time in contrast to the latter.'[1]

Sayyid Ahmad also had the unification of all Indians, regardless of religion, as his goal: 'Remember that Hindu and Mussalman are words of religious significance [;] otherwise Hindus, Mussalmans, and Christians who live in this country constitute one nation.' Unlike al-Afghani, though, he was self-consciously conformist in arguing that neither the Qur'an nor history bears out the assumption that only one Caliph should rule. In fact, we know that there were three Caliphs at one time – in Baghdad, Cairo, and Andalusia. Moreover, as far as the Ottoman Caliph goes, 'he is no doubt a Mohammedan sovereign and consequently we sympathise with him as Mohammedans – happy for his happiness and grieved at his troubles – yet he is *not* our Caliph either according to Mohammedan law or Mohammedan religion. If he has the rights of a Caliph he has them only in the country and over the people that he is master of.'[2] Such an explicit endorsement of pluralism as both natural and factual was distasteful to al-Afghani, who thought Sir Sayyid Admad too conformist, yet even he, for all his anti-imperialist fulminations, must be seen as a conformist when it comes to the necessity of the nation-state.

We may also see this coming to terms with the reality of nationalism, though not as cheerfully as in Sayyid Ahmad's case, in the thinking of Rashid Rida. This disciple of Muhammad 'Abduh and al-Afghani was concerned about Atatürk's intention to abolish the caliphate and the pre-eminence of the secular nationalists in Egypt, and thought that both of these developments were symptomatic of an Islamic malaise and at the same time intractable realities. Reform was needed, but, like his predecessors, he recognized that this could not be accomplished while Muslims were under colonial domination. The Arabs had a special role to play, for God has given his definitive revelation in their language and in their territory. Yet, having thus accepted Arab nationalism (and perhaps with one eye on his secularist critics), Rida took the next step somewhat hesitatingly: he acknowledged the need for the Muslim to be a loyal citizen of his nation as long as he remembers that he simultaneously belongs to a larger community.

Some believe that Rida was at best a 'negative' nationalist,[3] wanting to rid Egypt of the colonialists without accepting the principle of nationalism. But no matter how much he plumped for the revival of Islam around a single Caliph and aspired to overcome the divisions of the faithful, he made an important concession in a *fatwa* that Indonesian Muslims solicited on the question of Islam's compatability with nationalism:

The contemporary notion of patriotism expresses the unity of the people of different religions in their homeland, and their cooperation in defending the homeland they share. They cooperate to preserve its independence, to win it back if it was lost, and to develop it . . . The type of patriotism that should adorn Muslim youth is that he be a good example for the people of the homeland, no matter what their religious affiliation, cooperating with them in every legitimate action for independence . . .[4]

Although the explicit denigration of Islam by the secular nationalists horrified Rida, he was not, in truth, light years away from even such a 'positive' nationalist as the modern scholar and statesman Ahmad Lufti al-Sayyid. Also a student of 'Abduh, Lutfi al-Sayyid contrived at once to outrage and to mobilize his countrymen when he told them that the principle 'the land of Islam is the nation (*watan*) of all Muslims' was an imperialist contrivance. 'There is only one alternative, to replace it with the doctrine that is in accord with the aspirations of every Eastern nation with a defined *watan*. That doctrine is nationalism (*wataniyya*).'[5] Despite these obvious differences between Lutfi al-Sayyid and Rida, what is important here is that *both* advanced the conformist view.

Over time, indeed, the bulk of religious opinion came to coincide roughly with secular opinion on nationalism. This was because, as I have suggested before, a pronounced tendency has always been found among the Muslim *'ulama*, especially the Sunni *'ulama*, to acquiesce in the design of those who actually hold power. With regard to the subject of this book, the aim of those in power was first to create, and then to maintain, the national state apparatus. Even colonial rulers encouraged the emergence of national concepts such as 'Algeria' or 'India' in order to facilitate their rule over disparate tribes or principalities.

For example, in 1841, soon after General Bugeaud arrived to assume command of French troops in Algeria, his aides convinced him of the value of seeking a *fatwa* that effectively sanctioned French rule. This legitimation was especially important given that the *amir*, 'Abd al-Qadir, who was leading a *jihad* against the French, had declared that Muslims must not submit to infidel rulers and that Muslims who aided and abetted them became infidels themselves. He sought a *fatwa* from the *'ulama* of Fez to this effect, and though the result was not all he had hoped for, he continued to insist that Muslims who did not emigrate from conquered territory became part of *dar al-islam* again. The French, with the encouragement of the *amir*'s rivals in the Tijaniyya Sufi order, moved to counter the *fatwa* from Fez by inviting the more agreeable opinion of the *'ulama* in Qairawan, a city as renowned in Tunisia for its scholarship as Fez was in Morocco. Their *fatwa* endorsed obedience to the French at the same time as it coaxed the idea of 'Algeria' into making one of its first appearances: having resisted as much as could reasonably be expected, the Muslim tribes of Algeria were to submit to the French without becoming infidels so long as the French did not interfere with their practice of Islam or violate the honour of their women. The Tijaniyya formally accepted this opinion, and it was reported that the officials of al-Azhar, the most important Islamic university in the world, endorsed it. By their complaisance, the *'ulama* helped to stimulate the consciousness of people of disparate tribes and regions – as well as their own consciousness – that they all shared a common fate.[6]

In a similar way, the Indian *'ulama* helped to advance an incipient national self-consciousness by stressing the need to submit to the British. In the mid-nineteenth century, parts of India were in turmoil over the Wahhabi call to *jihad* against infidel rule. The Wahhabis, making a considerable impact in the rural areas of India, mobilized much of the peasantry, but the city-based intelligentsia quickly rallied to the defence of the Queen. Although the compliance of the *'ulama* throughout Islamic history has been more consistently seen among Sunnis than Shi'a, the Shi'i *'ulama* have also displayed this tendency. They did so in this instance when they argued that the Wahhabis were deviators from the right path, and that in any event *jihad* is permissible only when the Imam is present to give his approval. Several Sunni arguments, appeared, but the conclusion of the majority was the same as that of the Shi'a.

The *'ulama* of northern India argued that India was part of *dar al-harb* and therefore *jihad* was permissible, but that in this case, because the Christian rulers faithfully protected the Muslims and allowed them to practise their religion freely, they could not justifiably rebel – especially, they artfully added, since Islam required rebels to have a reasonable chance of winning. The *'ulama* of Calcutta disagreed that India was part of *dar al-harb* and that *jihad* was therefore legitimate in some circumstances. India, rather, was part of *dar al-islam* because it had been under Muslim rule and nothing significant had happened since then to affect adversely the practice of the faith there. Consequently, rebellion was simply out of the question.

As a British author wrote at the time, 'this result must be accepted as . . . satisfactory to the well-to-do Muhammadans, whom it saves from the perils of contributing to the Fanatic Camp on our Frontier, and gratifying to ourselves, as proving that the law and Prophets can be utilized on the side of loyalty as well as on the side of sedition.'[7] But even this author felt that the '*ulama* had gone too far in the desire to be acquiescent. According to classical theory, in his view, India could not be anything but part of *dar al-harb* because the formerly Christian *dhimmis* of the Islamic empire were now rulers who allowed pork and wine to be consumed; they had displaced the *shari'a* and its judges; and they had improved the status of women. It must be said, however, that if the '*ulama* were too acquiescent, it was not exactly for the reasons which the British observer gave. Even when Muslims ruled over non-Muslims, pork and wine were never entirely forbidden and were generally available to *dhimmis*; the legal system that the British introduced was not automatically in contradiction of Islamic law; and the status of women was subject to controversy and change in the empires of Islamic history long before the British empire.

In the event, three of the four main jurisconsultants of Mecca had no objection to the Calcutta statement and in fact backed it with *fatwas*. The Hanafi and Shafi'i *muftis* said that as long as the British allowed 'even some' of the Islamic practices to be observed, India was in *dar al-islam* and hence *jihad* was not permissible. The Maliki *mufti* said much the same thing when he observed that India would become part of *dar al-harb* 'only when all or most of the injunctions of Islam disappear therefrom',[8] and that this lamentable situation had clearly not resulted under British rule. Even so staunch a critic of the '*ulama* as Sir Sayyid Ahmad Khan agreed that Muslims must 'dispel from [their] minds any idea of disloyalty', and so great an admirer of the Ottomans as Shibli Nu'mani later agreed that Indians were lawfully subject to the British government and had a clear obligation to be loyal to the Christian Queen.[9]

One could of course argue that those who fought against the foreigners, such as 'Abd al-Qadir in Algeria or the mutineers in India, did more to encourage the idea of Algeria or India than the conformist intellectuals did. There is no doubt that the rebels were early nationalists, as no one can deny that *jihad* or mutiny has a wonderful way of concentrating the mind. Moreover, one can rightly point, as indeed I have, to such intellectuals as al-Afghani or Rida who argued against the imperialists and in that way, against their instincts, became nationalists. But it is important to recognize that those who did not rebel and in fact counselled obedience to alien rule *also* helped to focus attention on a particular patch of territory and a common fate: in explaining the obligation to submit to the infidels, these '*ulama* distinguished their part of *dar al-islam* from other parts. Rebellion certainly fired the imagination, but deference was not without its effects on self-identification.

'Consensus of speech' today

Opinion today is mainly conformist too. Conformists naturally differ in their precise arguments, but they fall loosely into three groups.

THE NATION-STATE AS A FACT OF LIFE

The first argues that the nation-state and Islam may be theoretically incompatible, but that national pluralism is a fact of life which cannot be ignored and must be accepted. The Indian philosopher and poet Muhammad Iqbal set the stage for this line of thinking today. He began with the assumption that Islam demands one unified community, and that it was European imperialism which had shattered 'the religious unity of Islam in pieces'. But he was a realist and a gradualist, and soon came around to the point of view that Islamic unity first required the independence of every Muslim territory. He had hoped that the solution for Indian Muslims would be to make them into a distinct community with their own identity and rights, but by 1930 the idea of communalism had moved into the idea of a fully separate territorial state: 'Self-government within or without the British Empire, the formation of a consolidated North-West Indian Muslim State appears to me to be the final destiny of the Muslims, at least of North-West India.' This kind of Muslim nationalism was justifiable because it would protect Muslims and give them some power while leaving their common spirit intact. In effect, a Muslim League of Nations would be preliminary to the *umma*.[10]

A contemporary member of this group of conformists, Datuk Musa Hitam, the Deputy Prime Minister of Malaysia, concedes that there is a tension between the ethics and the logic of a situation, between what ought to be done and what can be done. Ethics may demand that pluralism give way to the *umma*, but the logic of events is that there is no chance of this happening. 'The nation-state is reality, and politics is the art of facing reality.' Muslims must thus recognize that they will not act as one group in world politics, and that building the *umma* is not the answer to the world's problems. But Islam will be relevant in so far as it coincides with notions of social justice worked out in national contexts.[11]

Qadeeruddin Ahmed, former Chief Justice of Pakistan, believes that nationalism and Islam are incompatible in theory; the universality of Islam cannot exist so long as one's loyalties are divided. However, there is really not much incompatibility in practice because the modern individual is able to wear two hats, or be loyal to both Islam and his nation-state, at the same time. 'How many times does practical conflict exist between them?' he asks. In the long run perhaps, the larger Islamic identity will season national loyalties, but as yet undetected is any real movement towards Islamic solidarity. Rather, the individual must learn to be a good Muslim and a good citizen simultaneously.[12]

Faruq Jarar of the Ahl al-Bayt Foundation in Jordan says that Muslims will go on talking about unity, but that this discussion is simply theoretical. Islam and nationalism are not compatible as principles, yet reality has impinged. Arab Muslims must acknowledge the force of this reality, just as they must acknowledge that some of the greatest Muslim heroes have not been Arabs, and that the Arab 'Abbasid and Umayyad empires depended greatly on Persians and Christians to keep them running. Arab Muslims, in short, must face the world as it is and not as they would prefer it to be.[13]

Shaykh Muhammad Jbayr, an influential member of the *'ulama* in Saudi Arabia, told me in 1975 that Islam does call for one *umma* with one Caliph, and that this unity in fact prevailed in the early days of Islam. But the situation radically changed under the 'Abbasids, when division and dynastic rivalry became commonplace. Given the internal weaknesses, it was inevitable that the Europeans would colonize the region and create separate entities. The differences of custom, culture, and law which they have left behind are so great that even now Muslims are not able to unite. King Faysal wisely recognized this, and consequently lobbied for Islamic solidarity (*tadamun*) rather than unity (*ittihad*). A new generation, well-versed in the *shari'a* and Islamic political theory, may perhaps move towards unification, but this would take a long time to bring into place. For the foreseeable future, then, Muslims must realize that the foremost Islamic duty is working for justice, and that this can be done within the confines of the nation-state as well as within a broader community.[14]

Two other Saudis, both formally trained in international law abroad yet belonging to different generations, endorsed Jbayr's general viewpoint. Samir Shamma, a Jidda advocate, conceded that the theory espouses pan-Islam, but he argued strongly that it simply was not feasible today. 'After all, what do Arabs, Turks, and Persians really have in common?' In fact, we should be wary of states, such as Iran, that are advancing pan-Islam, since they are probably using it to mask their hegemonic designs on the region.[15] Sulayman al-Sulaym, now Minister of Commerce, emphasizes that the Islamic goal of 'world government' is well-established and valid, but, given the entrenchment of pluralism in the modern world, 'this goal doesn't even come to mind'. Muslims must be practical at the end of the day, and combine their own beliefs with the essentially European concept of the nation-state.[16]

THE NATION-STATE AS NATURAL

The second group of thinkers differs from the first by arguing that the nation-state is more than an unfortunate fact of life; it is a natural institution and only to be expected in the order of things. It is hardly surprising that statesmen, especially those who fought wars of liberation against colonial powers, are the strongest component of this group. President Sukarno reasoned with Muslim authorities in this way:

We shall found an Indonesian national state. I ask you the following question, Mr Ki Bagus Hadikusumo and other representatives of Islam. I beg your pardon for using the word nationalism. I am a Muslim myself. I pray, however, gentlemen, do not misunderstand me when I say that the first basis for Indonesia is nationalism. This does not mean nationalism in the narrow sense of the word, on the contrary, I strive after a national state . . . As Mr Ki Bagus Hadikusumo said yesterday, he is an Indonesian, his father is, his grandparents were Indonesians, and so were his ancestors.[17]

Later politicians do not seem to have thought that the question of Islam and nationalism is so sensitive; they seem to view the two as in natural harmony. Mohammed Fedhel Jamali, former Prime Minister of Iraq (and a Shi'i), for example, said that pluralism is sanctioned by the Islamic texts and desirable because it allows for diverse cultural contributions within the loosely conceived *umma*.[18] Mahathir Muhammad, the Prime Minister of Malaysia, believes that Islam accepts that there are valid differences among peoples. No centralized empire of Muslims is likely to come about because the *umma* consists of many races and cultures, which, the Qur'an says, God has created in order to make us know one another better.[19] 'Abd al-Rahman 'Azzam, former Secretary-General of the Arab League, also found that although Islam is predicated on the greater interest of humanity, which is above every particular interest, the Qur'an speaks of the reality of divisions of men into sects and nations. To be sure, the sovereignty of the individual states is not unlimited, for the *shari'a* is above everything. However, he accepted that the differences of geography, custom, and culture among the Muslim states reflect their differing needs, and condition their differing constitutional orders, but that this does not detract from the larger sense of fraternity that all believers share.[20]

As Minister of Islamic Affairs in Morocco and an important writer on modern Islam, 'Allal al-Fasi bridged the practical and theoretical worlds. In a sophisticated and intricate argument in favour of both the independence and the political liberalization of Morocco, he argued that the nation and the Islamic community are not incompatible at all. Islam is a religion of reason and in tune with the spirit of the times, but its endorsement of national divisions goes beyond gracious acquiescence in a *de facto* situation. Indeed, because Islam is synonymous with freedom, it virtually commands that individuals and collectivities of individuals be free. Rather like Ibn Khaldun, he saw a natural order of things in which freedom and sound thinking happily coexist, just as loyalty to one's family and loyalty to the nation coexist. By logical extension of this principle, there is no contradiction between loyalty to one's particular nation (*watan*) and loyalty to the Arab nation or indeed to Islam. With 'proper education', the citizen will come to understand this and to realize that the natural order of things is wise: loyalty to the nation checks the excesses of loyalty to the family ('the small nation'), loyalty to the region checks the excesses of loyalty to the nation, and loyalty to Islam checks all. 'Love' of the Moroccan nation is only to be expected, then, because it flows from the very tolerance that characterizes Islam, and because it is reasonable, a term al-Fasi frequently used, owing to a consciousness of simultaneous solidarity with larger communities – the Maghreb, the Arab nation, and Islam.[21]

Muhammad Hamidullah, an Indian lawyer and prolific writer on Islamic international relations, thinks that individual 'states' have always existed and are the basic political unit. Although Muslims constitute one nation, the Qur'an, scholarly opinion, and history, which records Islam's expansion into distant lands, internal rebellion, and 'prevalent international conditions', all testify to the validity of separate Muslim states in the international system.[22] Mohammed Talaat al-Ghunaimi, an Egyptian international lawyer, also does not believe that Islam proposes a monistic world order. On the contrary, quoting from the Qur'an to support his belief that Islam endorses political pluralism, he seems to suggest that the unity of the *umma* should really be taken to be 'social'. He goes on to conclude that 'if Islam tolerates division of the Islamic community into different states, Islam a fortiori must accept division of the world community among different states'.[23]

Ma'ruf al-Dawalibi, former President of the World Muslim League (Rabitat al-Alam al-Islami) and former Prime Minister of Syria, says that states jealously guard their sovereignty and are unlikely to give up any part of it, but that there is also Qur'anic justification of pluralism. The concept of *jihad*, moreover, is widely misunderstood or wilfully misrepresented. Rather than being an aggressive holy war, *jihad* is essentially any effort to establish good and suppress evil; but, when it does involve fighting, it is clearly meant to be self-defensive fighting. This was the message of the second, Medinan period of Qur'anic revelation. Even with regard to Israel today, *jihad* means protecting one's country against the aggressive expansionism of the Zionist entity. It certainly does not mean expanding the Islamic community by force of arms and must not be interpreted as an indicator of Islamic hostility to the present multi-state, international system.[24]

'Abdullah al-Munifi, an American-trained international lawyer and adviser to the Saudi Council of Ministers, similarly argues that sovereignty is not antithetical to Islam because the Qur'an advances a theory of self-defence whereby one community of Muslims may protect itself against a non-Muslim community or another Muslim community. Moreover, one can find political pluralism in the early rivalry between Mecca and Medina, or between 'Ali and Mu'awiyya. The territorial nation-state today similarly does not contradict the idea of the larger Islamic commonwealth: the nation-state is a part, fitting into the larger whole. The real question is: how do Muslims govern themselves within each state?[25]

Syed Zein Abedin, an expert on Muslim minorities at King 'Abd al-'Aziz University in Jidda, believes that the idea of a monolithic Islamic order is fallacious, and that it is undesirable: 'Many flowers must bloom in the Islamic world.' The *umma* remains a broad framework to be reckoned with, but it is not a political concept. Nation-states will continue to exist, and this fact will account for differences even among institutions that develop in the name of Islam; an American Islamic organization will differ from a Nigerian one. These local variations are no bad thing, though, for it is important for Islam to have good roots, or it will remain an abstraction.[26] Abdul Rahman Wahid, head of an Indonesian *pesantren*, or traditional religious school, and a leader of the Nahdatul Ulama party, similarly looks upon the nation-state and nationalism as both inevitable and acceptable. Nationalism must not become narrow chauvinism, but in fact it is being qualified every day. Participation in the non-aligned movement has internationalized its member states and has brought general questions such as North–South distributive justice to the fore. Nationalism is also being qualified by regional identifications, such as Arabism, and even such incipient sub-regional loyalties as that which may be developing among the Gulf Cooperation Council countries along the Persian Gulf littoral. The idea of the *umma* is of course important, but for the heightened awareness that it fosters among Muslims of what Islam means, not for suggesting the need for a single entity. This awareness is particularly crucial in our age, since Muslims must recognize more than ever their paramount Islamic duty – to overcome poverty and restore human dignity within each nation.[27]

An avowedly leftist variation also accepts the nation-state as fact and as divinely sanctioned. The thinking of Hasan Hanafi, professor of philosophy at Cairo University, is an example. Islam, unlike Judaism and Christianity, which are supernatural religions, is a natural religion. This means that it is universalistic but at the same time realistic – seeking new converts but adapting to local cultural differences and social circumstances. Islam's goal is not the accumulation but the affirmation of particular groups; particularism is the vehicle for universalism. It follows that if nations fall under foreign control, Islam advocates their liberation and itself becomes a national movement. Hanafi believes that another reason why Islam naturally espouses a theology of national liberation is its principle that men can hold deed to land only as long as they are obedient to God. Western imperialists, Zionists, and Muslim despots, therefore, lose all claim to the land that they may in fact control because they contradict God's will that 'freedom and justice have to be given to every human and to every community without any distinction of colour, race, or religion'. But Arabs themselves bear considerable responsibility for imprisoning the idea of the nation: Arab intellectual life itself is paralysed by submissiveness to authority; it eschews genuine self-criticism for apologetics; and it prefers flattery to plain speech, or, bluntly, it prefers hypocrisy. Arabs are out of touch with history and tend to glorify the past at the expense of the present, or look to the future and ignore the past, or concentrate on the present without regard to the future. The result is that nationalist thought, both particular and pan-Arab presumably, is undeveloped and shallow, keeping the individual from realizing his full potential and dignity and the Arabs from realizing their destiny.[28]

THE NEED TO REVISE THE NATION-STATE SYSTEM

In their enthusiastic endorsement of the nation-state and territorial pluralism, the intellectuals of this second group are reminiscent of Sayyid Ahmad Khan. In some respects, Hanafi's brand of conformism goes furthest along this road and best clarifies the difference with the third group of intellectuals. Hanafi thinks that Islam demands there be no attack on the idea that every people deserves its own nation-state; this position represents the *unqualified* triumph of the national idea. The writers of the third group, by contrast, think that Islam demands the modification of the idea of the nation-state system. It is not so much the individual state that is important, but the whole system of states. This approach thus represents the *qualified* triumph of the national idea – which, in a sense, is reminiscent of Rashid Rida's position.

Al-Sadiq al-Mahdi, for example, Oxford-trained descendant of the Mahdi, former Prime Minister and leader of the Ansar group in the Sudan, argues that although nation-states are the creations of Western colonialism, a great deal of the responsibility for their dominance now lies with the Westernized elites who seized the chance to propel themselves into power and to put their hand to creating a successful political community of their own. It was a type of internal colonialism, for, regarding Islam as rigid and inflexible, they advocated replacing the doctrine of *taqlid*, or imitation of early precedent, with progressive – that is, secular and nationalist – Western ways of thinking. Some groups, such as the Bahais, the Ahmadis, and the reformist Republican Brothers (who advocate the complete equality of men and women and of Muslims and non-Muslims, and the restriction of some aspects of the traditional *shari'a*), went so far as to reject Islam itself, he says, for the sake of foreign ideas. Others, such as the Nasirists, turned to socialism but so abused it that they created a police state.

Al-Mahdi believes that because the record of post-independence has been such a dismal one, the elites have gradually lost ideological ground to the masses, who have always looked upon Islam as the centre of their identity and their inspiration. One result has been a resurgence of 'traditionalist' thinking, a trend which threatens to revive *taqlid*. On the other hand, it would be unfortunate, according to al-Mahdi, if the Westernized elites were allowed to continue their secularizing programme; what is needed instead is a new synthesis that is both Islamic and modern. In international relations this synthesis would tell us that the present nation-state system is a system based on naked power. It needs to be reformed, however, not have its national base destroyed, and then it can be put to good effect, rather than serving as the sole god of men. International relations, in fact, needs to adopt the five Islamic principles: all men form a true brotherhood; justice is the supreme practical consideration; force is illegitimate except in self-defence; all agreements, regardless of the partners, are honoured; and all relationships, in the absence of specific agreements, are reciprocal.[29] The alternative that emerges, then, is an international system in which the persistence of the nation-state is accepted but its power qualified.

Kamal al-Sharif, Minister of Awqaf and Islamic Affairs in Jordan, believes that Islam and the nation-state are fully compatible, but at the same time that Islam has much to offer the prevailing system of nation-states. With its great respect of family, Islam can help nudge the system towards 'a family of nations' and thereby temper the harshness of existing sovereignties. The system would also benefit from the Qur'anic encouragement of friendliness towards, and tolerance of, neighbours. Moreover, if a 'Muslim bloc' of states were to emerge, then – because of its commitment to these Islamic values of respect of family and tolerance of others – it could play a constructive, even stabilizing, role in an era of inflamed rhetoric and conflicting ideologies.[30]

A number of Southeast Asian Muslims, too, belong to this third group of thinkers, who, while regarding the nation-state as compatible with Islam, call for a modification of the general system. Chandra Muzaffar, president of the Malaysian reformist organization ALIRAN, or the Society for National Consciousness, looks upon the nation-state as something that has always existed and not merely as a Western creation. It is a sociological fact of longstanding and universal application. But in modern times the state, with vast technological expertise at the disposal of its bureaucracy, has become immensely and dangerously powerful. Elites have become authoritarian, and, with the competition for scarce resources even more fierce, the separation between particular communities has become more pronounced. This separation occurs within countries such as Malaysia, with its growing communalist tensions between Malays and non-Malays, and between countries. Influenced by such writers as Iqbal and Tennyson, Muzaffar thinks that an alternative framework which emphasizes universalism over particularism is needed. Any ideology that leads man away from kowtowing to the state is valuable, but Islam is particularly so because it 'does not advocate an obscurantist sort of unity' and so can help in making technology a source of general good and not merely of benefit to some.[31]

Anwar Ibrahim, former leader of ABIM (Angkatan Belia Islam Malaysia, or

Muslim Youth Movement of Malaysia) and now Minister of Agriculture in Malaysia, says that the nation-state is a reality which must be accepted; national borders are not subject to change. Nationalism, however, is too narrow, being based on Western ideas, and thus must be qualified by the sense of belonging to something greater. It would be unrealistic to expect a universal Islamic government to emerge, especially from such tentative institutions as the Organization of the Islamic Conference and the Islamic Development Bank. Still, we must get to the stage at which the interaction of Muslims is based on something more than national interest.[32] Harun Nasution, rector of the Institut Agama Islamic Negeri, the Islamic tertiary education institute in Jakarta, echoes the general point, confining himself specifically to Indonesia. The great majority of Indonesian Muslims, he says, are nationalists, but they want a nationalism that is within the brotherhood of Muslims everywhere and is moderated by the habit of political cooperation with others.[33]

The process of culture change

However much these Muslim thinkers differ, they represent what I believe to be the majority sentiment of Muslims today. In effect, they represent the intellectual consensus of the age, the 'consensus of speech', which the law recognizes, along with the consensus of action, as a valid indicator of Islamic meaning. If we add to this, first, that the early theory makes some concessions towards pluralism and, second, that the weight of historical evidence, the consensus of action, falls on the side of pluralism (the subjects of the preceding chapter), it would seem that, for all three reasons, a strong case exists against the proposition that for Muslims the nation–state is an alien and heretical idea. Martin Wight overstated the case somewhat when he said that men in the modern world have been more loyal to the state than to religion, class, or any other political tie,[34] but there is much to this conclusion – even when it comes to Muslims.

A major reason why this is so is that the *'ulama* have traditionally been deferential in their action and conformist in their attitude towards prevailing ideas and institutions. In the twentieth century these tendencies have only increased in the Sunni countries of the Muslim world, while more and more people have acquired a voice on Islamic matters and broken the monopoly of the *'ulama*. Making the religious authorities a bureaucracy, thereby 'nationalizing' them or making them integral to the national establishment, probably accounts for both their greater deference to the state and the larger number of people today whose opinion may be considered authoritative. This point needs to be developed.

In many countries today, the *'ulama* are civil servants receiving regular salaries, pensions, and perquisites, and even where they are not, they are largely financially dependent on the state because of its funding of the religious schools. They also recognize that they cannot easily resist the power of modern centralized governments. This power has been brought home to them in several places by the systematic altering of their bases of support – the *madrasas* and other educational institutions, the *waqfs*, or religious endowments, and the *shari'a* courts. Egypt illustrates all these changes: *madrasas* have become part of the national educational network, and the university of al-Azhar, which is older than Oxford by two hundred years, underwent Nasirist changes and now teaches such modern subjects as the social sciences and English; the government has eliminated or taken over the administration of many of the endowments; and the jurisdiction of the *shari'a* courts has been whittled away by having many of their areas of concern transferred to the state court system. In Algeria, Jordan, Turkey, and Indonesia, to cite only a few more examples, Ministries of Religious Affairs control the administration of religious education and the mosques. Some governments have discovered that an especially effective way of controlling the *'ulama* is to set the training they must undergo before they can be certified and, once certified, to monitor closely what they can say in their sermons.

The situation of the Shi'i *'ulama* is not as clear because the Iranian revolution has turned things upside down – to the point at which the *'ulama* now actually govern. But in pre-revolutionary Iran, despite retaining considerable financial independence and significant political influence among the masses, the *'ulama* found themselves on the defensive. Reza Shah created a modern educational system alongside the *madrasas*, restricted and then abolished the *shari'a* courts, limited the *'ulama*'s control of *waqfs*, introduced state taxes that interfered with the collection of *zakat* and *khums* (one-fifth of income paid by Shi'a to the *'ulama*), and forced changes in Islamic style such as the unveiling of women. His son, Muhammad Reza Shah, continued to make reforms in women's rights and land ownership, which the *'ulama* opposed. Remarkably, both rulers found little overt opposition, partly because of the brutal demonstration of their power, and partly because of the attitude of Ayatollah Borujerdi, the 'source of imitation', who argued for an apolitical stance. Shi'i history shows that this conformist approach has dominated when governments were perceived to be hostile.

Whether Sunni or Shi'i, the very deference of the *'ulama* and manipulation by the government have contributed to the general criticism that is levelled against them. As I indicated in Chapter 1, they seem uncreative and moribund to many, but their lack of independence disappoints almost everybody. It is precisely this perception, which is common throughout the Muslim world, that legitimates the intellectual contributions of people who have not had the traditional training or experience of the *'ulama* but who nonetheless have impressive educational qualifications and the ability to articulate their views. Consequently, the number of people whose opinions may be considered authoritative is larger today than it was formerly. The irony, though, is that these intellectuals are usually the product of the national education system and are often employees of the government. Many, if not most, therefore, tend to be themselves dyed-in-the-wool conformists. In essence, they hardly differ at all from the older and more informally educated *'ulama* when it comes to the questions of nationalism and the nation-state.

The general point to note here is that the deference of the intellectuals to the political elite has worked to the consolidation of the national idea, as it did to the emergence of the idea, because the intellectuals have become dependent on the very structure of the powerful, centralized state and were largely educated by the apparatus of the state. In turn, once they identify with the state, they strengthen it: their views carry weight and – together with the *fatwas* and teachings of the *'ulama* supporting government policies – help to condition people, as the state educational system and propaganda apparatus more overtly do, into thinking that loyalty to one's nation is a natural and noble sentiment.

It is possible, of course, that the *'ulama*, and intellectuals generally, will become less compliant. Indeed, making the *'ulama* into a bureaucracy may have an unintended effect: the more they become part of the establishment, the more regular their input will be; and the more their training is standardized, the more self-consciousness they may develop, and thus the more likely to emerge as a distinct pressure group. But even if the *'ulama* were to dissent from official policy and resist governmental attempts to suppress their independence, it is unlikely that they would be anti-nationalist. Like all other Muslims, they have been caught up in culture change, and this has made territorial pluralism seem acceptable. Moreover, increasingly, new generations of *'ulama* have been born and raised in the independent nation–state and know nothing else.

The history of the Iranian Shi'i *'ulama* demonstrates this conformity to the long-established idea of the Iranian state. Institutionalization of the *'ulama* during the Safavid period only solidified their identification with the state or nation. Even during the less salutary periods of the Qajar and Pahlavi dynasties, conflict with the government did not translate into sentiment against the Iranian nation. On the contrary, the *'ulama* saw themselves as upholding the integrity of the nation against the Shah's follies when they agitated against foreign concessions in 1872–3 and 1891–2 and for constitutional reform in 1905–11. During the early 1960s, when the Shah launched his 'white revolution' and invited large numbers of foreign technicians into the country, Khumayni saw himself as defending both Islam and the nation:

It is incumbent upon me, according to my religious duties, to warn the Iranian people and the Muslims of the world that Islam and the Qur'an are in danger; that the independence of the country and its economy are to be taken over by Zionists, who in Iran appear as the party of Baha'is; and if this deadly silence of Muslims continues, they will soon take over the entire economy of the country and drive it to complete bankruptcy. Iranian television is a Jewish spy base, the government sees this and approves of it.[35]

This quotation reflects the historical pattern of Iranian Shi'ism's identification with Iranian nationalism, and points to the nationalization of the *'ulama*'s attitudes. Political cooptation and formalization of the *'ulama*'s governmental role have facilitated this attitude, but even when they have resisted cooptation, nationalization has taken place because of the general shift in Muslim thinking over time in the face of the historical record of pluralism.

The effects of this shift are similarly evident in Pakistan. A Baluchi leader makes no specific reference to Islam in his call for greater rights for Baluchis. Rather, he frames his appeal in national terms. He argues that his people deserve the same special recognition as is given to the other major ethnic groups – the Sindhis, Punjabis, and Pathans – within the Pakistani state.[36] Territorial pluralism is so unquestionably acceptable that every 'national' group should have clearly defined rights, but not to the point of damaging the conventional umbrella of the Pakistani nation-state.

In the case of the Palestinians, there is a more definably Islamic component to their discourse, which has been apparent ever since the revolt of 1936–9. Even earlier, from his Haifa mosque Shaykh 'Izz al-Din al-Qassam cast his fiery, anti-imperialist sermons in an Islamic mould. He preached against prostitution, drinking, and gambling and called for *jihad* against the related imperialisms of the British and the Zionists. This kind of speech had resonance among the peasantry and helped to awaken nationalist sentiment for the first time in the countryside. The Palestine movement became more than an elite phenomenon and now extended beyond the few aristocratic families of the cities.[37]

More recently, official Palestinian rhetoric continues to combine the terminologies of Islamic struggle and national struggle. In particular, a virtual twinning of key emotion-laden terms has developed. The word for revolution, *thawra*, is interchangeable with *jihad*; the word usually used for guerrilla, *fida'i*, is interchangeable with *mujahid*, the word for one who fights in a *jihad*; and the word for martyr, *shahid*, applies to all who die fighting for Palestine. A striking indication of the overlapping of terms is seen in the transformation of the traditional phrase *jihad fi sabil Allah*, '*jihad* in the path of God'. In Palestinian rhetoric it has now become *jihad fi sabil al-thawra*, '*jihad* in the path of the revolution'.[38] In the early years of the Iranian revolution, the common Palestinian–Iranian struggle against anti-imperialism became a noticeable theme. For example, Yassir 'Arafat said in 1979: 'This great Iranian people lives with us in one trench raising together the same emblems – all of us are fighters, all *mujahidin*, all revolutionaries (*thuwwar*) under one flag – the flag of our Islamic nation – against imperialism.'[39] It should be said, however, that the theme of a common struggle with Iran has been heard less as Khumayni's Iran has developed close ties with al-Asad's Syria, an opponent of 'Arafat's faction of the Palestine Liberation Organization (PLO).

None of these Islamic terms, probably, has an explicitly religious significance for most Palestinians, any more than the word 'crusade' has a specifically religious significance when it is used in Western parlance today. But unconscious benefits may be derived from the association of religious and secular ideas. For example, belief in the natural association, or compatibility, of Islam and the nation-state may help Christian Palestinians, worried about the excesses of the Islamic revolution in Iran, not to think of Islam as too threatening or alien. If this were so, the idea of the Palestinian nation-state would help to make Islam acceptable. The reverse situation seems more significant. It is likely that the explicit appeal to Islam in the 1930s made the difference in winning over people whose political vision had not yet included the clearly formulated idea of a Palestinian nation-state. But even today, when the word *watan* ('nation' or, more ambiguously, 'homeland'), is on every lip, the linkage of Islamic and secular categories probably helps Muslim Palestinians to affirm the essential rightness of the struggle for national self-determination. If so, Islam helps to make the idea of the nation-state acceptable.

The need to do this may be pronounced when it comes to older Palestinian men with minimal education and to the petty intelligentsia of villages who, perhaps more than the under-thirties and the city-based students and professionals, believe religion to be a governing influence in their lives.[40] However, the results of university elections on the West Bank suggest that many of the students also feel strongly about Islam. Muslim groups have consistently captured the majority of seats in student elections at Najah University since 1978, and in 1985 they won back from a Fatah-leftist coalition control of the Islamic University in Hebron and the Teachers' College in Ramallah. At Bir Zeit University, Muslim students captured 42 per cent of the vote in 1979, 38 per cent in 1981, and 30 per cent in 1985.[41] Some people think that the necessity of coalition voting always exaggerated the importance of Muslim groups in these elections. According to one official, out of Bir Zeit's Muslim student population, which is about 70 per cent of the total student population, only 2 per cent approximately are 'die-hard' Muslim activists.[42] Moreover, the popularity of Muslim groups at Bir Zeit has declined since 1979 (although their 1985 vote was higher than that of 1984). Nonetheless, there remains a strong element of Islamic sentiment in the West Bank population as a whole, as attested to by the elections at other universities and by the 1982 *Time*–PORI Institute poll of West Bank Palestinians, the only such general poll to have been published. This poll points to the value that many Palestinians – they are not more precisely identified – attach to religion: although 56 per cent of respondents wanted a secular, democratic state, a substantial 35 per cent wanted an 'Islamic state'.[43]

It is obvious that Islam figures prominently in the Lebanese opposition to the

Israelis in southern Lebanon. A number of Shi'i groups from Amal to Islamic Jihad have deliberately invoked the terminology of *jihad* and martyrdom. But even more interesting is the growing tendency of others to rely on Islamic categories to express essentially secular ideas. For example, the former Christian President, Sulayman Franjiyah, endorsed the idea of 'defensive *jihad*' as resistance against the Israelis.[44] The teenage girl Thana Muhaybili, who ended her life in a suicide mission against an Israeli convoy and instantly became an Arab heroine, referred to herself as a 'martyr' in a valedictory interview, and viewed her 'sacrifice' as her 'duty toward my land and people'.[45] The nationalist commitment to the freedom of her land and people is unremarkable; what is, however, noteworthy is that, as a purported member of the secular Syrian Social Nationalist Party,[46] she should have used religiously evocative language to express this commitment. At a time when Shi'i groups have especially captured the popular imagination and secular groups are less active, she would have been aware that the use of such terms as 'martyr' and 'sacrifice' would have automatically validated her – and her party's – commitment.

THE IMPORTANCE OF LANGUAGE

The Palestinian and Lebanese cases point to the general importance of language in culture change. It may be said that the language of Islam is no more than a veneer to essentially secular expressions, but this view would overlook the complex process of what anthropologists call linguistic acculturation. This is the process whereby a people extend the old meanings of words to new circumstances or new demands, so that alien or contentious ideas gradually become 'indigenized',[47] or come to seem entirely natural and unexceptional. As in the case of the Apachee Indians, who came to talk of the automobile as if its parts belonged to the human body, the emphasis is on a perceived similarity. But this perception occurs only in the broader context: the change in one word occurs when the related categories, and the structural relationship between them, are understood to be similar to another set of words and categories. In the example of the Apachees, using the word 'liver' to mean 'battery', for instance, seems only reasonable when the relationship between the chassis, front, and motor of a car appears to be similar to the relationship between the body, face, and viscera of a man.[48] In a similar but less precise way, using the word *jihad* to mean *thawra*, or revolution, seems reasonable when the relationship between one who fights in a *jihad* and the martyrdom that he may suffer appears to be similar to the relationship between a fighter for national liberation and the sacrifices that he is called upon to make.

In general terms, there seem to be three ways in which associations of similarity are found and developed. (1) The first way may be called metonymic: it is based on intrinsic association, the relating of like to like, specifically of a part to the whole. For example, 'crown' is used to mean 'king'. In this approach the part is a *sign* of the whole, as is also the case when a poet uses 'the Great Questioner' to suggest the general idea of God: 'greater glory in the sun,/An evening chill upon the air,/Bid imagination run/Much on the Great Questioner.'[49] (s) The second way may be called metaphoric; it is based on arbitrary association, the relating of unlike to unlike, things that have no intrinsic relationship to each other. This approach deals with *symbols* rather than signs, and an example is to refer to 'the noise of water' as 'the garbled voice of prophets'.[50] (3) The third way may be called quasi-metonymic; it is based on an arbitrary association becoming an intrinsic association, the relating of unlikes to each other but making them seem alike.[51] This approach makes *symbols into signs*, as can be seen in one novelist's evocative phrase, 'the minarets shone loudly'.[52] The implied arbitrary association between a minaret and something which radiates light and, in turn, something which gives off sound becomes a kind of intrinsic association, making the minaret a sign of the light and sound – Middle Eastern midday and the muezzin's call to prayer.

In everyday parlance we tend to be aware of the differences between signs and symbols, the metonymic and the metaphoric. For instance, we know that 'Whitehall' is a sign of the British government and 'Quai d'Orsay' is a sign of the French Foreign Ministry; they are parts of the whole. We also recognize the difference between referring to the American Presidency by a part, 'the Oval Office' (sign), and speaking of the President near the end of his term as a 'lame duck' (symbol).

But sometimes we move from one realm of discourse to another without even noticing it. Anthropoligists say that this transformation occurs in the midst of significant ritual and/or because of steady repetition, and sociologists add that often we are influenced by individuals because of the social roles that they play. In the United States newsmen and political analysts have done much to broaden the application of that great point of no return, Watergate. Bearing no intrinsic relationship to other public scandals, the word nevertheless has become a metaphor to cover them: Korean bribes of Congressmen, President Carter's tolerance of his brother Billy's questionable activities, or the pirating of President Carter's papers to prepare Ronald Reagan for debates with Carter. Over time, even a relatively brief time, the symbolic connotation and explicit comparison become superfluous: the incidents are described as kinds of Watergate (Koreagate, Billygate, Debategate) because the word has become equivalent to the misconduct of public officials. So persuasive has this transformation been that the term has been adopted elsewhere. For example, the scandal surrounding the South African Information Minister, Cornelius Mulder, over the misappropriation of secret funds at the disposal of his ministry came to be called Muldergate.

Over the considerable period during which I have been visiting Saudi Arabia, I have noticed precisely this dynamic at work among Saudi intellectuals when it comes to accepting the basic premises of the international system, particularly the idea of territorial and national pluralism. The most interesting feature is the absence of any marked difference between the traditionally educated *'ulama* and the more modern, often foreign-educated, intellectuals. They both have conformed to the idea of national pluralism and employ strikingly similar arguments. It is possible, however, to distinguish the ways in which the two groups argue according to the three approaches just outlined.

(1) For example, some Saudis argue on the basis of a metonymic, intrinsic, relationship between Islam and the nation-state. This approach is most clearly seen in their attitude to the international treaty. Everyone to whom I have spoken regards this as a valid legal instrument and as a sign of Islam. They say that it is indigenous to the Islamic order, either because the Qur'an and *sunna* speak of mutual relations, truces, and even an alliance (*mithaq*) among rulers, believing and infidel; or because *ijtihad* approves of any kind of agreement redounding to the public interest (*maslaha*). Although the traditionally educated *'ulama* tend to argue on the basis of the Qur'an and *sunna*, and the modern-educated intellectuals on the basis of the public interest, the lines are not clearly drawn and the two kinds of authority are equally acceptable. The pre-eminent international norm, *pacta sunt servanda* ('agreements must be kept'), is just as easy to accept. One representative Saudi argues that the importance of religious obligation to Muslims is the main reason why they honour all contracts, including international ones. The duty to fulfil the terms of a contract stems from an oath, voiced or unvoiced, which contractors make before God.[53] In short, these ideas are easy to accept because they are seen as intrinsic to Islam: the relationship is metonymic.

(2) Saudis also rely on metaphor to make the point that Islam and the modern system of states are compatible. They specifically react against the widespread view that Islam is expansionist and militant, and that the concept of *jihad* leads Muslims to reject the idea of peaceful coexistence among states. In support of their claim, some argue that the word *jihad* means 'self-defence', rather than 'crusade', but others – and this is a more important line of argument – say that the word does not mean 'self-defence' so much as 'effort', coming from the root verb *jahada*, 'to strive', 'to exert effort'. According to a Saudi trained in international relations, warfare may be involved in the idea of *jihad*, but to stress only this aspect, he says, is to rely heavily on medieval thought and to misconstrue early Prophetic history.[54]

In the view of an *'alim* (singular of *'ulama*) who likewise casts doubt on the premise that religious crusading is central to Islam, *jihad* must be seen principally as working for the good: i.e., as an attack on evil and an obligation to correct wrongdoing, resist corruption, and practise forbearance and equality. To do these things is to create a society that is at peace with itself. But according to him, because of the unquestioned desire for such a society, Saudi courts must sometimes enforce these duties – for example, when a son fails to care for his indigent father. In such cases, the general principle of respect for one's elders as essential for social harmony is upheld as *fard 'ayn*, or an obligation attendant upon the individual, and it is specifically seen as part of his 'greater *jihad*'. If *jihad* is to be made to refer at all to fighting, then this usage must be seen as the 'lesser *jihad*'.

Two other Saudis, both connected to the Meccan establishment, who gave me their views, agree that *jihad* means 'positive and peaceful effort'. One argues that there are two legitimately pacific efforts – liberation from false beliefs and advancement of social justice; the other emphasizes that society has an obligation to uplift the welfare of its people. Unlike the *'alim* cited above, these two imply that the *jihad* imposes *fard al-kifaya*, or collective responsibility, on the believers.

All three Saudis agree, nonetheless, that *jihad* is not the same thing as, or a sign of, war, but that, in its meaning of a more general obligatory striving towards the good and the suppression of evil, it is like, or a symbol of, peace, Going even further, they make a connection between sets of categories. As the greater *jihad* is thought to provide peace within society, it also thought to provide peace between societies or internationally: the use of the word *jihad* to mean international peace seems reasonable to them when the relationship between striving towards the good and social harmony, or domestic peace, appears to be similar to the relationship between striving towards the good and harmony between nations, or international peace.

(3) Saudis likewise rely on the metaphoric becoming metonymic to justify the acceptance of a system based on national pluralism. The early practice of Islam is so obviously like the present practice of pluralism that it comes to seem a form of current practice: symbol becomes sign. A Western-educated legal adviser to the government argues that the territorial nation-state fits into the larger framework of the *umma* and so does not contradict it. He argues, moreover, that political pluralism is indigenous, dating from the tension between Mecca and Medina from 622 to 630. Two other Western-trained Saudis see the notion of 'national interest' implied in that hallowed tenet of Islamic law, *siyasa shar'iyya*, which gives governors administrative discretion in cases when the public welfare demands it. Finally, a prominent *'alim* concludes that the principle whereby the *shari'a* applies to the believer no matter where he may live suggests that classical jurisprudence recognizes that territorial divisions will arise among the faithful.

All these Saudis link ideas from different contexts but would deny that they are being metaphorical. Early Islam, which takes on the aura of a golden era, still seems so alive and vibrant that it makes the modern idea appear as if it were intrinsic to the set of classical ideas. Here, therefore, is an example of quasi-metonymy at work: the nation-state seems more than merely a symbol of Islam.[55]

No doubt some of these arguments are contradictory or facile, but I feel sure that they amount to more than 'gratuitous and non-committal slogans'.[56] Rather, they represent a process of culture change, or assimilation, whereby Saudis have conformed to the principle of orderly pluralism as we know it in today's international system. They have done so by seeing in pluralism and Islam natural connections, of parts to a whole, or by finding that modern concepts have analogues in Islamic theory and practice, or better yet by believing that an equivalence of concepts exists. The third, dealing with quasi-metonymy, is the most interesting process, for sometimes the Saudis seem unaware that the connection between old and new is contrived, whereas at other times repetition makes the connection seem unconventional. At any rate, a transformation occurs, and what really is a symbol loses its lustre and becomes ordinary. I can find no discernible pattern as to when the Saudis rely on metaphor, metonymy, or a combination of the two, but I suspect that, as with all matters of language, much depends on comfortable expression rather than conscious choice.

Conclusion

We have noted a powerful and automatic dynamic at work over the years: people have a hard time disputing facts and they have a relatively easy time accepting them as the years go by. No matter how much they may think the reality diverges from the theory – and it must be remembered that this is not necessarily the case with the question at hand – the reality usually wins, even to the extent of affecting the way people think about it. The longer it is there, the more people begin to regard it as normal, natural, perhaps even desirable. If the classical theory at all lends itself to endorsing the factual record, then culture change is that much easier. This dynamic is what has taken place over the Islamic centuries so that the acceptance of territorial pluralism paved the way for the acceptance of national pluralism when the ideal of nationalism made its appearance in the nineteenth century.[57]

The role of intellectuals is especially important, particularly that of the *'ulama*, the formal arbiters of Islamic opinion. In the nineteenth century, Indian conformist *'ulama* supported the territorial *status quo* in order to preserve the religious *status quo*. In accepting British rule, in some people's view, they were not even 'negative nationalists'; that is, they were not even anti-imperialists. Today, with the imperialists gone, their intellectual descendants also support the territorial *status quo* to preserve the religious *status quo*, but increasingly less self-consciously and more automatically so. By and large they have become 'positive nationalists', disposed in favour of the nation-state.

There does not seem to be any significant difference between the traditionally educated and the modern-educated intellectuals. Both groups almost equally alternate among the three ways of arguing that I have described, and none relies exclusively on any one way. Moreover, society has conferred great respect on them, and consequently people defer to them and believe what they say. Perhaps somewhat like the stereotypical priest ('Law is the words in my priestly book/Law is my pulpit and my steeple'[58]), the *'ulama* and other intellectuals may not always possess fluency of logic, but they do have the weight of authority and the tradition of authority behind them.

My evidence in this chapter has come primarily from Saudi sources because it is with them that I am most familiar, but I have no reason to believe that these views are atypical. Indeed, it is significant that the Saudis, who are generally thought to have one of the most traditional of outlooks and conservative of approaches, have shown themselves to be so sensitive to – or defensive about – the concepts of modern international relations: the nation-state, the treaty, international peace. If they respond – both the traditionally educated and the modern-educated – in the way that I believe that they have, then it should not surprise us that this pattern of linguistic acculturation or adaptation exists elsewhere. In fact, throughout the Muslim world, one commonly hears and reads arguments similar to those advanced by the Saudis.

Thus the intellectual heritage of Muslims has certainly not stood in the way of their understanding and accepting the central modern idea of international relations. Yet, as I indicated at the beginning of Chapter 3, this is precisely what some writers on Islam argue. Indeed, many of them would doubtless counter my argument with the suggestion that the Muslim conformists have been engaging in narrow self-justification and, in as one writer put it, 'the sheerest sophistry'.[59] They might say that to argue that classical theory has indications of pluralism reads into the theory what the modern mind wants to see.

Apologetics is a frequent resort of modern Muslim scholars of Islam and one that many find irritating. Apologists characteristically affirm that Islamic ideas are not inconsistent with certain Western concepts that command current universal respect, such as democracy, constitutionalism, progress, or the nation-state.[60] They sometimes go further and argue that these Islamic ideas are actually superior to those advanced in the West – as when they claim that *jihad* means self-defence, or that Islam has qualities of tolerance and morality that are conspicuously missing in the Western-dominated international order.

There is no doubt that these statements betray a certain defensiveness, which is perhaps understandable in view of the attitude of non-Muslims. In the club of monotheists, Muslims have been made to feel like late-arriving interlopers; the 'family' has rejected them.[61] Western colonial armies easily defeated them, and much Orientalist scholarship left the disquieting implication that resurrecting *ijtihad* in the modern era was too little too late. Yet, regardless of the reasons for the defensiveness and of whether they are valid or not, apologetics is troubling to many people. They argue that it distorts the historical message of Islam by trying to locate 'good' ideas in the classical sources. This distortion in turn induces intellectual complacency, and almost certainly both tendencies stimulate Western disbelief and criticism.[62]

We can, however, take another view of apologetics. Rather than accenting the conscious side of it and seeing it as self-serving or dishonest, we can accent the unconscious side and see it as a stage in the complex process of culture change. My reading of the theory is that there are indeed indications of territorial pluralism, though naturally I would not subscribe to every argument outlined in this chapter. But the important point is this: even if no references to pluralism were to be found in the early sources, we would need to recognize that many Muslims think that they are there.

Reality constantly limits the ideal in history and this modifies what Muslims think that Islam is, or what 'the theory' says. Theory is certainly important, but it is important because Muslims feel the need to justify their conduct and belief by reference to some version of it. In doing so, theory has a way of changing in the direction of conduct and belief – a pattern seen in every religion, whatever the official expectation may be. But those who are sceptical about Muslim thought on international relations have underestimated this tendency, and as a result they have overestimated the degree of nonconformism that exits among Muslims.

5 Nonconformist thinking on the nation-state

Nonconformism, while not the majority's sentiment, has a distinguished place in Muslim thought on nationalism and the nation-state, and it continues to have many adherents. Although this is still unclear, it is possible that the present revival is stimulating nonconformist more than conformist thinking. What is indisputable is that, by its very nature, nonconformism has much in common with Islamic revivalism. The one consistent revivalist theme, which has emerged regardless of time or place, is that the cause of Muslim decline is the acceptance by many Muslims of inappropriate and alien innovations, or, more simply, their deviation from 'the straight path'. This reaction against *bida'*, or what is alien to Islam, has since the nineteenth century taken the particular form of a rejection of Western ideas and institutions that run counter to the Islamic message and distort it. Muslims themselves have been very critical of their own gullibility, and of the ease with which they are persuaded of the superiority of things Western. But, in the end, generous allowance has usually been made for these failings because of the obviously pernicious character of Western ideas and lifestyles. This pattern has been true of many issues, including international relations.

Twentieth-century Muslim thinking on international relations owes a great deal to the famous scholar of British India and, later, Pakistan, Abul A'la Mawdudi. In the late 1930s and the 1940s, he contended with the thorny question of whether a Muslim should be a Muslim nationalist, advocating a separate state for Muslims, or a nationalist Muslim, believing in one federal Indian state. Circumstances made him a Muslim nationalist, but he was nothing if not scornful of the ability of Western philosophy to make nationalism a natural and honourable sentiment. The terms 'Muslim nationalist' are as contradictory, he said, as 'Communist fascist', 'socialist capitalist', or 'chaste prostitute'.[1]

According to Mawdudi, in fostering nationalism, Westerners reveal the hollowness of their civilization: the nation–state, not God, is divine; material wealth, not spiritual welfare, is the goal; social strife and split personalities, not harmony and integrated personalities, are the result. In the name of nationalism, Hitler and Mussolini perpetuated their barbarities, and even the relatively more benign Americans set about 'exterminating' the Red Indians, and the Europeans enslaved millions of Africans.[2]

It is thus all the more damning that Muslims have come to be blind to the immoral tyranny of nationalism. They have done this, in Mawdudi's view, because their thinking has become intensely confused and contradictory. According to him, Muslims, especially Muslim elites, say that nationalism is the road to independence, yet they cannot see that their slavish aping of Western dress and cultural styles is hardly a sign of independence. They say they are working for their own national self-determination, yet they refuse to see that nationalism is selfishness writ large: that it leads to the denial of the self-determination of other peoples, and to domination over everyone else. It is no wonder that Muslims are in a new era of 'ignorance', *jahiliyya*, similar to that age of ignorance or darkness which preceded the advent of Islamic revelation. But, in a way, this *jahiliyya* is far worse because Muslims who know in their hearts that Islam has dispelled the darkness and replaced it with truth prefer, in the terms of the famous Platonic allegory, to sit in the West's cave and watch shadows dancing on the wall. His judgement was sharp: 'To declare allegiance to one creed and, at the same time, to support and advocate the cause of an opposite creed, only betrays a confusion of mind and a looseness of thinking, and those who do so, about them we are obliged to say that they are ignorant of Islam or of nationalism or of both.'[3]

Yet, critical as he was of his fellow Muslims who accepted nationalism, Mawdudi put the principal blame on Western imperialism. Political subjugation of Muslims was less important than 'the mental slavery' that the West imposed on them, leaving them 'cowardly and defeated mentalities', open to the nationalizing of God and His religion. The imperialists taught them that the only route to freedom, progress, and honour is through Western civilization, and, with the example of the political and ostensible cultural success of the Westerners before them, Muslims could be forgiven for concluding that the imperialists' lesson was the correct one.[4]

But they would still be wrong, Mawdudi felt, and they must come to understand that only Islam offers the alternative of selfless universalism to racialist, narrow-minded nationalism. Christianity cannot lead mankind to the world-state that Mawdudi thought necessary because it does not have a cogent political theory, and in practice it is racially prejudiced against blacks, as he believed was the case in Christian America and South Africa. Buddhism is totally aloof, unequipped to deal with the practical matters of life, he said, and Hinduism divides men into demeaning categories and castes. He left the possibility open that Marxism might achieve the universal state, as it suggests it will, but even if it were successful, the price – 'class struggle and the resultant bloodshed' – would be too high to pay.[5]

The only world philosophy remaining is Islam, according to Mawdudi, and it is for him a philosophy based on morality and spiritual unity, not on the force and political divisions that he saw in nationalism. To justify this conclusion, he quoted the Qur'anic verse, 49:13, which says that Allah divided men into nations and tribes so that they might come to know one another. Whereas other Muslims, such as some of those cited in Chapter 4, invoke this statement as justification of national divisions, Mawdudi used it to the opposite effect. According to him, the emphasis must fall on the second part of the verse, on knowing one another: Allah divided mankind into nations and tribes in order that similarities rather than differences would come to be appreciated, and a sense of kinship with the others rather than a sense of superiority over them would result. In fact, Islam endorses only one kind of superiority – in piety (49:13) – and the complete lack of discrimination on other grounds, such as race, language, or ethnicity, was the distinguishing characteristic of the early community of the Prophet and his four immediate, 'rightly guided' successors. Looking through distinctly rose-coloured glasses, Mawdudi thought that, despite qualifications of the ideal and the certain existence of divisions, Muslims held common citizenship in the Islamic *umma* until the nineteenth century, able freely to travel across what frontiers existed and willing to defend the Islamic common weal against all attack.[6]

In contrast, that great Muslim intellectual of the subcontinent, Muhammad Iqbal, moved far – and early – from his original antipathy to nationalism and enthusiasm for pan-Islam, and by 1929 was advocating a Muslim League of Nations.[7] Mawdudi also shifted his ground in the face of uncongenial realities, but not as much as Iqbal did or as early. In 1938, at Iqbal's invitation, he moved from Hyderabad to an East Punjabi religious community, and three years later he founded the Jama'at-i-Islami, which, after partition, became – as it remains today – a political force to reckon with in Pakistan and a political presence in India. It was designed to be an association of pious Muslims which would improve the education of Muslims generally and guide them to spiritual renewal, and was eventually to lead to the establishment of an Islamic state. But since the independence of Pakistan in 1947, the Jama'at has become both a moral force, teaching and influencing by example, and a political party, lobbying for specific constitutional changes and, when permitted, contesting for power. In the process, Mawdudi identified by osmosis with Pakistan (he moved to Lahore in 1947, when the partition unrest erupted), but he never lost sight of the larger *umma*. In 1965, on the eve of what he hoped would be the first summit of Muslim leaders, he wrote: 'I am particularly hopeful that my own country, which has consistently championed the idea of Muslim unity and has seen tangible manifestations of that unity during its recent conflict with India, will play a positive role in making this Summit a success.'[8]

Mawdudi talked, it is true, of the need to create 'a bloc of Muslim countries' and a Muslim International Court of Justice to resolve differences,[9] but he never lost sight for long of the greater unity of all Muslims as the prelude to the unity of mankind itself. In this, Mawdudi differed from Iqbal, who vigorously advocated the concept of Muslim nationalism, as he had pan-Islam before it.[10] Mawdudi was also unlike others who have argued that Muslims desirous of greater cooperation do themselves a disservice when they fail to understand the reality of nation-states, and thus the impossibility of unity; and he was unlike still others who have argued that it is in fact possible to be a good Muslim and a good citizen, regardless of what the abstract theory maintains. Examples of these lines of thought were given in Chapter 4. Mawdudi, by contrast, arrived at an understanding that Muslim nationalism was the best option in the circumstances, but he never settled for it.

In the famous 'sermons', *Khutabat*, that he gave in 1938, Mawdudi chastised the Punjabi Muslims for their failure to understand that Islam does not constitute an exclusive racial or political group but, rather, is open to any Brahmin or Englishman who accepts the tenets of the faith, just as the Islamic community is closed to any 'son of a Sayyid or Pathan' who is unfaithful.[11] His stinging rebuke to the Punjabi Muslims of the late 1930s anticipated his criticism of Muslim leaders thirty years later for failing to agree on the need for greater cooperation or even for a summit meeting. But for its bluntness, the earlier rebuke could have made his point well in the mid-1960s that the public squabbling between 'Abd al-Nasir and the Algerian President on the one hand, and King Faysal and the Iranian Shah on the other, over the desirability and the purpose of an Islamic summit was both unseemly and self-defeating:

Verbally you call each other Muslim brothers but in reality you observe all those distinctions which were prevalent before Islam. These distinctions have prevented you from becoming a strong wall. Each and every brick of yours is disjointed. You can neither rise together nor face a calamity together. If you are asked, in accordance with Islamic teachings, to break these distinctions and become one again, what do you reply? Just the same point: 'We cannot break the customs which have come down from our forefathers.'[12]

Indeed, in the 1960s Mawdudi talked of concrete steps for greater cooperation between independent Muslim states, such as a joint armaments industry, but he made it clear that he was still asking for unity: economic integration should be promoted; the teaching of Arabic as the Muslim lingua franca encouraged; more extensive communication between Muslims developed; and passports and visa restrictions among Muslim countries abolished. There is no doubt that he thought greater interstate cooperation, on the pattern of the Organization of African Unity or the European Economic Community, desirable and possible;

he referred to this as 'the union of Muslim States'. After all, he asked, are not Muslim states contiguous, and do they not share, in Israel, a common enemy as well as a common culture of prayer and ritual?[13] However, almost at the same time – though, to be sure, not as emphatically as he did in an era when independent Muslim states had yet to take hold – Mawdudi urged Muslims to overcome 'the diabolical conspiracy' of nationalism, and to realize finally that the doctrine of *tawhid* – 'One God, One Prophet, and One Book' – makes their future political imperative obvious.[14]

Arab Muslim thought

Mawdudi's writings, which were readily available in Arabic from the early 1950s, to some extent influenced Arab thinking of the 1950s and 1960s. This is particularly true with respect to the Egyptian Sayyid Qutb, one of the most important Muslim Brotherhood writers. Although the emotional power and uncompromising logic are Qutb's own, the premises of his argument owe a great deal to Mawdudi and, to a lesser extent, to the Indian writer Abul-Hasan 'Ali Nadvi, a disciple of Mawdudi and rector of the Islamic Academy in Lucknow, whose works have likewise had a wide reading in the Arab world.[15]

Sayyid Qutb has come to have one of the broadest followings of any Arab intellectual in this century, both because of a series of lucid and penetrating books that he wrote and because of the martyrdom that his execution by the Egyptian government in 1966 automatically conferred on him. His thinking is now widely known in the Indian subcontinent – and, indeed, elsewhere – just as Mawdudi's and Nadvi's ideas were known to him. As a wry commentary on human nature, the message that has won such popularity among Muslims is essentially unflattering to them and pessimistic: contemporary society is fatally flawed.

Qutb skilfully painted the picture of a self-absorbed and aimless society, in which individuality is valued above loyalty, achievement above character, status above honour, secular political success above fidelity to Islam. This is a society that has lost its moral compass. The blame lies mainly with the West, which, first, imposed the politically dead hand of imperialism and, then, proffered what it took to be the only model which could follow it but which in reality was the socially dead hand of Western culture. In the age of supposed national independence and anti-colonialism, he said, Muslims themselves must bear much of the responsibility for being attracted to this model and failing to see what it produces – crass materialism, social inequality, impersonal sexuality, superficial tolerance, and moral relativity – which he himself saw in the United States in 1949.[16] Clearly, this was a man who felt that he knew the West, and what he knew he did not like.

Muslims who are attracted to the Western lodestar thus inevitably lose their way and fall into a *jahiliyya* more execrable and perilous than the pre-Islamic *jahiliyya*. They have forgotten or disregarded what Islam teaches; and, unlike the earlier period, they are flirting with a full-blown philosophical alternative that seeks the supremacy of man rather than God and advances extremism of every kind rather than moderation in all things.[17] A central part of this philosophy that puts man above everything else is nationalism. The nation becomes the measure of everything, and the principle 'my country right or wrong' displaces the principle of submission to God. This new tribalism encourages men to fight for such unworthy goals as territory and prestige, and it will inevitably turn into imperialism.

According to Qutb, the Muslim should have no nationality except his belief, and his country should not be a piece of land but *dar al-islam*. Differing from the medieval jurisprudents who viewed the world as divided into two territories, *dar al-islam* and *dar al-harb*, Qutb seems at times to have thought of *dar al-islam* as only a spiritual community. But taken as a whole his writings must be seen as part of the general tradition that calls for the expansion of the Islamic community in material as well as spiritual terms. Any other sense of belonging – for example, to family, race, tribe, or particular territory – is the 'belonging of ignorance' ('*asabiyya jahiliyya*) and must be countered by the universalizing of the sense of belonging. And that will occur only when the *shari'a* becomes supreme everywhere and governs all aspects of life.[18]

A number of Sayyid Qutb's contemporaries argued along roughly similar lines, but were perhaps less uncompromising. For example, Muhammad al-Ghazzali, a member of the Muslim Brotherhood until 1953, seems to have believed that post-revolutionary Egypt could have an Islamic government, yet by and large he was critical of the institution of the nation-state. It is the product of Western imperialism and 'a return to the first *jahiliyya*'. Islam offers a stronger form of cohesion than kinship, he said, and, since there is one God, there is one community of faith (*umma*), which should eventually include all mankind.[19] To give another example, Sa'id Ramadan, also a member of the Muslim Brotherhood, went much further than Qutb or al-Ghazzali towards accepting the apparatus of the modern state, but he worried about the immoderate ideology that it spawned. Like the others, he credited the Muslim adoption of national ideologies to the cultural invasion of the West and feared that these ideologies have caused love of God to be replaced by love of country. In trying to reconcile his adherence to Islam with acceptance of the state, he made the arbitrary distinction between nationalism and nationality. Nationalism is an extreme ideology and is unacceptable; nationality, by contrast, is simply an administrative classification, a matter of exercising privileges and meeting the obligations of citizenship, and is acceptable. However, he worried that the idea of nationalism has become so popular and so displaced the idea of nationality that the Muslim has now come to believe his primary sense of belonging is to a particular race or ethnic group.[20]

A major reason why many Muslims have been passionately committed to the universal Islamic community is bitter disappointment at the experience of Arab nationalism. Committed Muslims have always had a certain ambivalence towards this idea. On the one hand, the Arab nation was to lead to the Arabs' liberation from Ottoman tyranny and European imperialism and to the creation of a core around which the larger community of Muslims would be formed. On the other hand, Arab nationalism was first and foremost promoted by people who were seen as secularists: i.e., those who, if they thought of Islam at all, did so as an afterthought and then usually as a means to legitimate the idea.

When, in 1931, the pan-Arab Congress proclaimed that the Arab nation was one and indivisible, it gave no formal role to Islam, even though the convocation took place in Jerusalem, the third holiest city of Islam.[21] The proponents of Arab nationalism hoped to convince their European masters, who for a century and more, had been suspicious or fearful of the 'fanaticism' of Islam, that a secular union would not be as unresponsive and antagonistic to their interests as they seemed to fear an Islamic union would be. Indeed, throughout the late 1930s and the 1940s one of the greatest exponents of Arabism, Sati' al-Husri, argued that although religion and history are important factors, language is the most important factor of all, given that Arabic is the only common element between Christian and Muslim Arabs.[22]

Despite its secularist beginnings, Arab nationalism came to have the endorsement of many, if not most, Muslim thinkers in the early 1950s. The Muslim Brotherhood in Egypt had already in the 1930s and 1940s supported the idea, mainly because it saw it as a way to oust, first, the British and, then, the Zionists, while at the same time moving towards the larger unity of Islam.[23] But the main intellectual justification was to come with 'Abd al-Rahman al-Bazzaz, a distinguished professor of law and later, in 1964, Secretary-General of the Organization of Petroleum Exporting Countries (OPEC). In 1952 he argued that Arab nationalism and Islam do not contradict each other because Arab nationalism is a 'belief and movement' and Islamic history is based on Arab history: the Qur'an was revealed in Arabic; the Prophet was an Arab; the early community of the Prophet and of his 'rightly guided' successors was situated in Arabia; within a few centuries Arabs had extended the Islamic empire from the Atlantic to the Indian subcontinent; and Arabs made capital cities such as Damascus and Baghdad impressive centres of erudition.[24]

This was an important argument, albeit a chauvinist one, but the more substantial point that he made was actually subtly – one might say, timidly – presented. It may be remembered that earlier I suggested that the theory of the Arab nation helped to rationalize the theory of particular nationalism (*wata-*

niyya): once a division of the *umma* was considered legitimate, other divisions were logically acceptable. Al-Bazzaz, however, went on effectively to reject this line of argument. *Wataniyya* and Islam do contradict each other, he implied, because glorification of one's own history outside of the Arab world would lead one to resent and perhaps to disparage the contributions of the Arabs to Islam, and this negative attitude would be inconsistent with the spirit of Islamic brotherhood. He failed to consider the possibility of differing loyalties among Arabs themselves, but even here we may surmise from what he said that local nationalisms are similarly contrary to loyalty to the larger Arab community, the heart of the Islamic community.

Later, in 1963, when al-Bazzaz was Iraq's ambassador to London and was soon to become Prime Minister of Iraq (1965–6), he was careful to say that his endorsement of Arab nationalism should not be interpreted as a denigration of the 'spiritual bonds' (*al-rawabit al-ruhiyya*) of patriotism that individuals have to their particular countries. Arab nationalism, in fact, could build on the idea of commitment to specific territory. But his main thesis was that nationalism can exist without land and a state: it is primarily a spiritual matter.[25] In failing to deal forthrightly with the obvious clash of different 'spiritual bonds' within the Arab world, however, al-Bazzaz left the distinct impression, both in 1952 and in 1964, that he was endorsing the Arab Muslim orthodoxy of the early 1950s: namely, that *al-qawmiyya al-'arabiyya*, Arab nationalism, was at once the bulwark against *wataniyya*, particular nationalism, and the stepping-stone to *al-umma al-islamiyya*, Islamic unity. Qutb himself was attracted to this view, and in 1953 endorsed Arab nationalism as virtually the historically mandated prelude to Islamic unity.[26]

Secular voices in disapproval of Arab nationalism had been heard before then, such as that of the Christian writer Antun Sa'ada, who in 1932 founded the Syrian Social Nationalist Party and was also advocate of a Fertile Crescent state centred on Syria. In 1940 he wrote that people were being deluded into thinking that the diversity which existed across the Arab world could be magically transformed and superseded by appeals to either a common language or a common religion.[27] Not long after Qutb endorsed the Arab nationalist idea, doubts began to set in among its Muslim supporters as well. The pan-Arabist government of 'Abd al-Nasir was becoming too secular, socialist, and authoritarian, and the Muslim Brotherhood, which had once supported the regime, was now proscribed and its vocal opponent, often clashing with it. Moreover, Muslims did not derive much satisfaction from the arguments of Christian Arab nationalist thinkers such as Michel 'Aflaq, the proponent of Ba'thism and one of the founders of the Ba'th Party, who argued that Islam is the foundation stone of Arabism and the greatest achievement of Arab civilization.[28] This concession to Islam was seen as perfunctory, and the general vagueness of nationalist plans, whether Nasirist or Ba'thist, on the details of how to achieve Arab unity was hardly reassuring to those who, while weak on details themselves, expected a steady, heavenly ordained progression towards the *umma*.

Muhammad al-Ghazzali did not ultimately lose faith in the idea of Arab unity and continued to regard it as the best route to Islamic unity. But the secularism of the Egyptian experience, particularly manifested in the doomed union with Syria from 1958 to 1961, convinced him that Islam had been manipulated, and that it would be merely a legitimating appendage rather than the very *raison d'être* of any larger union. The fault, to his mind, lay with grasping, self-serving Arab nationalists, and not with 'true' Arab nationalism.[29] However, a sobered Sayyid Qutb travelled the full distance of disillusionment within the confines of his Egyptian gaol. In the early 1960s he came to denounce Arab nationalism itself as alien to the divine scheme of things: 'Allah, the Omniscient and Wise, did not set His Prophet in that direction.'[30] Moreover, he said, *qawmiyya* belongs to the *jahiliyya* and, therefore, has 'completed its role in world history' and left the stage to Islam.[31]

Current thinking

Among the Saudis, this rejection of Arab nationalism was a common theme in the 1960s. 'Abd al-Aziz Ibn Baz, one of the leading members of the *'ulama*, vigorously denounced both the theory and the practice, and Faysal, locked in a political and military struggle with 'Abd al-Nasir and with several Nasirist officials at home, saw it as detrimental to plans for Islamic solidarity as well as a threat to the continued existence of Al Saud rule.[32] It was only with 'Abd al-Nasir's defeat in the 1967 war and the consequent hasty withdrawal from the Yemen, and the relatively greater confidence of the Saudi royal house which followed from these, that the criticism of Saudi Arab nationalism was muted. Since then, Arabism has come to be seen even as complementary to, and the twin pillar of, Islam.[33] Both the objection to and the approval of Arab nationalism, however, must be viewed as part of the same process of the advancement of a Saudi *wataniyya*. It is for this reason that, as I indicated in Chapter 4, most Saudi intellectuals are currently defenders of the nation-state idea.

But a dissenting intellectual line persists. In 1975 Muhammad al-Milham, a Yale-trained lawyer and academic and now a Minister of State, emphatically told me that there is 'a complete theoretical contradiction' between the nation-state and Islam and between international law and the *shari'a*. Both the nation-state system and international law are Western products, and they are predicated on such ideas as territorial sovereignty and national independence that are unknown to Islam. He maintained that although Islam does not allow for separate nation-states, there are Islamic principles, such as arbitration, that have been known to Muslims for fourteen centuries and that have relevance to present-day international relations. Yet the capability of Islam for self-renewal guarantees that this pluralistic system will be overcome and a unified world community established. The community will be 'an Islamic one', such as existed in early Islamic history.[34] Like al-Milham, Ibn Baz would not want to be seen as questioning the validity of a Saudi nation-state, but he too is hesitant to argue that practical reality must be indulged and the factual existence of national divisions accepted. Indeed, Ibn Baz was reported as saying in 1984 that Saudis should not travel excessively to the West because that can be corrupting, whereas the *umma* is 'the best nation mankind has seen'.[35]

Among non-Arab Muslims in the present period, South Asian thinkers have been particularly ready to grapple with the question of nationalism and to continue the tradition of articulate criticism of it. Southeast Asian intellectuals and activists, by contrast, have not agonized over it so much, or been so negative. This relative unconcern has probably come about because the spectre of inter-community conflict in Malaysia, Indonesia, and elsewhere has until recently encouraged a consistently strong official policy which seeks to de-emphasize religious issues in public life. Conversely, the South Asian concern with nationalism is not surprising in view of the perennial Pakistani debate over what constitutes an 'Islamic nation' and the turmoil that gave rise to Bangladesh's independence in 1971.

Fateh Sandeela, a Pakistani lawyer and commentator on Islamic affairs, argues that the sovereignty of the state can only be fictitious. But, more than that, the appropriation of sovereignty by the state has turned loyalty and law upside down. Rather than giving loyalty to God and obeying God's word, the individual has been made to think that he is loyal to God by being loyal to his state, and that God's law is operable only in so far as it is part of the state's law. 'The helplessness of the individual and of the Ummah was also enhanced by the division of the Ummah into innumerable states that tended to inculcate, not only exclusiveness and self-sufficiency, but also prejudice and petty-mindedness.' This divisiveness explains the silence of Muslims during the invasion of Lebanon in 1982. The only solution is to destroy the very idea of the nation-state.[36] In a similar manner, Akhtaruddin Ahmad, a Bengali lawyer and one-time Pakistani government minister, argues that sovereignty belongs only to God, and that the distortion of this truth has led men to fight for 'mere territorial integrity'.[37]

A more nuancé argument is presented by Fazlur Rahman, director of the Central Institute of Islamic Research in Pakistan from 1963 to 1969 during the Ayub Khan period (1958–69) and now Professor of Islamic Studies at the University of Chicago. He distinguishes between social nationalism and political nationalism. The former involves the cohesiveness of a group, and the latter involves loyalty to a nation-state. According to Rahman, the Turkish or Egyptian peasant can be a social nationalist, experiencing a sense of common ties of culture, language, and history with other Turks or Egyptians, without losing the sense of belonging to a greater Islamic whole. But when he becomes a political nationalist, his loyalty and identity become secular and clash with the Islamic ideal. The distinction strikes me as arbitrary and not borne out by practice. Nevertheless, unlike so many others, Rahman does not try to score debating points against the West, and he does hold out hope of a moderate compromise. As long as the ideology that puts the nation-state above everything else is avoided, it is possible to have a multi-state system that is compatible with the larger loyalty to Islam. However, a distillation of Rahman's thought on nationalism would leave something very much like Maududi's thought on the subject: nationalism, in the sense of identification with the nation-state, is predicated on secularism; and 'secularism destroys the possibility of the unity of the *umma*'.[38]

Kalim Siddiqui, director of the Muslim Institute in London, is less charitable and less subtle. He does not pull his punches, especially when criticizing fellow Muslims. They, particularly the academic community, have too docilely accepted the Western idea of the nation-state, he says. Muslim nation-states are like all the others – based on selfish interests, dedicated to the rivalries of power, and devoid of moral sensitivity. International relations need to be reformed so that the prevailing rules of diplomatic intercourse can be abandoned in favour of rules that discriminate between aggressor and victim and between believer and infidel. Moreover, he says, national frontiers should disappear to allow Muslim unity in the form of several regional groupings.[39]

KHUMAYNI'S THINKING

Siddiqui acknowledges the influence of the most noteworthy contemporary exponent of the non-conformist view, Ayatullah Khumayni. Khumayni is in an awkward position, for as the Iranian head of state he cannot disavow the idea of the nation-state, but as a revolutionary Islamic leader he cannot make his commitment to the national idea too strong or his commitment to the *umma* too weak. Perhaps this accounts for the various strands in his thinking.

Three strands are identifiable. First, some attachment to one's homeland is permissible and even natural, but when such attachment leads to conflict between Muslims, nationalism contravenes the Qur'an and helps the imperialists.[40] Second, Islam is, in any case, stronger than nationalism for it stimulates fiercer loyalty, thereby strengthening the righteous nation: 'A military man or a revolutionary guard who prays in the bunkers can resist like a lion.'[41] Third, it is important to strengthen the righteous – that is, Iranian – nation so that it can lead the movement for unity of the Muslims and, more important, of the world.

But whereas a former Iranian foreign minister spoke of Iran as the catalyst for transforming the Islamic countries and the world, Khumayni put his emphasis on world leadership: 'Islam is a sacred trust from God to ourselves, and the Iranian nation must grow in power and resolution until it has vouchsafed Islam to the entire world.'[42]

One may argue that for all his millenarianism Khumayni has implicitly joined the prevailing consensus and accepted the territorial nation-state. He refers to the development of the Iranian nation, talks of exporting the revolution beyond his borders, identifies his great enemies, the United States and the Soviet Union, in territorial terms, and ceaselessly condemns Iraq for violating Iranian territory and infringing its borders. With regard to the last, he has repeatedly said:

[Saddam Husayn] attacked Iran from land, sea and air . . . Each day they drop bombs or missiles on to Iranian cities and on the defenceless people . . . Our nation . . . will resist until it achieves its legitimate demands . . . We have never violated the rights of the people of Iraq and although our forces can hit Baghdad or Basra, they will not do so . . . We are brothers of the Iraqi nation and regard its soil as sacred . . .[43]

Other Iranian religious leaders have echoed these themes time and again, and have spoken in the same vein of defending the nation. Ayatullah Montazeri, for example, has said that the nation would bear the shortages that result from the war and foreign embargoes, and that Iranian honour demands that neither Washington nor Moscow be allowed, along with Iraq and other enemies of the revolution, to weaken the nation and the revolution.[44]

But it is the more fiery nonconformist rhetoric that seems to have resonance and predominate. During the hostage crisis, notable for the government's flouting of international conventions, the Foreign Ministry was nonetheless attacked for the inherent conservatism of its diplomacy. Moreover, in commenting on the reason for Saudi Arabia's denunciation of Khumayni's call for a universal state, Iranian radio sacrificed subtlety to directness, suggesting that it might be 'because this awaited universal Islamic state will demolish all tyrannical thrones built on the corpses of the oppressed and the sword of justice will claim all charlatans, agents and traitors'.[45]

There is in fact a coherent world-view behind comments such as these. Khumayni and his followers, believing that the world is corrupt and in a state of *jahiliyya*, say that Muslims and non-Muslims alike have succumbed to the immorality of Western culture and the political tyranny of the superpowers. The United States bears greater responsibility than the Soviet Union for manipulating Third World countries such as Iran and setting up false gods before Muslims, but both superpowers are satanic: 'These world-devourers who bear glittering names and chant slogans claiming to defend human rights, to seek peace and tranquility in the world and to support workers and farmers, are attacking the oppressed masses of the world and are adding to corruption, terror, murder and theft all over the world.[46] In international politics these two powers are clearly the *mustakbarun*, the oppressors, and the Third World, including the Muslim world, is the *mustad'afun*, the oppressed.

The world will overcome this fundamental rift and the oppressed finally meet justice, according to Khumayni, only upon the reappearance of the Twelfth Imam, who, according to the Imami Shi'i rite, went into occultation in 940 and, as *sahib-i zaman*, or 'master of the age', will re-emerge in the fullness of time. But in the interim the righteous believers should not slide into passivity; rather, they have a responsibility to overthrow corrupt and un-Islamic regimes and to spread the Islamic message across the world. Though the Imam is still absent, the Muslim community can be galvanized to this task by the *'ulama*, and in fact, according to Khumayni's doctrinal innovation, the *'ulama* have the right and duty to lead the community – or at least the paramount *'alim*, such as he is himself, has the right and duty to lead in their name.[47]

The Islamic revolution in the 'Muslim nation of Iran' must be preserved at all costs, Khumayni says, because in our era it is the core of the *umma*.[48] There are other 'progressive and Muslim countries', such as Syria and Libya[49] (which doubtless earned this tribute for their support of Iran in the Iran–Iraq war), but national distinctions and boundaries should count for nothing. According to Khumayni, the idea of territorial divisions is the fruit of 'deficient minds', and this revolution must be waged among people and movements, not elites and nation-states.[50] Though this concept may seem to be ideologically aggressive, it is really a 'defensive *jihad*' against the ideological warfare that the West and its Arab surrogate, Iraq, are waging against Islam.[51]

The best defence against evil ideas, however, is apparently the export of correct ideas. Khumayni is unapologetic about the need to spread the message of his revolution and feels that with ideas such as those, there is no need to resort to bombs and terrorism to get the message across, despite what many people in the West may say.[52] This divinely inspired 'call' (*da'wa*) has unity as its end, both spiritual and material. Muslims should unite around 'the sovereignty of Islam and the Koran' and in monolithic opposition to 'the front of blasphemy'; they should also form a political union that obliterates prior national divisions and serves as the prototype of the world state.[53] The obstacles to both kinds of unity are formidable, however, and ultimately Khumayni is not a simple determinist. He cautions that Muslims are divided between Sunnis and Shi'a[54] and into various schools of law, and that the imperialists have engaged in shameless exploitation, both directly in the era of colonialism and now indirectly via the Zionists. Muslims are truly at 'the crossroads of happiness and ruthlessness', he says: they can choose 'the straight path' of God and unity in His name, or 'the crooked path' of Satan and national divisiveness.[55]

KHUMAYNIST GROUPS

An extensive network of groups in the Middle East and beyond is inspired by Ayatullah Khumayni and partly influenced by Tehran. The exact connections are obscure,[56] but what does emerge clearly is that several groups share the current Iranian regime's world-view. For example, Hizbullah (the Party of God) and al-Amal al-Islami (Islamic Amal) in Lebanon, and Hizb al-Da'wa al-Islamiyya (the Islamic Call Party) and Munazzamat al-'Amal al-Islami (the Organization of Islamic Action) in Iraq, espouse the creation of Islamic republics in Lebanon and Iraq along the lines of Iran.

Most of their attention is focused on the political, economic, and social injustices that they face in their own countries but, – like Khumayni – they are prepared to believe that the nefarious hand of the United States in particular, and the West in general, is behind the injustices. Consequently, they are willing to use violence to overthrow the regimes based on *jahiliyya* and to usher in rule for and by the oppressed. Husayn al-Musawi, the leader of Islamic Amal in Lebanon, which broke away from the more mainstream Amal organization in 1982 and which is virtually the military arm of Hizbullah,[57] told an American television interviewer in 1984: 'As a nation and as Moslems . . . yes, we do not object to fighting the Americans . . . For us death is easier than smoking a cigarette if it comes while fighting for the cause of God and while defending the oppressed.'[58]

But Khumayni's followers in the Arab world, like Khumayni himself, display both millenarianism and pragmatism, able by turns to threaten violent upheaval in order to make way for the *umma* and to work within the system in order to make one country of the *umma* – their own country – truly Islamic. In doing so, however, they display their willingness to accept the framework of the nation-state even as they work in the long run for its replacement. Al-Musawi, for example, has said that coexistence with Christian forces, including even the Phalange, is a necessity if the unity of Lebanon is to be maintained.[59] Shaykh Muhammad Husayn Fadlallah, the spiritual if not the actual leader of the Hizbullah,[60] has repeatedly argued that gradualism, not revolutionary change, is what Lebanon needs: 'We told them [Iranian intellectuals and scholars] that Lebanon was different, that we do not have sufficient and necessary conditions for an Islamic Republic.'[61] Al-'Amal al-Islami in Iraq, which broke away from al-Da'wa in 1980 after the Iraqi government executed the influential religious leader Muhammad Baqir al-Sadr, is more uncompromisingly committed to armed struggle, but it too sees its role as a national one – to overthrow the Ba'thist regime and establish an Islamic state in Iraq.[62]

In the case of Lebanon in particular, Shi'i *mullas* and Shi'i groups became between 1983 and 1985 the rallying point for the resistance against the Israeli occupation of southern Lebanon. The leadership that they displayed earned them a great deal of respect throughout the country and in the Middle East generally, and even such secular organizations as the Syrian Social Nationalist Party took inspiration from their example and used religiously emotive terminology while themselves engaging in suicidal missions against the Israelis.[63] The Hizbullah has argued that even though its struggle is an Islamic one, it is at the same time a national struggle of resistance.[64] But, as one Lebanese Shi'i has put it, the Shi'a have come to an accommodation with the idea of Lebanon by way of 'negative consensus': as Shi'a they have emotional bonds with both Iran and Iraq, yet the war between those two countries has left them bereft of a home for their real loyalty. Having nowhere else to turn, they have made a minimal acceptance of Lebanon but have not positively identified with it.[65] I am not entirely convinced that this is the dynamic that is at work, but I have no doubt that the Shi'i groups which I have mentioned – though not necessarily the majority of the Shi'a – do in fact look beyond Lebanon to the *umma* for the focus of their loyalty.

Al-Musawi told a Paris-based Arabic journal that he and his colleagues follow neither Iran nor the Arab nation, but God and His religion. Nationalism and race are to be rejected as obstructing the sense of brotherhood that Islam instils.[66] Shaykh Fadlallah says that sectarianism of any kind is 'tribalism' (*'asha'iriyya*), and that nationalism, although an understandable reaction to Ottoman imperialism, is nonetheless incomplete and no substitute for Islam.[67] The Hizbullah has accented the focus on the Islamic community of believers by calling on the Christians of Lebanon to embrace Islam.[68] In Iraq as well, al-Da'wa denounces nationalism as racism.[69]

Conclusion

Despite obvious differences, there is a remarkable coincidence of themes in the writings of the nonconformists. First, running throughout is an unmistakable note of pessimism. Muslim society has gone badly wrong, and if radical action is not taken soon, spiritual and political catastrophe will certainly result. Second, Muslims have descended into a new *jahiliyya* that emphasizes nationalism, just as the pre-Islamic *jahiliyya* emphasized tribalism. Given the automatic association with the universally reviled pre-Islamic era of ignorance, this application of *jahiliyya* has great negative force and is meant as a powerful indictment. Third, part of the explanation for this sorry state of affairs is that Muslims have been seduced by Western ideas and culture, and therefore deserve considerable blame. But if one consistent villain emerges in the piece, it is the West. Seen as a monolith, it is the purveyor of bankrupt and immoral ideas as well as being the arch-imperialist. Fourth, the solution is to reject things Western, including the idea of the nation–state, and to return to God's rule on earth and to the notion that Muslims constitute one community (*umma*). The medieval jurisprudential bifurcation of the world appears as a sub-theme whereby *dar al-islam* should expand at the expense of *dar al-harb*, or, in its ironically semi-secular new formulation, 'the party of the oppressed' (*hizb-i mostaz'afan* [*mustad'afun*]) should triumph over the 'oppressors' (*mustakbarun*).

In all this, there is surprisingly little difference between Sunni and Shi'i nonconformists. Khumayni does acknowledge that the final triumph of good over evil can come only with the reappearance of the Imam, and bends over backwards to accommodate his idea of the export of the revolution with the only idea of *jihad* allowed to him in classical Shi'i thought – that of defensive *jihad*.[70] But apart from this and certain differences on the details of how to govern the *umma*, Khumayni and his followers sound remarkably like Mawdudi or Qutb in their assault on the nation-state idea.

Yet it would be wrong to leave the impression that this assault represents the mainstream of Muslim, whether Sunni or Shi'i, opinion. I believe it does not. Moreover, even Mawdudi eventually came to an accommodation with Pakistan, believing that it would be the first step in building the *umma*. This kind of begrudging acceptance has meshed with the general response of Muslims, whereby the reality of pluralism has gradually and steadily made its mark on their consciousness.

A prominent international figure such as Khumayni, with his fevered anti-Western rhetoric and emphasis on the universalism of the faith, seems to belie this point. He tends to suggest that the goal of all present-day Muslims is to return to the medieval juristic hostility towards *dar al-harb* and to give primary political allegiance to the *umma*. But even this kind of thinking, as we have seen, coexists with nationalist thinking, and often in practice takes second place to it. Particularly when charged with running a society, these idealists become realists – of sorts – who recognize that the nation-state is a functional institution. Thus Khumayni is able to say – in almost the same breath – that what counts is the battle between Islam and blasphemy, not that between Iran and Iraq, but also that national borders must be defended from the attack of blasphemous Iraq.[71] In effect, Muslims see the nation-state as part of the modern landscape while keeping their mind's eye fixed on the far horizon. It is impossible to predict what will be the long-term impact on the Muslim majority of the minority's ardent faith – that the seemingly unattainable is attainable.

6   Development and the Muslim nation-state

In the past two decades or so, a variation on conformism has emerged, influenced by nonconformism. This variation accepts the institution of the nation-state, but rejects the specific Western form that it has taken. It is a kind of conformism in that it accepts the nation-state idea; it is influenced by nonconformism in that it is critical of the Western model of the modern state. This criticism is levelled not so much at the model itself as at Westernization, or the course that economic, political, and social development has followed in the West. The Muslims who voice it are saying in effect that a modern state with a modern economy and society, and with effective political institutions, is fully compatible with Islam, and in fact is demanded by Islam's pre-eminent commitment to social justice.

This self-image flies in the face of the general Western assumption that Islam retards change and inhibits development. Cromer's experience of Egypt, for example, convinced him that Muslim societies were 'politically and socially moribund', and immersed in a 'gradual decay' that 'cannot be arrested by any modern palliatives however skilfully they may be applied'.[1] Modern social scientific literature has developed this general line of argument.

The view that Islam retards the process of development, and thus debilitates nation-building, owes much to Marx and something to Durkheim, both of whom argued that development and secularization are closely connected.[2] More recently, Manfred Halpern set the standard for contemporary social science – until the Iranian revolution, that is – when he spoke of 'Islamic traditionalism' as anachronistic (incompatible with modernization) and dangerous (tends to give way to violent extremism). The unhappy example of the Muslim Brotherhood locked in mortal combat with Egypt's 'Abd al-Nasir obviously influenced him, and led him to conclude that 'to be traditional . . . is to remain unrelated to modern political choices'.[3] This view has crept into a great deal of writing on Islam and builds on the implied notion that fatalism, the supposed closing of the door of *ijtihad* in the tenth century, and scriptural literalism are substantial and nearly insurmountable defects in Islam *per se*.

Malcolm Yapp offers an intellectually elegant variation of this argument. He says that the revival of Islam is dependent on the rate of a society's development: that is, the rate of economic growth and 'mobilization' or movement of people to the modern sector of the economy and society. When people are too quickly brought into the modern sector to be assimilated, they are dissatisfied, will press for economic and political changes, and will find in Islam a powerful language to articulate their demands. He goes on to say that because Islamic reassertiveness depends principally on the pace of economic development – though there are other factors at work, such as the kind of political development – we may conclude that the revival is a kind of hiccup in the progression of history: 'the transition may be more uneven than was supposed but the association of modernity with secularism, at least in the sense of the divorce of religion and politics, is still evident.'[4]

It is of course true that *de facto* secularism has often developed in Islamic history; I have argued this myself in Chapter 1. But it is a different matter to leave the impression that religion stultifies public life and that modernity, or the process of development, requires secularism. This would be tantamount to saying – as indeed some do – that Muslims face the stark choice of 'Mecca or mechanization'.[5]

Muslim views of development

Although the idea of development is often approached in terms of technological advancement, I will use the word in a broad and commonsensical way to mean the increase of economic, social, and political diversification and complexity. This implies greater degrees of efficiency at meeting people's needs, though, of course, the practical result may not live up to the ideal.

I think this is what Muslims have in mind when they talk of development, although, it must be noted, they differ widely on what exactly can change in Islam, what needs to be developed, how these changes are to be accomplished, and whether development should be done within the national context. Yet it is itself significant that there is remarkably wide agreement among Muslims, of all factions, that they have not fared well in terms of economic, social, and political development, and that this poor record has been due to excessive dependence on the West as well as to their own passivity. If the situation is to improve, Muslims must take charge of their lives and become more active in improving society.

Ayatullah Khumayni makes the same general point on development but characteristically puts it in terms of an historical imperative: 'In Islamic history we have not fought a single war that has had a purpose other than the building of our society and halting those who did not want to let that society develop.'[6] The society to which he refers is the *umma*, but even those who are loath to be bracketed with the Ayatullah and who are concerned more immediately with their particular society than with the broad Islamic one would agree nonetheless that Muslims have an obligation to be activists and to work for development. The Syrian Muslim Brotherhood, for example, in its manifesto of Islamic revolution for Syria, reminds Muslims that 'the establishment of God's rule on earth' depends on man's efforts and that, if a society of economic, social, and political justice is to be built and maintained, Muslims must see to it themselves.[7]

If there is any agreement among the many voices calling for a strategy of development to counter what is seen as an excessively Westernized approach, it is not on details but on the general principle that Islamic values should suffuse all planning schemes. A case in point is the argument put forward by the prominent Pakistani economist Khurshid Ahmad, Deputy Amir of the conservative Jama'at-i-Islami Party and former Minister of Planning and Development. As a disciple and translator of Mawlana Mawdudi, Ahmad starts out with the assumption that the nation-state is incompatible with Islam and that national-ism is an alien imposition on Muslim life. But he goes on to stress that Islam calls for unity, not uniformity, and that therefore political pluralism is tolerable as a fact of life – though it is not finally desirable – so long as the larger framework of Islamic cultural unity is kept in mind. The Muslim nation-state becomes more acceptable – 'legitimate' is the word he has used – when it follows its own light and not that of the West.

This means that each Muslim nation-state must make the *shari'a* supreme, develop a political system based on *shura*, or consultation, and commit itself to the path of economic growth and gradual change. With regard to the last point, Ahmad believes that it is imperative for Muslim planners, no less than Western observers, to understand, first, that Islam is not opposed to change (rationality is its most important characteristic) and, second, that not everything Western has to be rejected. The planner has to consider what the society needs, what Islam has to say on the matter, and whether the Islamic framework will allow a Western solution to these needs.[8]

Kamal al-Sharif, Minister of Awqaf and Islamic Affairs in Jordan (and former Egyptian Muslim Brother), says that one of the important effects of the revival is not that it is turning Muslims against the West, but that it is 'removing impurities' and providing 'immunity' against harmful alien ideas. It is equally important, therefore, to encourage the operation of traditional values in the society, such as the collection of *zakat* and the creation of interest-free banking in deference to Islam's prohibition on *riba* (usury). Muslims should even try to improvise, combining modern banking practices with traditional ideas. An example is the

Jordanian government's decision in 1982 to allow banks to offer 'partnership' (*muqarrab*) bonds, whereby in place of guaranteed interest the investor undertakes to share with the bank's other investors in the losses as well as gains of the investment.[9]

Other Muslims are not as sanguine about the ability of Islam to generate its own approach to modern economics. Abdurrahman Wahid, a prominent intellectual associated closely with the Nahdatul Ulama Party in Indonesia, thinks, for example, that all the efforts to create interest-free banking are too clever by half. After all, he says, 'economics is economics', and such devices as partnership bonds are merely a way to earn interest on an investment without using the name 'interest'.

Rather, Wahid believes that Islam's principal contribution to building a modern society lies in its ability to provide a 'theology of human growth'. But this positive contribution can happen only if Muslims rise above the self-complacency that leads them to think that the answer to every problem is the application of traditional Islamic law. On the contrary, he thinks, Muslims must develop a new consensus on what the law means today. For example, would it not be right in conditions of overpopulation and mass poverty for the community to come to accept the validity of birth control, even though some Muslims seem to be hostile to it? When a new consensus is worked out, he feels, it will be easier to integrate Islamic law into national law. This integration can only advance the cause of national development, which, without doubt, must be the highest priority.[10]

It is clear that Wahid represents a revisionist line and thus differs from the others by being highly critical of the way Muslims have approached the question of development. But he may be taken as representative of the nearly unanimous opinion that an Islamic strategy of development has as its end the creation of a modern nation-state that is true to indigenous, not Western, values. Wahid is aware that nationalism and religion may be at odds doctrinally (where, for example, do loyalties ultimately lie?) and practically (government and church inevitably find themselves in political competition). But he concludes that the real contribution of religion is to draw on the strength of its transcendent values, such as 'justice' and 'equality', and on the appeal that these values have for the masses. In this way, he says, religion can make the nation focus on development above all, thereby helping the nation to meet its moral obligation to the people.[11]

There are differences of approach and emphasis, but three general points emerge from the comments of these Muslims: (1) Islam is compatible with economic, political, and social change; (2) Islam requires social justice, and this imperative implies the need to change within a broad framework of traditional values; and (3) rejection of the West means rejection of social and cultural

Westernization, and (though Khumayni would not subscribe to this) not necessarily rejection of the historically Western institution of the nation-state or of the fruits of Western technical and material development.

The compatibility of Islam and development

The poor reputation that Islam has acquired for not being able to adapt to new circumstances is not entirely undeserved, for Muslims have put strong emphasis on the need for *taqlid*, or imitation, since at least the tenth century. But, as I showed in Chapter 1, since the late eighteenth century, there has been a growing body of opinion among Muslims that *taqlid* was one of the main causes of their weakness and stagnation. In the nineteenth century, Al-Afghani took this idea a long way by arguing that the early community of Islam made provision for progress, and that believers could recapture that spirit if only they would accept that science and faith are consistent. Rashid Rida went further in arguing that the community has the authority to create positive or man-made law as long as this law does not contradict, and is subsidiary to, the *shari'a*. Some people would say that he made an arbitrary distinction between man-made and God-made law and that the idea of the *shari'a* implicitly covers evolution. Still, most Muslims prefer to follow the formula that God is the sole legislator but that there can be such a thing as supplementary man-made law to allow the community to keep pace with or to address social changes as long as these do not specifically contradict the *shari'a*. This is what was meant when the Iranian constitution of 1906–7 said that the *'ulama*, as guardians of the constitution, were to take 'the requirements of the age' into account.[12] In effect, most Muslims would be unable to disagree with the essence of Muhammad Iqbal's comment that 'the claim of the present generation of Muslim liberals to reinterpret the foundational legal principles, in the light of their own experience and the altered conditions of modern life, is . . . perfectly justified'.[13]

Indeed, even many conservatives or so-called fundamentalists, who object strenuously to the idea that further legislation is possible, in practice accept that there are well-established procedures by which legal changes can be made. These procedures fall into five main categories. First, many accept that one can pick and choose (*takhayyur*) among the legal schools in order to make a judicial ruling or frame a regulation, rather than relying exclusively on one school of thought. Second, they also accept the principle of *siyasa shar'iyya*, which since at least the eleventh century has allowed Muslim rulers to supplement the basic law with administrative decrees. Third, and related to this, is *takhsis al-qada*, whereby the sovereign is allowed to create and reform institutions or prescribe penalties when these are lacking in the main sources of the law. Fourth, it is generally accepted that rules can be made so long as they are in the public interest (*maslaha*). Finally, there is a built-in flexibility in the legal categories that can be employed. The law classifies permissible acts into those that are recommended (*mandub*) and those that are censurable (*makruh*). It has become common for Muslims to translate these ethical judgements into legal commands. For example, the laws of personal status in several countries have severely limited the husband's privilege of repudiating his wife, always considered *makruh* or a reproachable act.

THE CASE OF SAUDI ARABIA

There is much scholarship on how these procedures have allowed legal reform in several countries of the Muslim world, but there has been almost no comparable work on Saudi Arabia. Saudi Arabia's practice is particularly instructive, since many people believe that its Hanbali jurisprudence prevents it from adapting to new situations. This view is far from the truth. The Saudis maintain that they are not out of touch with 'the requirements of genuine civilization',[14] and there is a great deal of evidence that they use all the five methods that I have just described to create a modern system such as would exist in other countries. I have deliberately chosen to focus on the example of Saudi Arabia on the grounds that if an ostensibly conservative country such as this can use such legal procedures to revise the law, any country of the Muslim world can do so. (Egypt, Syria, Tunisia, Pakistan, and others have in fact done this.[15]) It is worth looking at these procedures in turn.

The Saudis have certainly relied on *takhayyur* (or picking and choosing among the orthodox legal schools) – despite some initial resistance from the *'ulama*. When King 'Abd al-'Aziz tried to make it possible for the *'ulama* to pick and choose, they opposed this step, since they feared it would mean the effective triumph of the Hanafi school, which in fact prevailed in the Hijaz.[16] He therefore deftly ruled that jurists were to rely primarily on the main texts of the Hanbali school but were to call on other texts if Hanbali law was silent or unclear on a given issue. Today the invocation of non-Hanbali principles is relatively common. The Mining Code, for example, reflects the greater clarity of Maliki teachings that minerals are not subject to private appropriation in any circumstance; the state's possession of them is subject to neither 'cancellation' nor 'devolution' over time.[17] But the lack of juristic unanimity on this point, as well as the understandable special interest in petroleum and natural gas and the need to have foreigners extract them, probably explain why the code excludes these two resources. In effect, the code gives Saudis some control over their economic future without automatically precluding foreign involvement, on which they have been practically dependent.[18]

The Saudis have also relied on *siyasa shar'iyya*, administrative discretion, and in this way have reconciled Muslim sensitivity over the permissibility of legislation with the obvious fact that the *shari'a* does not cover every detail of social and political life. They have preferred, for instance, to use the term *nizam*, 'decree' or 'regulation', in place of *qanun*, or 'law'. The objections to the idea that legislation is possible have largely disappeared, but the use of this linguistic convention assures that the Saudi government appears to be operating within permissible bounds.

Siyasa shar'iyya has proved useful in dealing with the conditions of modern economics. In 1931 the government promulgated a Commercial Code, and this was replaced in 1954 by the Regulation on Commerce, which is based on the nearly universally accepted – and liberal – Ottoman commercial Code. Other examples include the Labour and Workmen Law and the Social Insurance Law, both of 1970. The latter is interesting for its ostensible abandonment of the traditional patterns of inheritance. It lists only the widow, orphans, brothers, sisters, and parents as 'heirs' and 'possessors of right' in the question of inheriting the insurance benefits, and notably says nothing about male agnatic relatives becoming claimants. Moreover, it fails to distinguish among the collaterals (i.e., among germane, uterine, and consanguine brothers and sisters), and it says that before the deceased's father can inherit he must be over sixty years of age and 'unable to work' – both points contrary to the classical principles of inheritance[19] but in keeping with the view that the general social welfare in a modern economy must be the first consideration.

The Saudis have likewise resorted to *takhsis al-qada*, which permits the sovereign to reform legal institutions in the interest of assuring public order. As noted, this type of administrative discretion is closely associated with the well-accepted right of the ruler to prescribe the way to deal with offences whose punishments are not specified in the main legal sources. Saudi Arabia has an established record of such administrative innovations. Over the years it has created a multi-tiered *shari'a* court system[20] and has joined all other Muslim states in providing for an appellate mechanism: the ruling of the individual *qadi* (judge) may be subject to the review of the Court of Cassation and the Supreme Judicial Court. The Saudis have also been innovative in areas outside the *shari'a*. The most important has been the Board of Grievances (*diwan al-mazalim*), which has been in operation since 1955 and, following 'Abbasid precedent, handles complaints of administrative injustice.[21]

There are many examples of administrative tribunals that are not as comprehensive in function or as rooted in history but are instructive nonetheless. One must suffice here. The Labour and Workmen Law provides for the establishment of both a commission of first instance and an appellate body to hear and resolve labour disputes and to impose appropriate penalties. The judgement of the Supreme Commission is final, though of course appeal to the Board of Grievances is possible. Although these boards are administrative innovations, they do not operate wholly outside the influence of the traditional law. The chairman of the commission of first instance must hold a degree in *shari'a*, and at least one of the remaining two members must have a degree either in *shari'a* or in 'jurisprudence' (*al-huquq*).[22] Moreover, the Labour and Workmen Law demonstrates how the Saudis are able to be creative in combining old and new ideas. It expressly forbids the commissioners to abstain from making a ruling whenever they are convinced the law is silent, and it enjoins them instead to rely at such times on, first, principles of the *shari'a*, and, then, local rules, judicial precedents, the principles of justice and of usage, and equity (*qawa'id al-'adala*).[23] This law provides a remarkable collection of standards that support and facilitates the work of one administrative tribunal which it trying to help the regime to meet social demands.

The Saudis have found opportunity, too, for applying the broad idea of *maslaha*, public interest or welfare. The Mining Code, which follows the spirit of the United Nations Resolution on the Permanent Sovereignty over Natural Resources and declares state ownership of most mineral resources in the soil and subsoil, on land, and in the air, was possible largely because of this idea. The government went to great pains to stress that it was not a new law, but only a way to avoid 'considerable economic losses' that might arise without it and to put the kingdom in line with 'most modern codes'. In actual fact, it was of course new legislation, and the reason why it was even conceivable was that the government was seen to have a fundamental obligation to serve the public interest. In fact, with regard to this piece of legislation, the government noted that *maslaha* was the very 'anchor' (*manat*) of all principles applicable to Muslims.[24]

Finally, it may be argued that the Saudis appreciate the modern juristic practice of turning what is recommended (*mandub*) and what is censurable (*makruh*) into legally binding commands and prohibitions. Their abolition of slavery seems to fall into this category. In 1936 the government ended the slave trade, but it was only in 1962 that it altogether abolished the practice of holding slaves and provided for their manumission.[25] Although the Qur'an allows the possession of slaves, it does not commend the practice. It encourages the conditional freeing of slaves (24:13), stresses that to use one's wealth on their behalf is an act of piety (2:177), and gives manumission as the first example of the 'steep road' to virtue (90:12–13). In turning the morally recommended into the legally required, therefore, the 1962 decree allowed the Saudis to meet the demands of the modern international consensus without appearing to break radically with the traditional framework.

These examples of Saudi adaptability, however, should not be taken to mean that conservatives are uniformly happy with all the laws that have been introduced. Indeed, in several Muslim countries, conservative voices have been clearly heard in criticism of laws framed in an earlier, more self-consciously liberal era. Criticism is made both because the content of these laws is seen as deviating from traditional Islamic principles, and because those who promulgated them are seen as being over-Westernized and secular.

Family law, covering matters of marriage, divorce, and inheritance, is a particularly sensitive area. The Ottoman Law of Family Reform set the tone for liberal reform as far back as 1917 (although when Atatürk came to power he dismissed both this and Islamic law generally as reactionary), and a number of liberal codes followed. These have been under attack recently in several countries, including Pakistan, whose 1961 law is being reconsidered in the context of a general codification of *shari'a* law, and Iran, whose 1967 law (revised in 1975) has been revoked. Yet in neither country has the reaction been part of an attempt to enforce the notion that all legislation is impossible. On the contrary, in Pakistan, President Zia ul-Haq has reinvigorated the Islamic Council of Ideology precisely to propose new legislation in keeping with the Qur'an and *sunna*[26] – or, rather, his interpretation of them. Moreover, by creating an appellate *shari'a* court to pass judgement on whether individual existing laws are consistent with Islam, he has implicitly accepted that not every piece of legislation is void.

In Iran, Ayatullah Khumayni says that Islamic government differs from all other forms of government in that only God can legislate, but he principally argues that the legal scholar (*faqih*) is the proper ruler of an Islamic society. His task is to implement whatever laws are permissible, but he also has a duty to exercise *ijtihad*: 'Ijtihad has always existed, does and will exist, and it must be considered that the problems that have arisen today differ vastly from the problems of former times, and there are different interpretations of the laws of Islam.'[27] The practical line, thus, between implementation and legislation tends to become blurred, and recognition of this reality is made in the constitution of the Islamic republic: the Majlis (Parliament) is empowered to enact new laws as long as the Council of Guardians, made up of *faqihs*, certifies that these laws are in keeping with Islam. It has approved a new banking law, for example, that Islamizes the old banking system but does nothing significant to impair its operation.[28] That proposed legislation on trade nationalization and land reform was rejected in 1982 by the Council of Guardians testifies merely to the political objections to these bills rather than to any general conclusion that they are outside the areas on which the government can legislate.

The first conclusion to draw from this discussion is that even supposedly conservative regimes are able and willing to adjust Islamic law to changing circumstances. They therefore seem willing to accept that there is a distinction between divinely ordained law and divinely inspired law: the former is immutable, the latter capable of revision as later inspirations occur. This is the distinction which Sayyid Qutb made when he said that the *shari'a* is beyond amendment, but that *fiqh* (the body of rules developed from interpretation of the *shari'a*) can be changed as the situation warrants.[29]

Given this legal flexibility in practice, a second conclusion follows: nothing intrinsic to Islam prevents the development process from taking place. We must, however, concede that Muslim conservatives, like conservatives anywhere, want to slow down the process and to reshape development plans so as to ensure that the rush to change does not eliminate fundamental traditional values. In Pakistan and Iran, they have managed to delay the implementation of some of these plans, and in Indonesia they ardently attacked the idea that development of the economy needed to be accompanied by changes in marriage law. But the conservatives have been unable to derail the development process, and, by and large, they have not wanted to.

The need for social justice

The revival of traditional values that began in the late 1960s forced Muslims to go further than merely to claim that Islam allows development: many now argue that Islam *requires* it. The Indonesian Abdurrahman Wahid, in speaking of religion's role as moral guide to the nation, put his finger, I think, on what is at work among many Muslims: it is the idea that Islam demands social justice, and that to realize this and work for it are the true tests of the committed Muslim today. Although Westerners tend to think – and not always unreasonably so – that the typical Muslim stance is to be *against* something, there has been a growing recognition among Muslims in recent years that Islam must be *for* something. In a way, many Muslims have come to take heart from the experience that they themselves have had of what is wrong with society, just as the peasant girl, Zuhra, does in one of the novels of the Egyptian writer Najib Mahfuz. Having gone to Alexandria to find the good life, she is bitterly disappointed. But a wise old man, 'Amir Wajdi, tells her that it has all been useful: 'Those who discover something of what is *not* good for them may have already, in a magical sort of way, come to discover what is truly good for them.'[30]

Yet, as the story implies, it is easier to know what is not good than what is good – or, in the current language of Muslims of all opinions, what is not authentic rather than what is authentic (*asali*).[31] We have seen that Western and purely secular ideologies do not seem authentic to a great many Muslims. But the problem is to decide what is authentic. Here there is no precise agreement, although we can detect one idea looming out of the intellectual haze – social justice, much as the old man with his 'troubled heart' in Najib Mahfuz's story was drawn to the chapter of 'the Beneficent' in the Qur'an (55:1–13: 'He has set up the Measure; do not exceed it, but weigh with justice, and do not fall short . . . For His creatures He has set down the earth, wherein are fruit and palm-trees, husked grain and scented herbs . . .').

A new consensus may be emerging that if God's call to mankind means anything today, it is a 'call' (*da'wa*) to uphold the fair deal of the Qur'an – a society both balanced and just. Indeed, the very idea of *da'wa*, a concept which the Qur'an mentions (14:44), seems now to have acquired broader connotations.

TRANSFORMATION OF DA'WA

The word is generally associated with missionary activity because of the idea that Muslims have an obligation to proselytize among the non-believers, and Muslim writers have sometimes distinguished it from other activities. However, the differences between such activities as *tabligh*, 'transmitting information' about Islam, *takallum*, 'speaking' about Islam, and *tadhkir*, 'reminding' of what Islam stands for, are barely distinct in practice. More important in practice are three points. First, the distinction between these activities, which are clearly aimed at Muslims in order to make them better Muslims and do not have conversion of non-Muslims as the objective, and *da'wa*, which is aimed at non-Muslims and does have conversion as an objective, has been blurred, although not entirely erased. As a result, all activities with a pedagogical intent are often subsumed under the idea of *da'wa*. Second, the educational character of *da'wa* has been transformed. Teachers now help their students acquire modern skills as well as explain to them what they believe Islam is. Third, for many Muslims the range of *da'wa* activities has broadened beyond the educational and propagative to include social welfare activities such as health care. Whereas *da'wa* once applied primarily to the conversion of non-Muslims, it now includes the idea of the education of Muslims and, more importantly and recently, social welfare activities for Muslims. In short, the balance of emphasis has largely shifted to fellow Muslims.

The slogan *din wa dunya*, 'religion and the world' (or *din fi'l-dunya*, 'religion in the world'), captures the spirit of this new and extended *da'wa*, whereas the standard formulation *din wa dawla*, 'religion and state', with the implication of Islamic law applying to everything, seems antiquated and beside the point to many Muslims. Ashfaq Ahmad, an academic and member of the Islamic Society of Papua New Guinea, provides an example of this new way of thinking:

Da'wah work [as traditionally understood] must be supplemented with the social, cultural, and economic development of the country. A substantial amount of funds should be allocated to be spent in these countries for health, education, and better living conditions for the people living there in the form of grants, aids or loans . . . The spirit of service and brotherhood should inculcate and permeate all the activities of development, so that people may appreciate the difference between da'wah work and colonialism.[32]

It must be said that although this quotation, in making colonialism the bogyman, illustrates an important new way of thinking, it also points to an old theme of Third World thinking.

The World Assembly of Muslim Youth (WAMY), or al-Nadwa al-'Alamiyya li'l-Shabab al-Islami, which has its headquarters in Mecca but which has several hundred member branches throughout the Muslim world, is an example of the educational *da'wa* organization. Its Assistant Secretary-General, Abu Bakr Bagader, says that it is, properly speaking, not yet a *da'wa* group, and he prefers to call it a cultural organization. But its aims – helping young Muslims to 'think seriously in modern terms' and to contribute to the development of their societies – are in keeping with the broad notion of *da'wa* that, first, blurs the distinction between the conversion of non-Muslims and the education of Muslims and, then, focuses on the encouragement of Muslims to be better Muslims in today's world. The fact that this Saudi-controlled organization sees as its *raison d'être* to help Muslims deal with modern conditions and, in Bagader's words, to 'integrate science with humanism' is a sign of how widespread the consensus is that *da'wa* must be relevant. WAMY, however, is a relatively limited organization in that it restricts it activities to sponsoring religious study camps for young Muslims between the ages of fifteen and thirty, and to holding conferences on such themes as the propagation of the faith and the nature of recreation in Islamic societies.[33]

In Nigeria the Jama'atu Nasril Islam (JNI), or Society for the Victory of Islam, sees itself as having a number of functions: to propagate the faith; to 'encourage intellectual religious activities'; to establish schools where Islamic and 'other subjects of general education' are taught; and 'to establish and run Hospitals and Dispensaries of all categories for the care of the sick'.[34] The educational mission has taken on particular importance, since the government's Universal Primary Education scheme has had the effect of reducing the number of students who attend Qur'anic schools, particularly in the countryside.[35] The JNI still operates a religious school, although the general primary schools and the secondary school, Sabah College, which it had set up, have now been taken over by the government. Other *da'wa* groups are active in this field too. For example, the Ansarul Islam Society, or Followers of Islam Society, has recently set up an Arabic Higher Education Institution in Laduba in the Nigerian state of Kwara State.[36] But the JNI is the largest body and is active in other fields, such as health care: it has created an Aid Group that operates similarly to the Red Crescent or Red Cross, and, according to Alhaji Abubakar Mahmud Gummi, the chairman of the JNI and former chief *qadi* (judge) of northern Nigeria, there are hopes of expanding the services to include health clinics.[37]

In Indonesia Muhammad Natsir, a former prime minister, created in 1967 the Dewan Da'wah Islam, or Council of Islamic Da'wa, to help advance the establishment of an Islamic state. Towards this general end *da'wa* activities came to include not only the sponsorship of educational programmes and the coordination of the activities of religious schools and *pesantrens*, the traditional schools, but also help towards the construction of new hospitals. According to Natsir, in 1981 there were 550 hospitals in Indonesia, of which 135 were private and Christian and only 12 private and Muslim. The Dewan does not actually build Muslim-controlled hospitals but, rather, sets up foundations to channel funds for their construction, supplies technical training for the personnel, and gives general advice, as it did in South Sumatra. To Natsir's mind, then, *da'wa* means 'field service',[38] as it does to a great many other Indonesian Muslims. For example, a group of students and faculty at the Bandung Institute of Technology, known as the Salman group, has been very active trying to create viable cooperatives. It has been successful in running a bookshop, building a residence hall, and publishing textbooks and translations of a wide selection of works, ranging from the writings of Sayyid Qutb and Khurshid Ahmad to Godfrey Jansen's *Militant Islam*.[39]

The Angkatan Belia Islam Malaysia (ABIM), or the Muslim Youth Movement of Malaysia, is, like WAMY (to which it is affiliated), primarily concerned with educational matters. It provides two years of pre-university coursework not only in Islamic subjects, but also in such subjects as English, for approximately a thousand students who aspire to enter university, and it also organizes special training seminars and occasional colloquia on such topics as Islamic education and the *hajj*.[40] Its former president, Anwar Ibrahim, now Minister of Agriculture, to whom I referred in Chapter 4, prefers not to call it a *da'wa* organization, for, he says, that would imply it has a missionary role. However, he may object merely because he thinks that people still associate it with groups whose almost exclusive concern is with ritual. His view is that an 'Islamic organization' such as ABIM should engage in a broad range of activities, including exerting pressure on the government to effect land reforms, to clamp down on corruption, and to be more tolerant of the non-Malay population. He argues that organizations of this kind should also set up cooperative societies, as ABIM has in fact done, in order to run retail stores and other enterprises for the economic benefit of its members.[41]

The most established *da'wa* organization in Malaysia, however, is Pertubohan Kebajikan Islam Malaysia (PERKIM), or the Malaysian Muslim Welfare Organization. Unlike ABIM, PERKIM clearly envisages its principal task to be the conversion of non-Muslims, particularly the Chinese, to the faith, and claims considerable success at it: 60,000 in the Malay peninsula, 100,000 in Sabah, and 80,000 in Sarawak since independence in 1957. But it also runs an institute for the training of missionaries, a vocational training institute in collaboration with accounting and business firms, and five health clinics throughout the country. There have been plans to open a hospital and an Islamic bank in cooperation with Dar al-Mal, the international Islamic banking house set up by Saudi Arabia's Prince Muhammad.[42]

DA'WA AND POLITICS

But the picture of *da'wa* is more complex. In fact, as *da'wa* becomes more active and preoccupied with creating the conditions of social justice, there is greater and greater difficulty in separating its pastoral role from politics. This political role leads some people to conclude that the new *da'wa* work is effectively becoming subversive, barely concealing the aim of toppling impious princes and, in that way, undermining the already weak institution of the nation-state in the Muslim world. Indeed, there seems at first glance some evidence of this.

A good case in point is the Dewan Da'wah Islam in Indonesia. Muhammad Natsir is remarkably open in acknowledging that the organization, while ostensibly devoted to its educational and medical services, is in fact the new vehicle for the old, now banned Masjumi Party. 'I limit myself, constrain myself, to social activities,' he says, 'but how can one say *da'wa* is not political? People cannot stop still and cease to be politicians.'[43] The *da'wa* people can be political in perhaps three senses: lobbying for an alternative political order; being 'fifth columnists', helping to infiltrate the establishment; and openly rebelling, seeking to overthrow the government.

There is no doubt that in Indonesia many people feel strongly about the first political sense of *da'wa*, arguing that Indonesia should ideally become an Islamic state, or, failing that, at least an 'Islamic order' or society in which Islamic values are more diligently applied. Not everyone believes that the issue of an Islamic state is a burning one,[44] or perhaps feels that it is prudent to be so candid in light of the sensitivity generated by the Dar'ul Islam revolt of Kartosuwiryo in West Java from 1948 to 1962.[45] Still, most Indonesian Muslims believe that agitation for greater Islamization goes to the heart of what Muslims should be doing today and recognize that this demand inevitably puts them at odds with a government committed to the secularization of the Pancasila. Natsir, for instance, goes the full distance. When he says that 'it is too mathematical to conclude that because the majority of Indonesians are Muslims, there should be an Islamic state', he is of course being ironic and means exactly the opposite: if we lived in a logical and just world, Indonesia would indeed be an Islamic state. Many Muslims would disagree with Natsir's identification of an Islamic state with a 'theistic democracy', question what he means by it being an 'open society', and specifically object to his view that it should involve freedom of religion and genuine 'communication with non-Muslims'. Many in fact would regard his conceptualization as entirely too ambiguous, if not emasculated. But, to Natsir's mind, the fact that few people agree on what the idea of an Islamic state means in practice is less important than that most people are instinctively and consistently drawn to it.

Lobbying does not always consist of 'holding the torch '[46] for an Islamic state. *Da'wa* people may sometimes think that the establishment of such a state is impossible or even undesirable, but they may feel strongly about particular state policies and seek to influence whether or not they are adopted. For example, *da'wa* groups in Egypt, many inspired by the sermons of the charismatic Shaykh 'Abd al-Hamid Kishk, were responsible for the modification of President al-Sadat's 1979 proposed reform of family law (covering the rights of women in marriage and divorce), although the President and his wife largely had their way. The Supreme Court struck this law down in 1985, however, and the Mubarak government has replaced it with a watered-down version that, while not pleasing all the religious people, is accepted by many of them to be less offensive than the 1979 version. Muslim activists in Kuwait have supported bills before Parliament that would prohibit women from taking part in advertisements and stop the Ministry of Interior from interfering in controversial *shari'a* cases. They have been unsuccessful so far in amending the constitution to make the *shari'a* the sole source of law, but they have prevented women from acquiring the right to vote.

Various groups in Malaysia have lobbied successfully for the introduction of the daily prayers into national television and the establishment of an Islamic university. They have also lobbied, less successfully, for changes in the official policy whereby the *bumiputra* ('sons of the earth'), or Malays, are given economic preference over non-Malays. ABIM and ALIRAN (Persatuan Aliran Kesedaran Negara), in particular, have argued that this policy works to the advantage of urban Malays only, while the rural population is being further impoverished and the non-Muslim urban population – most non-Muslims are urban – is further aggrieved. Moreover, they say, this kind of discrimination is at odds with the spirit of Islam.[47]

In Turkey, according to the London-based, Arab-owned magazine *Arabia: The Islamic World Review*, *da'wa* groups publish at least four magazines, with about 100,000 readers. It does not specify whether this figure represents the individual or the combined readership, and in any case the figure is small, but the underlying point is clear and indisputable: in Turkey interest in Islam has discernibly increased. For several decades now, *da'wa* groups have exploited their greater popularity to pressure the government into building more mosques, restoring religious subjects to the national educational curriculum, reopening training institutes for the training of *imams*, and opening schools exclusively for women.[48] The value that the Turkish government places on membership of the Organization of the Islamic Conference and its policy of strengthening economic and political ties with the Middle Eastern countries may partly explain the government's responsiveness to the Muslim demands.

But, in both the Turkish and the Malaysian cases, the success of *da'wa* groups may be partly due to their close association with well-established and legal parties, such as Partai Islam Sa Malaysia (PAS), or Milli Selamat Partisi, the National Salvation Party, in Turkey. In Kuwait, although they do not formally constitute a political party and in fact differ a great deal from one another, a number of Muslim activists – there were at least five out of fifty members in the 1981–5 sitting – are actually in Parliament and thus have a greater say than might otherwise be the case. Nonetheless, one must acknowledge that this group's ability to influence events is limited, and in the 1985 election the number of clearly identifiable Muslim activists was reduced.[49]

Let us turn to the second general way in which *da'wa* work may be said to be political: when it becomes a 'fifth column' and undermines the established political order from within. Natsir seems to believe that this subtle kind of subversion may already be occurring in the post-1945 'new generation' of military officers in Indonesia. The 1945 generation is retiring and withdrawing from the scene, and the colonels and brigadiers who are replacing them are showing signs that they are more interested in Islam than their predecessors. Natsir told me, for example, that some officers ask the Dewan Da'wah and other groups for books to read on Islam; some of these men have even concluded that if London could devote an entire year to an Islamic festival, as it did in 1976, then perhaps there is something to Islam after all! Here is at least one example of how the Islamic revival owes something to the bandwagon effect.

Even more subtle and virtually imperceptible infiltration seems to occur as *da'wa* groups prove their worth and show that they are doing effective and good work in the community. In a country such as Indonesia, where there are few official concessions to Islam despite the overwhelming preponderance of nominal Muslims in the population, groups that are seen to advance social justice and that at the same time deliberately defer to Islamic ideas may have the effect of encouraging doubts about the secular state itself.

For example, the Institute for Consultation and Legal Aid for Women and Families in Jakarta, known from its Indonesian name by the acronym LKBHUWK (Lembaga Konsultasi & Bantuan Hukum Untuk Wanita & Keluarga), is an organization of women lawyers and social workers under the direction of a military officer's wife, Nani Yamin. Its purpose is to help women with the legal, social, financial, and psychological problems that arise from their particular family situations and from the general circumstances of a developing society. It pays lip-service to the Pancasila, but the Islamic framework is obvious: the national council of religious authorities, Majelis Ulama Indonesia, is one of its sponsoring agencies and it regularly consults leading *'ulama*; the office itself is located in a mosque whose officials provide information on, and generally serve as a conduit to, the organization; and, in the disposition of a case, 'the client is always made to realize the importance of faith, so that peace is attained in life'.[50] Given these religious associations, it seems odd that the institute's main purpose is to attack the traditionally restricted role of women.[51] Moreover, in so far as this restricted role is usually considered a consequence of

Islamic tradition, one might be tempted to think of LKBHUWK as an ally of the development-oriented secular regime and in opposition to the traditional '*ulama*, despite what its generally deferential language might suggest.

Yet, in fact, LKBHUWK's leaders have been careful not to question the authority of the '*ulama*, or to ascribe illiberalism to Islam. If anything, we might reasonably think of them as being in league with the religious people against the 'New Order' government. Indeed, built into the institute's activities may well be a challenge to the government, precisely because the institute appeals to Islam to liberate women and otherwise to resolve the social injustice of the development process. It is saying in effect, 'Islam can help us develop', but beneficiaries may hear this message as, 'The government should pay more attention to Islam', or even, 'It is no longer acceptable that the government remain secular.'[52] In a way, then, *din wa dunya* may merge into *din wa dawla*: the search for social justice on earth may merge into 'the bringing of God's rule to earth'.[53]

This sense of divinely appointed mission may lead to the third type of political *da'wa* – outright, revolutionary opposition. The contemporary situation has indeed given rise to groups that feel tainted by exposure to the corrupt world and invoke plagues on the houses of both Western secularism and establishment Islam. It is tempting, though it would not be accurate, to give them all the label Takfir wa'l-Hijra. It is tempting because all these groups share the belief that their fellows, who pretend to be Muslims but who in fact are not, must be excommunicated or declared infidels (*takfir*), and that they themselves must emigrate to a truly Islamic society of their own making (*hijra*).

It would be inaccurate because the term Takfir wa'l-Hijra has a specific historical connection with Egypt in the 1970s and should not be made to cover a broad phenomenon across the Muslim world. Moreover, although the ideology of the various groups is roughly the same, their approaches differ in certain key respects. For example, Gilles Kepel shows that the so-called Takfir wa'l-Hijra in Egypt in the late 1970s actually consisted of two factions that differed in their interpretation of what to do in response to Sayyid Qutb's and others' condemnation of modern society as belonging to the *jahiliyya*. The members of one faction, which may be called 'the group of spiritual separation' (*jama'at al-'uzla al-shu'uriyya*), believed that they should dissimulate their views while in a weak position and that they did not need to withdraw entirely from society. The members of the other faction, 'the group of complete separation' (*jama'at al-infinsal al-kamil*), believed that they should not participate in or cooperate with the institutions of the *jahili* society at all.[54] However, complete separation underwent a transformation, to become total war with society, and it was advocates of this type of confrontational separation, led by Shukri Mustafa, who kidnapped and murdered the Egyptian Minister of Awqaf in 1977.

The important point here is that even the 'complete separaters', those who seek to withdraw from society, have ended by declaring war on society. There is thus a continuum between the Takfir wa'l-Hijra groups and those that may be conveniently described as al-Jihad: both are broadly nonconformist, but the latter have evolved a more deliberate policy of confrontation. To those such as 'Abd al-Salam Faraj and Khalid al-Islambuli, who were executed for the assassination of al-Sadat in 1981, if *da'wa*'s purpose is to call people to Islam, that must pre-eminently mean being called to an Islamic state. If an anti-Islamic regime is in the way, then there must be *jihad* against it and against the tyrants who suppress Muslims. An anti-Islamic regime creates an 'atheist state', against which there is a clear moral obligation to wage holy war.[55]

This line of thought follows the contours of Qutb's view that Islam is more than a 'defensive movement'. It is 'a spontaneous and exuberant movement (*haraka*) for the freedom of mankind on earth'; *jihad* is designed to stop any limitations on that freedom.[56] Qutb spoke, first, of the need for a moral revolution and, then, of the need to seize power, but his disciples put all their emphasis on the second part. With them, *da'wa* is taken one further step away from the conversion and pedagogical notions: it means working against social injustice *and* working against political injustice within Muslim societies. At the same time *jihad* is taken a further step from the notion that has become conventional in the contemporary period: fighting against political injustice at home is the prime duty of Muslims and even takes precedence over fighting the Zionist enemy outside. Other groups in the Muslim world follow roughly these lines of thinking, but are Khumaynists in inspiration and orientation, as I showed in the last chapter. It is clear that the line between *da'wa* and revolution is sometimes blurred, that *din wa dunya* may give way to something that we may call *din wa haraka*, 'religion and the movement'.

If I were to leave it here, it would seem that *da'wa* is in fact undermining regimes in the Muslim world in one way or another, thus perhaps undermining the weak structures of the states themselves. But we must not lose sight of other factors. For example, it is true that the blurring of the concepts of *da'wa* and *jihad* which I have just described is still an infrequent occurrence, and that *jihad*-ist groups are still a small minority, although larger than the 'complete separaters'. Moreover, governments have tremendous resources at their disposal and are actively seeking to keep *da'wa* within bounds. They can do this in three main ways.

First, they can create their own organizations and sponsor their own *da'wa* activities – what may be called the Trojan horse strategy. The Prime Minister's office in Malaysia, for example, set up a *da'wa* organization to educate government employees and, since 1978, has sponsored *bulan dakwah*, or 'missionary month', to combat what it believes to be extremist 'false *da'wa*' (*dakwah songsang*). The Ministries of Education and Defence also have their own *da'wa* groups, and the Yayasan Dakwah Islamiah Malaysia, or Islamic Da'wa Foundation of Malaysia, coordinates official *da'wa* activities and keeps an eye on other *da'wa* activities in the country.[57] Similarly, the Egyptian government, particularly through its Ministry of Awqaf, regularly buys and distributes *da'wa* literature and holds conferences throughout the country.[58] It has even managed to induce the redoubtable Shaykh Kishk, imprisoned as recently as 1981 for his fiery criticisms of official policy, to write a regular column in the government-sponsored weekly newspaper *al-Liwa al-Islami*.[59]

Second, governments can try to control *da'wa* by providing funds to nominally independent organizations, thus effectively suborning their independence. One sees this approach in Thailand, where *da'wa* activity has become very popular – and noticeable, especially to a government that is worried about the effect of having thousands of people gathered in the name of Islam in the troubled southern region.[60] The Jordanian government seeks to keep *da'wa* groups in line by providing money and other help to such organizations as the Young Women Muslim Association, which is under royal patronage.[61] The Kuwaiti government in the early 1980s was giving the Islamic Reform Society (Jam'iyyat al-Islah al-Islamiyya) 10,000–14,000 Kuwaiti dinars (roughly, US $3,500–$5,000) a year.[62] Though hardly a princely sum, the subvention is an indication of the government's view that it is better to have a hand in the work of these 'social' organizations, as they have come to be called, than to leave them entirely to their own devices.

And, third, governments can closely monitor *da'wa* activities and try to intimidate such organizations into political inactivity. This is clearly what is happening in Nigeria, where the Jama'atu Nasril Islam (JNI) has been warned repeatedly to stay away from politics and from any action that might be construed as political, lest further acts of millenarian violence be encouraged in Muslim areas, such as those that occurred in December 1980, February 1984, and April 1985. Through these warnings, the government has managed to taint the JNI by association with the Maitatsine uprisings, even though the JNI is basically a mainstream organization which considers that Maitatsine was a complete heretic. In Egypt, policy has fluctuated. Under 'Abd al-Nasir, the government proscribed the Muslim Brotherhood and then later, under al-Sadat, allowed it some activity – even encouraging it as a counterweight to leftists – although always keeping a close watch on it. But even al-Sadat's more lenient approach hardened when the Brotherhood's main publication, *al-Da'wa*, began to attack his peace treaty with Israel and his secular rule.[63] Its right to publish was suspended in 1979, as was the right of a similar Muslim publication, *al-I'tisam (The Safeguarding)*.

Both the Malaysian and the Indonesian governments have restricted the manoeuvrability of overtly political Muslim organizations. For example, in 1983 the Malaysian government forbade the operation of a new party, Partai Negara Islam Malaysia. In 1984 it arrested several leaders of PAS for allegedly encouraging subversive activities and proscribed PAS rallies in several states.[64] Similarly, the Indonesian government, from the mid-1960s on, began to ban the old Muslim parties, notably the Serakat Islam, the Muhammidiyya, and the Nahdatul Islam (NU), and in 1972 it forced them into a government-led amalgamation, now known as the United Development Party or PPP (Partai Persatuan Pembangunan).

Both governments have also introduced legislation to control 'social' organizations and to prohibit their engaging in political activity. In 1982 the Malaysian government, under Mahathir, rather clumsily moved to amend the Societies Act of 1966, which had already been amended in 1981 so as to restrict the operation of many kinds of social and religious organizations. The even more restrictive amendments of 1982, however, had to be dropped after strong and broad-based popular opposition was expressed. There is nevertheless a widespread suspicion among *da'wa* groups, as well as among the more broadly organized groups such as ALIRAN and the Consumers' Association of Penang, that the government will before too long try again to control their freedom of action. The Indonesian government has been more successful in imposing its will on social organizations. The law governing these organizations was already restrictive, but in 1983 the government of President Suharto wanted to impose Pancasila on them as the basic principle, and not – the case previously – as simply one of the principles, guiding them. Understandably, this move prompted disquiet, even soul-searching, among Muslim groups, which were being asked in effect to make Islam a subsidiary commitment. By 1984, however, most groups had fallen into line.[65] If the concept of *taqiyya*, which is particularly associated with the Shi'a and is usually translated as 'dissimulation', is taken more generally to mean acceptable caution in the face of unfavourable political realities, and taken to have broad appeal among Muslims, it might help to explain the motivation of these Sunni Indonesian groups.[66]

The heavy hand of government has produced apoliticism throughout Islamic history, and this effect is often seen today. For example, an important group within the NU in Indonesia, the so-called Situbondo group, has readily accepted the supremacy of Pancasila and has made what very many Muslims would regard as a contrived separation of *shari'a* from '*aqida*, or law from faith.[67] It argues that the former is the government's province and the latter the individual's, and that individuals should defer to the government's will as long as it does not harm personal faith.

But the opposite political effect, politicization, is at least as likely, and it is by no means certain that government efforts to control *da'wa* will be successful. For example, the very creation of an official *da'wa* establishment tends to work both ways: it subjects the *'ulama* and other religious people to some degree of regulation and standardization, but it also gives them regular access to politicians and an institutionalized platform from which to make their views and wants known. Bureaucratization leads to the muting of publicly expressed independent ideas, particularly when the Ministry of Religious Affairs distributes either the texts of mosque sermons or the guidelines for them. However, at the same time bureaucratization magnifies the *'ulama*'s voice within government circles and gives them an opportunity to make their views known on certain policies. This occurs in Saudi Arabia, where the *'ulama* have ostensibly had an impact on the direction and pace of social changes.

It may be easier for governments to control Sunni groups, however, than Shi'i groups. The Shi'i practice of tithing, whereby the Shi'a give one-fifth of their income, or *khums*, to the *'ulama*, gives Shi'i officials and institutions financial independence; this practice is not shared by the Sunnis. Moreover, Shi'i mosques, schools, and mourning centres, or *husayniyyas* (named after Imam Husayn, the martyred grandson of the Prophet, for whom there is ritualized mourning every Muharram, the first month of the Islamic calendar), may be built virtually without government money. These buildings, along with the traditional *diwaniyyas* in the Gulf (private assembly halls where Muslim men, whether Sunni or Shi'i, can meet for nightly discussion sessions), provide places where Shi'a can express their beliefs in the midst of what they may perceive to be a hostile environment. The Kuwaiti government has occasionally intervened directly in mosque affairs (as it did in 1979, when it expelled a Shi'i *imam*), and the Lebanese government has tried to exercise some degree of influence over the Shi'a by recognizing the Supreme Shi'a Council and creating the Council of the South (Majlis al-Janub). The purpose of creating the latter, which gave recognition to the predominance of Shi'a in the southern part of the country, was to raise the standard of living in the south and thereby draw it more fully into Lebanese society. If this had been accomplished, it would have given the government a measure of influence – though not really control – over the Shi'a there. Generally speaking, however, Shi'i institutions serve as a kind of buffer against crude governmental interference, and this protection is advantageous both to basically conformist organizations such as al-Jam'iyya al-Islamiyya al-Ijtima'i, or Islamic Social Society, in Kuwait, and to nonconformist, militant organizations such as Hizbullah, or Party of God, in Lebanon.

These sectarian differences notwithstanding, there is perhaps an irony in government efforts to control *da'wa* groups: sometimes the more the government officially sponsors groups and seems able to exercise control over them, the more politicized they become. There are distinct dangers to opening the Pandora's box of official sponsorship and cooptation. Politicization is an obvious development in societies in which most avenues of political expression are closed. Because few political alternatives to the Islamic groups exist, they become valuable for the aggregation and articulation of political opinions and demands. In other words, they become the functional equivalents of political parties. This politicization also happens in countries such as Morocco, Tunisia, and Malaysia, where institutional provision has, in fact, been made for some political participation and expression of opinion, but in countries where it is largely missing, such as Indonesia and Syria, the *da'wa* groups become very important, or potentially very important, spokesmen. Individual mosques can be razed – indeed, many were in the Syrian city of Hama in 1981 – but there are always others. In addition, innocuous-looking associations may quickly become politicized. A built-in problem for all governments is the difficulty of objecting to any group that frames demands by explicit reference to the paramount symbol of 'Islam'.

A more certain irony is that many of the young activists who have challenged the political and religious *status quo* are themselves products of the controlled religious environment. Even the engineers and scientists, who, profiles suggest, make up a significant share of the activists,[68] learned Islam as children and teenagers at the feet of officially appointed instructors and *imams* whose own education at al-Azhar in Cairo and elsewhere was largely designed by government and was relatively conservative. Moreover, some activists are radicalized by their experience in government-sponsored *da'wa* organizations, particularly those with a social welfare orientation. This appears to have been the case in Egypt.

When the activists appear on the scene, however, there is very often a curiously stubborn – some would say, imprudent – refusal on the part of governments to take this for what it is: indictment of their own plans for Islam. Rather, the government puts blame on precisely those *'ulama* who have been faithful servants of official Islam. In Egypt, for example, General Makhluf, the prosecutor of Shukri Mustafa and his group, made it clear who was ultimately culpable for the rise of Islamically oriented political activism. Students, he said, should have more exposure to a vibrant and relevant version of Islam.[69] This subtle, yet barbed, criticism of the *'ulama* must be seen as ironic, given that most of the *'ulama* have been doing the government's bidding for a long time.

However, this view points to the lack of simplicity of the picture: governments seek to control *da'wa*, but effectively concede that they will not be entirely successful at it. At the same time, *da'wa* can very quickly become politically charged, yet real power is likely to remain in the hands of the General Mukhlufs, not the Shukri Mustafas. In short, the political calculations are complex.

Westernization and the nation-state

It is thus too simple to say that *da'wa* is revolutionary and that it will undermine the institution of the state in the Muslim world. Taking the second part first, I accept that many people would challenge the assumption that subverting regimes is tantamount to undermining nation-states. Assuming this, they would say, is a basic error of political analysis – equating governments with the states themselves. They might point to the thrust of my own argument that people are increasingly identifying with the national unit, and thus that it has an existence independent of the government. All this is true enough and is one reason why the simple idea of *da'wa* undermining states is not acceptable.

Yet, in a very real way, there is something in the idea. Governments and states are intimately connected in countries with a relatively short history of independence and weak economies, as is the case in the Muslim world generally. Strong governments have made nation-states and held them together, and weakened governments may adversely affect national unity or territorial integrity, as is potentially true of Indonesia or Pakistan. To my mind, therefore, it is not so much the connection between regime and state that is in doubt as the probability of *da'wa* becoming politically revolutionary. As I have indicated, there is a distinct strand of thinking in contemporary Islam that calls for the radical overthrow, some would say purification, of the *status quo*. This strand is consistent with the nonconformist views on the nation-state outlined in the last chapter: revolutionary *da'wa* sees as its end the replacement of the nation-state with the universal *umma*. Theory apart, *da'wa*'s new manifestation of social activism is clearly a short remove away from political activism, even zealotry and bigotry, and although this transformation will not always happen or inevitably be violent, it does suggest that the field will not be left to official Islam unchallenged.

In the end, what is important are probabilities. Given the vast resources of modern governments to coopt and to suppress, there is a strong probability that this political activism will not become so violent and revolutionary as to threaten the existing order. I suspect that most governments will win through. And, in doing this, they will foster increasing identification with the nation-state in whose name they purport to speak.

But it is not simply a question of Muslims being coerced into identification with the nation-state. The feeling that something has gone wrong, and that Muslims need to take charge of their fate, translates into a search for Islamic social, economic, and political activism. This search has taken the form of the rejection of the Westernization of society but not of the institution of the state itself; rather than total rejection, then, there has been a partial rejection. Putting it the other way around, there has not been a complete acceptance, but rather a qualified acceptance – i.e., acceptance of the 'Islamized' nation-state or, more simply, the Muslim nation–state. A typical expression of this attitude comes from Ahmad al-Sabahi Awadallah, leader of the Umma Party in Egypt: 'We want an Islamic generation based on Islamic law, but not a Western generation. It is necessary to purify the good Egyptian community [of] evil.'[70]

The *da'wa* activities that I have described are important as the manifestation of a desire on the part of many Muslims to take charge of their destiny and become better Muslims. These activities are significant because they show that Muslims can use Islam imaginatively to deal with modern problems, and, in doing so, contribute positively to the process of nation-building. This factor is at the heart of the current revival, though it runs counter to what many observers hold to be true of either Islam or its revival.

A good example of misunderstanding is found in V. S. Naipaul's account of his travels around the Muslim world, *Among the Believers: An Islamic Journey*. He visited a Central Javanese *pesantren*, Pondok Pabelan, and came away 'confounded' by what purported to be unstructured education but was in fact structured, and by what called itself Islamic and yet had more to do with development than with religion. Agreeing with an Australian visitor who had asked, 'What does Islam tell you about Indonesia and what to do about poverty?', Naipaul negatively concluded that such 'modern' concerns as the ecological balance have become part of the 'new Islam' simply because it sounds right. 'What message did Islam have for the villages?' he asked, and his implied answer was 'practically none'.[71]

Naipaul's version of Pondok Pabelan, however, barely matched what I saw when I visited the *pesantren* in November 1982. Indeed, what impressed me was the degree to which the students (*santris*), teachers (the *kiyayi* and *ustazs*), and villagers were engaged in mutually beneficial educational cooperation and in community development. The main emphasis in the *pesantren* falls on religious study, which is more extensive than that found in the *madrasa*, or non-residential Islamic school. The daily routine is built around the five prayer-times, and even between times one cannot miss the sounds of Arabic as students learn recitation of the Qur'an (*tajwid*) and the finer points of the Arabic language. But there are features which are more striking. One is that other, more secular, subjects such as mathematics, history, biology, and English are taught. In this respect the *pesantren* does not differ from either the state school or the *madrasa*; what is significant is that an education that prides itself on developing the moral sense of Muslims, as does *pesantren* education, makes non-religious subjects an integral and important part of the curriculum. But, unlike the other types of school, there is an even more discernible emphasis on teaching such practical subjects as carpentry, electronics, auto mechanics, and farming for the boys, and sewing and cooking for the girls.

Another striking feature is the close, one might almost say symbiotic, relationship between *pesantren* and village. People to whom I spoke went to great lengths to say that student and peasant are partners in development. Indeed, the students run a cooperative shop, which sells small items of daily use for the benefit of the students and the adjacent villagers; the cafeteria is also run as a cooperative. Both students and villagers work together in cultivating the rice paddies, harvesting crops, and fishing in the ponds that they have built together. The *pesantren* members have shown the villagers how to diversify their crops, particularly introducing cloves and oranges, and the villagers have shown the students how to make handicrafts. Village women help to prepare food for the *pesantren*, and *santris* have helped the villagers to build new houses with stronger walls and better ventilation.

However, there are ways in which the *pesantren* is more helpful to the village than the village to the *pesantren*. The *kiyayi*, for example, acts much like the parish priest, not only taking care of the religious side but serving as marriage counsellor and welfare worker as well, even perhaps helping to shape political views. Probably the most important way in which the *pesantren* has been of help is to have induced the village to accept a health clinic and medical services. Although the government provides these, it was not until the *kiyayi*, *ustazs*, and *santris* welcomed them, that they seemed worthwhile to the villagers.[72] The result is a palpable improvement of the social welfare of the villagers – but also, it must be noted, a roundabout legitimation of the apparatus of the nation-state that provides the services.

The effect that Pondok Pabelan is having is thus evident, but it is still possible to wonder what is Islamic about it. I have dwelt on Naipaul's reaction to the *pesantren* in order to clarify just this point. His views reflect the habit in the West – and even in certain Muslim circles – of interpreting too narrowly what Islam is. In this particular case, he looked for a doctrinal basis to the *pesantren*'s activities and, finding none, concluded that whatever one may say of the community, one could not really say that it was an *Islamic* community. Yet a view such as this presupposes that there is an accepted standard by which one can gauge what is Islamic practice and what is not. I doubt that there is one, any more than there would be in Christianity, for example. Can one say that the Catholic Worker Movement in North America was less Christian because of its professed agrarian socialism, or that liberation theology in Latin America is un-Christian because of its leftist political radicalism? Clearly this conclusion would be questionable, given both the strong and self-conscious feelings of their adherents that they were and are following Christ's message, and the ultimate incapacity of any

Christian to specify exactly what Christ's social and political message was or is today. In every religion, the traditions of Scripture are applied anew in each generation, thus guaranteeing that differences of interpretation will appear. What counts in any time is that people believe they are following God's message and acting in His spirit. The view which fails to take note of this suffers from looking for the text of dogma rather than the motivation of people.

Such a view suffers further from making the assumption that Islam is no more than faith, ritual, and doctrine, and simply is not consistent with developmental economics. Most Westerners, if not most Muslims, believe that the West can be equated with technological advancement. Many Westerners, in particular, also believe that because the Islamic revival is espousing 'the emotional rejection' of things Western,[73] Islam must be anti-technology and anti-development. If they observe innovative activities such as those which occur at Pondok Pabelan, therefore, they naturally become confused – which is what happened to Naipaul, as he himself readily admits. But the problem lies in the preconception, and not in any supposed contradiction of practice with the real nature of Islam. As I showed earlier in this chapter, Islamic law and institutions are capable of change and adaptation.

Students of Islam, whether Western or Muslim, who approach the question too narrowly of what Islam is, will suffer a double disappointment, then. On the one hand, they will expect too much – a doctrinal basis for Muslim activism. Yet an Islamic brand of development may be said to occur simply when Muslims manage to advance their society and their economy without betraying what they perceive to be Islamic values. On the other hand, they will expect too little – a negative, inflexible response from Muslims. But there is nothing about Islam that prohibits Muslims from seeing the utility of and adopting Western skills, and there is no reason why they should appear to be less Islamic if they do so, even as they criticize Western values generally.

It would be useful to know how representative this Indonesian example is, and to measure any trend in that direction. I do not have this precise information. Moreover, Manning Nash reports that *dakwah* groups in Kelantan in Malaysia are suspicious of modern, and even of traditional, formal education and uninterested in economic enterprise. The little economic activity that exists is designed to keep the community going, and there is a distinct feeling that to be too involved in commercial transactions would endanger the soul. Rather than immersing themselves in the world, these people want to transcend a world that is seen as 'trivial, sensual, ephemeral, corrupt, and neurotic'.[74]

But, as I have shown, the theme of withdrawal from the corrupt world (*takfir wa'l-hijra*) may be a short step away from the theme of the need to change the world. In its most extreme manifestation, condemnation of the world leads to violent and spasmodic *jihad*, but a more common result is the generally non-violent and deliberate search for the just society. Nash himself says of the Kelantan *dakwah* that 'the younger members not only hold the present social order in contempt, they tend to be more actively opposed to it and willing to see social change. They have a shorter-range view compared to the older core's long-range salvation idiom.'[75] I have the clear impression from travelling in the Muslim world that although the conversion and pedagogical work of *da'wa* continues apace, and although many *da'wa* people prefer to withdraw as much as possible from the world, more and more young people are being attracted to and are helping to articulate an alternative, activist version of *da'wa*. This version may not incorporate all the details of the community at Pondok Pabelan, but it stresses the general need of practical work for social justice.

Many of the Muslims who adhere to this version would argue that justice can prevail only in the *umma* of believers, but even with them there is generally the practical, albeit begrudging, recognition that for the foreseeable future they must operate within the national framework. the Malaysian regional *dakwah* groups are no exception. Their emphasis on the nation-state is enhanced precisely because of the seeming inadequacies of national Islam: i.e., rivalry between the federal and state government on religious matters; ethnic tension between Muslim Malays and the non-Malays; the weakening of a formal, alternative Islamic party to that of the ruling coalition; and the cooptation of national *dakwah* groups by the government. By default, then, unofficial *dakwah* groups assume national significance.

It would be wrong of course to leave the impression that the commitment to social justice is something new in Islam; it is not, as the chapter of the Beneficent (55) in the Qur'an attests. Nor would it be correct to say that *da'wa* lacked a social or political dimension before. But there is a recently developed consciousness that working to develop one's society according to indigenous values and ideas is central, not marginal, to *da'wa*. This consciousness may be having the effect, whether intended or not, of increasing identification with the idea of the nation-state, though not its particular, Westernized form.

7 Conclusion

The discussion of *da'wa* groups in the preceding chapter omits one major element: the transnational character of *da'wa*. Often organizations based in one country, such as Saudi Arabia or Libya, reach beyond the national borders and influence *da'wa* work in other countries. Financial transfers and the exchange of literature, information, and training are usually involved. This kind of *da'wa* activity appears to be on the increase, and many Muslims sincerely believe that in time, and as a consequence of continual cross-border movement of people and ideas and the development of group-to-group cooperation, national loyalties will eventually decline and attachment to the *umma*, the community of believers, will strengthen. That hardy perennial, pan-Islam, will thus be achieved. The historical experience, to my mind, suggests that this optimism is misplaced, but, in any event, I have deliberately omitted such transnational concerns so as to give them full treatment in a companion volume.

The concern in this book, rather, has been the debate over whether Islam on the one hand, and nationalism and the nation-state on the other, are compatible. The classical and medieval theory does not refer to nation-states of course, and the main emphasis is on the unity of the believers, but there are indications that territorial pluralism is acceptable in theory. It is widely believed that the best indication of this acceptance is found in the Qur'anic verse that God divided mankind into nations and tribes for the purpose of better knowing one another. One can also point to medieval writers, such as al-Ghazzali, Ibn Taymiyya, and Ibn Khaldun, whose visions of the Islamic legal order incorporated the reality of divisions and multiple centres of power.

Clearly more important, however, is the consensus that has evolved over the centuries that Islam tolerates, even endorses, territorial pluralism. The historical record is overwhelmingly the record of pragmatic adaptation to diversity, and to the fact that diversity occurs as much among Muslims as between Muslims and non-Muslims. Rather than unmitigated hostility between *dar al-islam*, the believing realm, and *dar al-harb*, the infidel realm, in fact there have been, first, regular diplomatic relations, including professions of eternal peace, between the believers and the infidels; and, second, significant disagreements, including bitter wars, between organized collectivities of the believers themselves. The territorial and political differences between Muslims have also entailed their adoption of the mechanics of international relations – regular exchange of envoys and the conclusion of formal treaties. The seamless unity of *dar al-islam* has been as great a legal fiction as the bifurcation of the world into hostile camps.

This historical record constitutes the 'consensus of action' (*ijma' al-fi'l*), which in turn has influenced the development of the intellectual consensus, or 'consensus of speech' (*ijma' al-qawl*) of jurisprudential provenance. Predictably, statesmen and other Muslims with some direct experience of government have readily conformed to the idea of the nation-state. But others, across a broad spectrum of opinion and representing both traditional and modern styles of education, have similarly argued that the nation-state is not an alien development. Language has played an important role in facilitating the acceptance of such key ideas of modern international relations as territorial sovereignty, the international treaty, and peace among nations. Although there is some theoretical justification for accepting these ideas, the process by which Muslims have come to conform to the concept of the nation-state and its ancillary ideas is actually one of culture change. Like Islam itself, the 'theory', while having a basis in Scripture and the interpretative texts of theology and law, is ultimately what Muslims believe it is; and what they believe it is has a great deal to do with their conduct or what they do in practice. Through this subtle process, the originally Western idea of the nation-state has come to seem natural.

This is not to say, however, that the nonconformist view is ungrounded in theory or has run its full course in practice. Quite the contrary, there is ample textual support for the view that Muslims – indeed, all men – are equal in God's sight and commanded to rise above their differences and to form a single community; and there is a long and still vibrant tradition of Muslim agitation against nationalism and the nation-state. The most recent manifestation of this agitation has had Shi'i inspiration, but there are no significant differences between Sunnis and Shi'a on this question, or between Arab and non-Arab Muslims. Feeling that Islam's decline is due chiefly to the adoption of Western ideas and culture, all express pessimism and suggest a radical restructuring of the world order.

These nonconformists, in my judgement, are in the minority. They do not seem to have moved the Muslim consensus significantly towards the nonconformist position in spite of the current revival, which dates at least from the late 1960s and owes much of its power, it must be acknowledged, to dissatisfaction with the rocky process of development, unresponsive political institutions, and the failure to mount an effective military challenge to Israel. There is no doubt that this sense of disenchantment, even of grievance, translates for many Muslims into rejection of the state. But two factors explain why it is unlikely that this will become the prevailing trend.

First, all Muslims are born, live their whole lives and die in nation-states, thereby guaranteeing that their education, sense of security, livelihood often-times, and political attitudes eventually will be cast in the national mould. This pattern applies also – especially, some would say – to the *'ulama*, who are important influencers of opinion and conduct. It is not going too far to say that in the process Islam itself has become a national value; it has become nationalized. Second, Muslims have responded more positively to the challenges of development than by simply rejecting the idea of the state, and have worked for the creation of Muslim nation-states. These would be hybrid institutions – nation-states without Westernization, Islam without the *umma*. Here, to the extent that these Muslim nation-states have come into existence, it is truer to say that, rather than Islam becoming a national value, the nation-state becomes an Islamic value.

The core assumption is that Islam requires social justice, and that, since social justice is inseparable from the way society develops, Islam requires development of a certain – i.e., Islamic – kind. The obvious presupposition is that Islam permits the process of development. Indeed, most Muslims of various views and backgrounds accept that changes of the legal and institutional framework provided for by the *shari'a* and *fiqh* occur in fact, and that these changes are permissible. An important way in which Muslims work for the transformation of society is through *da'wa* activity. Since the start of the current revival, this has intensified, and is increasingly directed at helping Muslims to become better Muslims rather than at converting non-Muslims. This type of *da'wa* is intellectually and practically part of the general conformist 'consensus of action' (because development is accepted as occurring within the national framework) and it generally redounds to the benefit of the prevailing political order. However, *da'wa* activity may lead to revolutionary political activism that could have the effect – and, depending on the group, even the intention – of weakening national institutions and promoting the nonconformist line.

But, for the foreseeable future, it is not likely that this will often occur. Nevertheless, the yearning for some larger political identity – pan-Islam or Arab nationalism – may coexist along with particular nationalist sentiments. Empirical surveys among Arab university students, for example, point to both Islam and Arab nationalism as being more important loyalties than one-country nationalism.[1] The appeal of these transnational ideas needs to be examined in some detail. In brief, however, it can be said that the history of Arab nationalism during the past four decades shows that, despite contradictions of logic, the aspiration for broader unity does not automatically entail the rejection of identification with, and loyalty to, one's particular nation-state. A process of mental compartmentalization – of distinguishing between long-term and short-term goals – may be at work, yet it remains the case that many Muslims dream of something greater while at the same time identifying with their particular homeland out of habit, pragmatism, or desire, or a mixture of all three.

The persistence of nationalist sentiments is due to the long history of conformism and to culture change, but such Western writers as those whose views were outlined in Chapter 3 – as well as a great many Muslim writers – ignore these factors and emphasize instead what they perceive to be the imperatives of doctrine. As I have argued throughout, this approach has its distortions. The tendency is seen most clearly in the common assumption that religion and state, *din wa dawla*, are inseparable in Islam. Many writers are led to conclude from this assumption that Scripture requires the unity of the believers, and thus that there is neither justification nor legitimacy for the idea of the nation-state. But even when they acknowledge the reality of territorial division within *dar al-islam*, they are led to conclude that the nation-state is very troubled in the practice of the Muslim world. There are three such conclusions, all following from the *din wa dawla* assumption.

First, it is concluded that the unity of religion and politics rules out the kind of ideological freedom and institutional flexibility necessary for the development of the social, economic, and political system. This conclusion means in turn that nation-building is hindered and that the nation-state lacks the opportunity to take root. The obvious inspiration for this point of view is a belief that out of the separation of church and state in the West there have developed strong and dynamic forms of parliamentary democracy and an equally dynamic institutional framework that not only allows, but positively encourages, continual change and development. Not only is this belief utopian when it comes to the West, but its translation to the Muslim world gives a blinkered and defective view of that world. Nothing in Khumayni's rhetoric or practice, for example, suggests that he intends to arrest the process of economic and social change, although he intends unquestionably to control and redirect the process. The conservative Arab Gulf states, as well, are certainly not against economic development, for they regularly provide great amounts of money in aid or loans to many countries for development purposes. Moreover, Muslim societies may not have repro-duced liberal democracy, but Islamic history shows that nothing is intrinsic to Islam which precludes the establishment of effective political institutions of its own, or specifically prohibits the tribal and Qur'anic (42:38) concept of *shura*, or consultation, from becoming an effective political institution suitable to complex, modern societies. Some people believe that even if Islam were capable of such flexibility, once practised it would lead to the death of Islam. There is the argument that the 'glass' of traditional faith cannot be mended if broken,[2] or that changes only induce 'secularist corrosion'.[3] But most Muslims act on the assumption, and I think justifiably so, that the stuff of Islam is both more pliable and more durable than these pessimistic views would suggest.

Second, there is the belief that the unity of religion and politics produces tyranny within and leads to aggression externally. Indeed, unflattering images come to mind at the thought of religious politics. Simon Ockley, the eighteenth-century author of *The History of the Saracens*, reported that 'a reverend dignitary asked me if, when I wrote the book, I had not lately been reading the history of Oliver Cromwell?'[4] The experience of the English and French revolutions has only confirmed the almost innate suspicion that Westerners have of the Muslim experience. They believe that religious zealotry of all kinds demands enemies to be eliminated, or, in the words of Büchner's fictionalized Robespierre, that 'virtue must rule through terror'.[5] In commenting on the Iranian revolution, George Shultz, the American Secretary of State, said in 1985: 'The brutalities of Khomeini's regime against the Bahai show what happens to individual liberty when the state tries to control the thoughts and beliefs of its citizens, when it obliterates the distinction between the secular, political realm and the spiritual realm.'[6]

This view tends to obscure the fact that the religious and political spheres are, in practice, separate in the great majority of Muslim countries. The political elite becomes relatively secularized and seeks to dominate the religious establishment. Even when the political elite avows Islamic principles, as in Saudi Arabia, Iran, and Pakistan, it acts in ways which are more readily identifiable with more secular motivations. Any tyranny that exists is thus not due to the zealotry of religion in general, or Islam in particular, but to other, political, factors. More disturbing, however, is the frequent assumption that internal tyranny spills over into the international arena. The tyrannical state is the aggressive state; the Islamic state is the warrior state. The first assumption has had much currency in the modern literature of international relations,[7] and the second assumption underlay much of the European anxiety over the Ottoman empire.[8]

In singling out tyrannical, and thus by definition religious, states, this view is prejudiced in favour of liberal democratic states, which have had their own share of warmongering. Moreover, with specific reference to Islam, it is certainly true that the millenarianism of Khumayni has the built-in imperative of exporting the revolution. But it would be wrong to generalize from this one case and assume that any putative Islamic intolerance inevitably leads to intolerance internationally or to anti-Westernism. In the language of political science, this assumption would confuse levels of analysis: that is, it assumes that what applies at one level, domestic politics, is automatically transferred *in toto* to another level, international politics. A connection may well exist between the two, but one should not assume that it is preordained, automatic, or complete. Daniel

Pipes, however, argues in just this way. He says that the imposition of the harsh penalties of Islamic law, which are abhorrent to Western values, 'strengthens some of America's most profound antagonists, creating a dynamic that usually sours relations'. From the perspective of American relations with the Muslim world, 'although fundamentalist Islam is preferable to totalitarian ideologies, it is worse than almost any other political program'.[9] I think that the political calculations of Muslims are more complex than this view would suggest.

Third, belief in the unity of religion and politics leads to the conclusion that emotion prevails in the making of political judgements. A long artistic and literary tradition in the West has made the East seem sensual, mysterious, and often illogical.[10] Muslim civilization is particularly emotional, it is argued, because of the depth of commitment to a religion that requires complete submission to God and because of the promise of paradise to those who fall in a *jihad*.[11] As a result, it is thought, faith and passion govern the action of Muslims, and not hard political calculations. This view led in an earlier time to the fear that appeals to *jihad* would produce anti-Western solidarity among Muslims. For example, this was the message behind the Colonial Office's memorandum to the British Cabinet in 1922, when it spoke of a 'chain of possibly hostile influences' and of the Muslim world in a 'distracted state': 'Turkey, Arabia, Persia, Afghanistan, Turkestan and India are all fermenting with unrest. Great Britain, with her 60,000,000 Mahommedan subjects in India, has a special reason to fear a great Mahommedan combination throughout Asia directed against the West.'[12]

In the contemporary context, the emphasis on the emotional solidarity of Muslims has led to neglect of the idea that Muslims have national interests and that these interests often differ. Islam is seen as an emotion-ruled monolith that moves with one purpose. This point of view is present in Pipes' argument just cited, as it is found in the argument of Raymond Aron and Cyrus Vance, cited at the end of Chapter 2, both that the Muslim world is riding a revolutionary wave[13] and that it would have united in war against the West in the event of a successful rescue mission of the American hostages in Iran. But appeals to Muslim unity during the Khilafat Movement in the Indian subcontinent in the 1920s, and more recently in the Arab struggle against Israel since 1948 and the opposition to the Soviet Union's invasion of Afghanistan since 1979, have notably failed to produce the desired result.[14] The problem with assuming a unified response is that it conceals the reality of the entrenched national differences and differing national interests among Muslims which I have discussed throughout the book.

Several views of the Muslim world, then, assume that the nation-state is either impossible in theory, or so inherently contradictory to Islamic values that it will be very troubled in practice. But the fact of the matter is that, in Islam, the nation-state is no less possible, or no more fraught with problems, than it is in the non-Muslim world. Indeed, over centuries of historical experience and the evolution of theory, Muslims have largely freed themselves of a model which denigrates territorial pluralism and demands monolithic unity. In the process, another, rather different, consensus has emerged which says that the nation-state is, or can be, an Islamic intitution.

Chronology of the Muslim World

622   The Prophet Muhammad migrates from Mecca to Medina; this is his *hijra* ('exodus') and the beginning of the Islamic era.

628   Muhammad concludes the Treaty of Hudaybiyya with the Meccans.

630   Muhammad conquers Mecca.

632   Muhammad dies; Abu Bakr becomes his successor, or first Caliph.

633–7   Muslims conquer Syria and Iraq.

639–42   Muslims conquer Egypt.

644   Uthman becomes Caliph.

656   'Ali succeeds to the caliphate after the murder of the Caliph Uthman.

657–9   Conflict occurs between 'Ali and Mu'awiyya, governor of the Syrian province.

661   'Ali is murdered; Umayyad dynasty begins.

680   Husayn, the Prophet's grandson, and other partisans of 'Ali, or Shi'a, are killed at Karbala.

709   Muslims reach Spain.

711   Arab Muslim raids go into the Sind.

ca 720   Schools of Islamic law begin to take shape in the late Umayyad period.

750   Umayyad dynasty falls; 'Abbasid dynasty begins.

ca 750–950   The major schools of law establish themselves during the 'Abbasid period.

756   An Umayyid *amir* ('Abd al-Rahman) becomes independent ruler of Cordova.

788   Idrisid dynasty in Morocco begins.

799–800   Aghlabid dynasty in Tunisia begins.

825   Aghlabid conquest of Sicily begins.

901–6   Carmathians are active in Syria, Palestine, and Mesopotamia.

910   Fatimid Caliphate begins in North Africa.

929   Governor of Cordova ('Abd al-Rahman III) adopts the title of Caliph.

932   Buwayhid dynasty is established in Persia.

945   Buwayhids occupy Baghdad.

969   Fatimids conquer Egypt; Cairo is founded.

ca 970   Seljuk Turks enter the eastern territories of the 'Abbasids.

1021   Ghaznavids establish their capital at Lahore.

1030   Umayyad Caliphate in Spain breaks up into smaller principalities.

1055   Selijuk Turks capture Baghdad.

1070–80   Seljuks occupy Palestine and Syria.

1096   Christian Crusaders arrive in the Levant.

1099   Crusaders take Jerusalem.

1171   Saladin declares an end to the Fatimid dynasty, and sets up the Ayyubid dynasty in Syria and Egypt.

1187   Saladin defeats the Crusaders and recaptures Jerusalem.

1192   Treaty concluded between Saladin and Richard I of England.

1220   Mongols conquer the eastern territories of the 'Abbasids.

1250–60   Mamluk Sultanate emerges in Egypt as Ayyubid dynasty decays.

1258   Baghdad, the 'Abbasid capital, falls to the Mongols.

1287   Sultan of Pasai sends envoys to China.

1292   Marco Polo reports on the Arab Muslim penetration of Sumatra.

1400–1   Timor invades Syria.

1453   Ottoman Turks, descendants of Osman I (1288–1320), conquer the Byzantine capital of Constantinople.

1501   Shah Isma'il comes to power in Persia and makes Shi'ism the state religion; Safavid dynasty begins.

1517   Ottomans destroy the Mamluk Sultanate and conquer Egypt and Syria.

1612   The Ottoman Sultan grants capitulatory privileges to the Dutch Republic.

1526–30   Mughal dynasty begins with the reign of Babur.

1535   Treaty of alliance concluded between the Ottoman Sultan, Sulayman the Magnificent, and Francis I of France.

1619   The Dutch, via Dutch East India Company, install themselves at Batavia (Jakarta).

1628   Garrison of Algiers concludes treaty of peace with France.

1639   Ottomans take Iraq from Persia and conclude treaty demarcating the frontier between the two empires.

1683   Ottomans fail again (having already done so in 1529) to take Vienna.

1699   Treaty of Carlowitz provides for Ottoman cession of territory to the Austrians.

1718   Territorial adjustments between Austria and Ottoman empire are set in Treaty of Passarovitz.

1722   Safavid dynasty collapses in Persia.

1744   An alliance concluded between the Islamic reformer, Muhammad Ibn

'Abd al-Wahhab, and a local *amir*, Muhammad al-Sa'ud, in the Najd; this leads to the establishment of the first Sa'udi state.

1774   The Ottoman Sultan concludes the Treaty of Küçuk Kaynarca with the Russian Empress, Catherine II.

1779   Turkic Qajars establish a dynasty in Persia.

1801   Treaty of alliance between the Persian empire and Britain, the first formal alliance of the Persians with a European power.

1803   Wahhabi reformism is introduced to Central Sumatra.

1804–20 Fulani *jihads*, led by Uthman dan Fodio, take place in West Africa.

1805   Muhammad 'Ali becomes the independent ruler of Egypt, though nominally under Ottoman suzerainty.

1809   Sokoto becomes the seat of the Fulani Caliphate.

1819   The Sultan of Aceh concludes trading agreement with the British.

1820   British conclude a treaty with *shaykhs* along the Persian Gulf.

1830   French invade and occupy Algeria.

1831–40 Egyptians reoccupy Syria.

1839   – British take Aden.

       – Ottoman Sultan issues the Hatt-i Sherif of Gülhane, a decree that makes administrative reforms and applies them to Muslims and non-Muslims alike; this ushers in the period of reform known as the Tanzimat.

1857   Sepoy Mutiny occurs, marking formal end of Mughal empire and solidification of British rule over India.

1881   French occupy Tunisia.

1881–85 Mahdist revolt in the Sudan.

1882   British occupy Egypt after the revolt of al-'Urabi.

1888   Brunei enters into protectorate relationship with the British.

1898   First issue of *Al-Manar* (*The Lighthouse*), devoted to Islamic reform, appears in Cairo under the general editorship of Rashid Rida.

1905–11 Constitutional Revolution in Iran; the constitution is promulgated in 1906.

1908   Young Turk Revolution in the Ottoman empire.

1911   First Indonesian Muslim group, Sarekat Islam, formed.

1911–12 Italians invade Libya.

1912   The Muhamidiyya, a reformist Islamic organization, comes into existence in Indonesia.

1916   Sharif Husayn of Mecca proclaims 'the Arab revolt' against the Ottomans and declares himself king of the Arabs.

1917   British Foreign Secretary, Arthur Balfour, in letter to Baron Rothschild, commits Britain to the establishment of a Jewish national home in Palestine.

1918   Ottoman control of Arab lands ends.

1919–25 Khilafat Movement operates in the Indian subcontinent, seeking to preserve caliphate.

1920   Mandates within League of Nations system established, Syria and Lebanon being entrusted to France, and Palestine, Trans-Jordan, and Iraq, to Britain.

1923   Kamal Atatürk proclaims Turkish Republic.

1924   Caliphate abolished and the last Caliph (Abdülmecid) sent into exile.

1925   – Reza Khan becomes Reza Shah in Iran, and Pahlavi dynasty begins.
        – 'Abd al-Raziq's book *Al-Islam wa usul al-hukm* (*Islam and the Principles of Government*), arguing that Islam does not require union of religion and politics, appears in Cairo and causes sensation.

1928   Hasan al-Banna creates Muslim Brotherhood in Egypt.

1932   – 'Abd al-'Aziz proclaims his country the Kingdom of Saudi Arabia.
        – Britain terminates its Iraqi mandate.

1936   Anglo-Egyptian Treaty recognizes Egypt's independence.

1937   Sa'dabad Pact of Afghanistan, Iran, Iraq, and Turkey is signed.

1941   – Syria and Lebanon become nominally independent as their mandates end, although real independence comes only in 1945.
        – Reza Shah abdicates under external pressure and is succeeded by Muhammad Reza Shah.
        – Mawlana Mawdudi establishes the Jama'at-i-Islami in Lahore.

1942   Japan invades and occupies Indonesia.

1943   – Japanese bring all Indonesian Muslim organizations under one umbrella organization, Masyumi.
        – Lebanese conclude an unwritten National Pact that distributes power along confessional lines.

1945   – League of Arab States established.
        – Indonesia becomes independent.

1946   Trans-Jordan becomes independent.

1947   India and Pakistan are partitioned and gain independence.

1948   Palestine mandate ends and the State of Israel comes into existence; the first Arab-Israeli war occurs.

1949   Dar'ul Islam revolt of Kartoswiryo begins in West Java.

1951   – Muhammad Mussadiq becomes Prime Minister of Iran, nationalizes British oil holdings, and poses challenge to Shah's authority.
        – Libya becomes independent.

1953   – Anti-Ahmadi riots in Pakistan.
        – Shah of Iran, attempting to remove Mussadiq from office, briefly flees the country when pro-Mussadiq demonstrations occur, but soon regains power with the help of the CIA.

1954   Muslim Brotherhood is proscribed in Egypt, and shortly afterward is allowed to operate legally again.

1955   Baghdad Pact of Iraq, Iran, Pakistan, Turkey, and Britain signed.

1956   – Sudan, Tunisia, and Morocco become independent.
– Second Arab-Israeli war, with British and French participation.

1958   – United Arab Republic is established as the union of Egypt and Syria.
– Short civil war occurs in Lebanon.

1959–65 Sukarno presides over 'Guided Democracy' period in Indonesia.

1960   – The Turkish military overthrows the elected government, dominated by conservative Democrat Party, and writes new, more liberal constitution.
– Nigeria and Mauritania become independent.

1961   – United Arab Republic dissolved.
– Kuwait becomes independent.
– Muslim Family Law Ordinance promulgated in Pakistan.

1962   Algeria becomes independent.

1963   – A land reform bill is introduced in Iran, angering the *'ulama.*
– Sabah and Sarawak join the Malayan federation and bring Malaysia into existence.

1964   Ayatullah Khumayni sent into exile for activities against the Shah.

1965   – Members of Muslim Brotherhood in Egypt arrested.
– Sulayman Demirel's Justice Party, successor to the Democrat Party, wins parliamentary majority in Turkey.
– Attempted coup in Indonesia leads to considerable bloodshed.

1966   – Sayyid Qutb executed in Egypt.
– Suharto comes to power in Indonesia and inaugurates New Order regime.

1967   – Third Arab-Israeli war, ending in loss of the Sinai peninsula, West Bank, Golan Heights, and Gaza strip to Israel.
– South Yemen becomes independent.

1967–70 Biafran secession brings civil war to Nigeria.

1969   – Ja'far al-Numayri comes to power in the Sudan.
– Mu'ammar al-Qadhdhafi comes to power in Libya.
– Deranged tourist sets fire to the Al-Aqsa Mosque in Jerusalem, but Muslims believe the Israelis did it or at least could have prevented it.
– First Islamic summit takes place in Rabat in response to the Al-Aqsa fire.
– Musa al-Sadr becomes head of the Higher Shi'a Council in Lebanon.
– Major communal riots in Malaysia.

1970   – First Islamic Foreign Ministers' Conference takes place in Jidda.
– Hafiz al-Asad assumes direct control of Syrian government.

1971   – Zulfikar Ali Bhutto comes to power in Pakistan after a disastrous war with India brings Bangladesh into existence as separate and independent country.

– The military ousts Demirel from power in Turkey.

– General election in Indonesia, in which Islamic groups become main opposition to the secular regime.

1972   Charter of the Organization of the Islamic Conference signed.

1973   – Fourth Arab-Israeli conflict.

– In Turkey, coalition government is formed of the left-of-centre Republican People's Party and National Salvation Party, an Islamic party; Bulent Ecevit becomes Prime Minister.

– A marriage law proposed in Indonesia, and Muslim groups outraged at this attempt to bypass the relevant Islamic law.

1974   – Pakistani government declares the Ahmadis to be non-Muslims.

– Salih 'Abdullah Sirriya leads an attack of Muslim radicals on the military academy in Heliopolis in Egypt.

– Turks invade Cyprus after Greek-dominated Cypriot National Guard overthrows President Makarios.

– Shi'i Harakat al-Mahrumin (Movement of the Disinherited) set up in Lebanon.

1975–6 – Amal (acronym meaning 'Hope') set up by Musa al-Sadr in Lebanon.

– Another civil war is fought in Lebanon for 18 months.

1976   Syrian troops move into Lebanon to restore order at request of Arab League.

1977   – Coup brings Zia ul-Haq to power and commits Pakistan to *nizam-i islam* ('Islamic Order').

– Egyptian Minister of Awqaf and Azhar Affairs is murdered by the Takfir wa'l-Hijra group.

– President al-Sadat makes unprecedented visit to Israel.

1978   – Musa al-Sadr disappears in Libya.

– Camp David Accords between Israel and Egypt signed under American auspices.

1979   – Shah leaves Iran after widespread disturbances; Ayatullah Khumayni receives tumultuous welcome in Tehran on his return from exile in France.

– President Zia formally promulgates an Islamic Order, including a provision for *zakat*, in Pakistan.

– Second Nigerian republic begins with Shehu Shagari as President.

– Some 100 hostages taken at American embassy in Tehran.

– Grand Mosque in Mecca attacked by a group of Islamic zealots led by Juhayman al-'Utaybi.

	– Soviet Union invades Afghanistan.
April	– Muhammad Baqir al-Sadr, paramount Shi'i leader in Iraq, executed
1980	by Saddam Husayn's regime.
	– Fighting between Muslim groups and Copts breaks out in Egyptian city of Assyut.
Sept.	– The military overthrows civilian government in Turkey and imposes
1980	a law-and-order regime.
	– Iraq invades Iran's Khuzistan province, and a general war between Iran and Iraq begins.
Dec.	In Nigeria major religious riots erupt in Kano, and the self-proclaimed,
1980	but pseudo-Muslim, prophet Maitatsine is killed.
Jan.	The remaining American hostages in Iran are released
1981	
June	President Bani Sadr removed from office in Iran, signalling the
1981	paramountcy of the *mullas* of the Islamic Republic Party.
July	Members of the Mouvement de Tendance Islamique arrested in
1981	Tunisia.
Sept.	President al-Sadat of Egypt suspends publication of main Muslim
1981	Brotherhood journal, *al-Da'wa*.
Oct.	President al-Sadat assassinated by Muslim zealots in Cairo.
1981	
Dec.	Shi'i-dominated group tries to overthrow government of Bahrain.
1981	
Feb.	Muslim Brotherhood uprising in the Syrian city of Hama is put down
1982	by al-Asad regime with great loss of life.
June	Israel invades southern Lebanon.
1982	
Oct.–	Maitatsine-type riots in Maiduguri and Kaduna in Nigeria.
Nov.	
1982	
Oct.	Ahmadis lose their status as Malays under the federal constitution in
1982	Malaysia.
Nov.	Malaysian government introduces requirement that all colleges and
1982	universities have syllabus on Islamic culture.
Sept.	President al-Numayri introduces Islamic law as the law of land in the
1983	Sudan.
Oct.	241 US marines and 58 French soldiers killed in truck bomb explosions
1983	at the US and French military headquarters in Beirut; group calling itself the Islamic Jihad Organization claims responsibility.
Nov.	Motherland Party of Turgut Özal wins parliamentary majority in
1983	Turkey.

Dec. 1983	Civilian government overthrown by the military in Nigeria.
Feb. 1984	– Brunei becomes independent. – Maitatsine-type riots break out in Nigerian city of Yola.
March 1984	Islamic Jihad Organization threatens to attack the British, French, Italian, and American embassies in Jakarta.
April 1984	– A national unity government is formed in Lebanon that includes Amal leader Nabih Berri. – Pakistani government imposes severe restrictions on the Ahmadis.
Aug. 1984	Islamic Jihad Organization claims to have mined Red Sea after explosions cause damage to several ships.
Feb. 1985	Elections for a national assembly held in Pakistan.
March 1985	President al-Numayri arrests members of Muslim Brotherhood in Sudan.
April 1985	– President al-Numayri overthrown in military coup. – Fighting breaks out between the police and Maitatsine followers in Nigerian city of Gombe.
May 1985	– Assassination attempt is made on the life of the Kuwaiti *amir* (Shaykh Jabr Ahmad al-Sabah); Kuwaiti government identifies the attacker as member of the radical Shi'i group *al-Da'wa* in Iraq.
July 1985	Egyptian parliament approves a new marriage law that preserves the right of men to polygamy but makes some liberal reforms.
Sept. 1985	Four Russians are kidnapped in Lebanon by a group calling itself the Islamic Liberation Organization; one killed, three released.
Dec. 1985	Martial law imposed in Pakistan.
Jan. 1986	A Nigerian delegation attends the 16th Islamic Foreign Ministers' Conference in Fez as observers, and applies for full membership of the Organization of the Islamic Conference.
March 1986	Muslim unrest and violence in Sabah state of Malaysia against the Christian-led government, which Muslims regard as biased against them.
April 1986	Two Britons and one American are murdered in Lebanon, where they have been held hostage; Islamic Jihad says this is in retaliation for the American air attacks on Libya.

Glossary

'alim (pl. *'ulama*) learned religious authority

aman guarantee of safe passage

'aql 'reason': reasoning by syllogism, one of the four sources of law in Shi'ism

asala 'authenticity': the idea that Muslim societies should be based on Islamic, not Western, values

awqaf (s. *waqf*) religiously endowed properties entrusted to the *'ulama*

ayatullah 'Sign of God': major Shi'i official

baraka 'blessing': grace associated with Sufi saint

bida' innovations that are unacceptable

bumiputra 'sons of the earth': term used by Malaysian government for ethnic Malays

dar al-harb 'realm of war': infidel territory

dar al-islam 'realm of Islam': Muslim territory

da'wa 'call': broadly, educational and cultural activity; narrowly, missionary activity

daruri 'necessary': a criterion used in jurisprudence for the elaboration of legal rules

dhimmi non-Muslim subject of Islamic state

dira grazing area of nomads

diwan al-mazalim 'board of grievances': designed to handle complaints of bureaucratic injustice not covered by the usual *shari'a* courts

fatwa religious-legal opinion

faqih legal scholar

fiqh 'understanding': body of rules gradually developed from interpretation of the *shari'a*

firman royal or imperial edict

gharbzadegi 'Westoxification': poisoning of Muslim societies by the West

ghayba 'occultation': disappearance from sight of a Shi'i Imam

hadith 'tradition': record of what the Prophet said or did *hajj*   Pilgrimage to Mecca and Medina; one of the five 'pillars' of Islam

husayniyya   mourning centre of Shi'a in commemoration of martyrdom of Imam Husayn

ijma'   consensus

ijtihad   independent reasoning or judgement

ikhtilaf   divergence of juristic opinions and doctrines

imam   prayer leader

Imam   divinely inspired leader of community after Muhammad, in Shi'i belief

iqta'   land grant made by Caliph

istihsan   juristic preference, especially based on considerations of equity

istislah   consideration of the 'public interest' (*maslaha*) in the elaboration of legal rules

jahiliyya   'days of ignorance': pre-Islamic period

jihad   'striving': holy war

khalifa   'successor', viceregent, Caliph

khums   'one fifth': portion of income Shi'a give to *'uιama*

kiyayi   head teacher at *pesantren*

madhhab   school of law

madrasa   Islamic school

mahrumin   'disinherited': term used in Lebanon and elsewhere to refer to the economically, socially, and politically deprived

al-majiri   West African system of Islamic education by itinerant scholars

makruh   censurable act under Islamic law

mandub   recommended act under Islamic law

marja'-i-taqlid   'source of imitation': highest Shi'i official

maslaha   'public interest': a criterion used in jurisprudence for the elaboration of legal rules

mufti   religious-legal official empowered to deliver *fatwa*

mujaddid   'renewer': one who appears from time to time to restore Islam to purity

mujahid (pl. *mujahidun*)   'one who strives': fighter

mujtahid   one who exercises *ijtihad* or independent judgement

mustad'afun   term used by Iranian revolutionaries to mean the 'oppressed', the downtrodden

mustakbarun   term used by Iranian revolutionaries to mean the 'oppressors'

nasikh wa'l-mansukh   'abrogating and the abrogated': doctrine of revision in revelation

nizam   decree or regulation

Pancasila   'the five principles': official Indonesian ideology elaborated by Sukarno; the principles are: belief in one God; respect of human values; democracy; social justice; and nationalism

pesantren   traditional religious school in Indonesia

qadi   judge in Islamic court

qawmiyya   nationalism, particularly regional nationalism, such as Arab
nationalism

qibla   direction of prayer: that is, Mecca

qiyas   analogical reasoning or deduction

riba   usury

salah   prayer; one of the five 'pillars' of Islam

santri   strict Muslim; student at traditional religious school in Indonesia
(*pesantren*)

sawm   fasting; one of the five 'pillars' of Islam

shahada   'testimony' or profession of faith: 'There is no God but Allah and
Muhammad is His Prophet'; one of the five 'pillars' of Islam

shahid   martyr

shari'a   'path': divinely ordained law

siyasa shar'iyya   administrative discretion of ruler under Islamic law

sufi   mystic

sunna   'custom' based on the example of the Prophet as enshrined in the *hadiths*

tajdid   'renewal'

takhayyur   legal eclecticism

takhsis al-qada   administrative discretion of ruler under Islamic law

taqiyya   'caution': predominantly Shi'i practice of obscuring one's faith in
adverse times

taqlid   'imitation': strict adherence to legal precedent

tariqa   'way': Sufi brotherhood

tasjil   deed to land title granted by Caliph

tawhid   'oneness': doctrine of the absolute unity of God

'ulama (s. *'alim*)   learned religious authorities

umma   'nation': universal Islamic community

wataniyya   local nationalism, such as Egyptian (*watan*=country or nation)

zakat   alms-giving; one of the five 'pillars' of Islam

Notes

1 Interpreting Islam in the modern world

1 For example, Muhammad ibn al-Hasan Shaybani's *Kitab al-siyar al-kabir*, and sections of the works of the great Sunni jurists, such as al-Shafi'i's *Kitab al-risala*, or of the Shi'i jurists, such as Qadi al-Nu'man's *Da'a'im al-islam*.

2 For example, Muhammad Faraj, *al-Salam wa'l-harb fi'l-islam* (Cairo, Dar al-Fikr al-'Arabi, 1960); Muhammad Abu Zahra, *al-'Alaqat al-duwaliyya fi'l-islam* (Cairo, al-Dar al-Qawmiyya li'l-Tiba'a wa'l-Nashr, 1964); Muhammad al-Habib ibn al-Khujah, *al-Jihad fi'l-islam* (Tunis, al-Dar al-Tunisiyya li'l-Nashr, 1968); Subhi Mahmassani, *al-Qanun wa'l-'alaqat al-duwaliyya fi'l-islam* (Beirut, Dar al-'Ilm li'l-Malayin, 1972); and Muhammad 'Itani, *al-Nidal al-musallah fi'l-islam* (Beirut, Dar al-'Awda, 1973).

3 For example, Julius Hatschek, *Der Musta'min: ein Beitrag zum internationalen Privat- und Völkerrecht des islamischen Gesetzes* (Berlin, Walter de Gruyter, 1919); A. Sanhoury, *Le Califat: son évolution vers une Société des Nations Orientales* (Paris, Paul Geuthner, 1926); David Santillana, *Istituzioni di diritto musulmano malichita* (Rome, Istituto per l'Oriente, 1926) especially Vol. 1, Book 3; Nagib Armanazi, *Les Principes Islamiques et les rapports internationaux en temps de paix et guerre* (Paris, Picart, 1929); Mohamed Adbullah Draz, 'Le droit international public en Islam', *Revue Egyptienne de droit international*, 5 (1949), 17–27; and the unpublished thesis, Hans Kruse, 'Islamische Völkerrechtslehre' (University of Göttingen, 1953).

4 Khadduri's main contribution is *War and Peace in the Law of Islam* (Baltimore, The John Hopkins Press, 1955), but he has also provided an invaluble service by translating Shaybani's *Siyar* as *The Islamic Law of Nations* (Baltimore, The Johns Hopkins Press, 1966).

5 For example, Muhammad Hamidullah, *Muslim Conduct of State* (Lahore, Sh. Muhammad Ashraf, 4th edn rev., 1961); Mohammad Talaat al-Ghunaymi, *The Muslim Conception of International Law and the Western Approach* (The Hague, Martinus Nijhoff, 1968); the unpublished doctoral thesis, which is available from University Microfilms, Abdul-Hamid Abu Sulayman, 'The Islamic Theory of International Relations: Its Relevance, Past and Present' (University of Pennsylvania, 1973); and Marcel A. Boisard, 'The Conduct of Hostilities and the Protection of the Victims of Armed Conflicts in Islam', *Hamdard Islamicus*, 1 (Autumn 1978), 3–17.

6 J. Harris Proctor (ed.), *Islam and International Relations* (London, Pall Mall Press, 1965).

7 For example, R. K. Ramazani's two volume study of Iranian diplomacy: *The Foreign Policy of Iran: A Developing Nation in World Affairs, 1500–1941* (Charlottesville, University of Virginia Press, 1966) and *Iran's Foreign Policy, 1941–1973: A Study of Foreign Policy in Modernizing Nations* (Charlottesville, University of Virginia Press, 1975). Also see Ali Mohamed Fahmy, *Muslim Sea-Power in the Eastern Mediterranean from the Seventh to the Tenth Century A.D.* (Alexandria, Tipografia Don Bosco, 1950); Dorothy Vaughan, *Europe and the Turk: A Pattern of Alliances, 1350–1700* (Liverpool, Liverpool University Press, 1954); Muhammad Hamid Allah, *Majmu'at al-watha'iq al-siyasiyya li'l-'ahd al-nabawi wa'l-khilafa al-rashida* (Cairo, Lajna al-Ta'lif wa'l-Tarjama wa'l-Nashr, 2nd rev. edn, 1376 A.H./1956); Donald Hill, *The Termination of the Hostilities in the Early Arab Conquests, A.D. 634–656* (London, Luzac, 1971); Rudolph Peters, *Islam and Colonialism: The Doctrine of Jihad in Modern History* (The Hague, Mouton, 1979); 'Frontière Nell' Islam: Etnie, Divisioni Confessionali e Confini Imperiali Nell' Asia Musulmana', published as a pamphlet by *Le Monde Diplomatique*, 6 (1981); and Martin Kramer,

Islam Assembled: *The Advent of the Muslim Congresses* (New York, Columbia University Press, 1985).

8 *The Canberra Times*, 9 September 1984.
9 Of course, the other side is sometimes heard. See, for example, Isma'il R. al-Faruqi's article, 'Islam and the Tehran Hostages', *The Wall Street Journal*, 28 November 1979.
10 Thomas Carlyle, *Lectures on Heroes, Hero-Worship and the Heroic in History*, edited by P.C. Parr (Oxford, Clarendon Press, 1925), pp. 65–6.
11 These roles are institutionalized in the Iranian constitution in Principles 107–12: *Constitution of the Islamic Republic of Iran* (New Delhi, Iranian Embassy, March 1980), pp. 45–7. For another translation of the constitution, see *The Middle East Journal*, 34 (Spring 1980), 198–9.
12 This paragraph deals only with the Imami Shi'a, who constitute the predominant school in Iran. In general, I must say that I have deliberately not made distinctions among the '*ulama* in this section, nor have I precisely defined who may become '*ulama* or how. This is because the answers are not clear and there are many conflicting views. It is sufficient for the purposes here to note that the '*ulama* have had definite roles to play throughout Islamic history and that, although they differ among themselves on defining and applying *ijtihad*, they all in fact practise it.
13 N.J. Coulson, *A History of Islamic Law* (Edinburgh, Edinburgh University Press, 1964), p. 86.
14 See, for example, H.A.R. Gibb, *Mohammedanism* (London, Oxford University Press, 2nd edn, 1953), p. 104; Joseph Schacht, *An Introduction to Islamic Law* (Oxford, Oxford University Press, 1964), pp. 70–1.
15 Alfred Guillaume, *Islam* (Harmondsworth, Middlesex, Penguin, 2nd edn rev., 1956), pp. 97–8.
16 Muhammad ibn Muhammad al-Ghazzali, *al-Mustafa min 'ilm al-usul*, vol. 2 (Cairo, al-Matba'a al-Amiriyya, 1907), p. 342.
17 Omar Farrukh's translation of Ibn Taymiyya's *Kitab al-siyasa al-shar'iyya fi islah al-ra'i wa'l-ra'iyya: Ibn Taymiyya on Public Law and Private Law in Islam* (Beirut, Khayats, 1966), p. 183. The eleventh-century Hanbali writer, Ibn 'Aqil, said: 'It is not possible for an age to be devoid of a mujtahid.' See Wael B. Hallaq, 'Was the Gate of Ijtihad Closed?', *International Journal of Middle Eastern Studies*, 16 (March 1984), 22.
18 Hallaq, 'Was the Gate of Ijtihad Closed?', p. 4.
19 However, Hallaq cites al-Juwayni in the eleventh century arguing that *mujtahids* may contradict the opinion of the great legal ancestors of the orthodox schools: *ibid.*, p. 14.
20 Juan R. Cole, 'Imami Jurisprudence and the Role of the Ulama: Mortaza Ansari on Emulating the Supreme Exemplar', in Nikki R. Keddie (ed.), *Religion and Politics in Iran* (New Haven and London, Yale University Press, 1983), pp. 33–46.
21 See, for example, Muhammad ibn 'Ali al-Shawkani, *al-Qawl al-mufid fi adillat al-ijtihad wa'l-taqlid* (Cairo, Mustafa al-Babi, 1928).
22 See John L. Esposito, *Islam and Politics* (Syracuse, Syracuse University Press, 1984), pp. 45, 216.
23 Al-Sadiq al-Mahdi, 'Islam – Society and Change' in John L. Esposito (ed.), *Voices of Resurgent Islam* (New York and Oxford, Oxford University Press, 1983), pp. 235–6.
24 Speech opening the Academy of Islamic Jurisprudence in Mecca, 7 June 1983: *Khitab jalala al-malik fahd bin 'abd al-'aziz, malik al-mamlaka al-'arabiyya al-sa'udiyya, fi iftitah a'mal al-mu'tamar al-ta'sisi li-majma' al-fiqh al-islami* (Mecca, Munazzamat al-Mu'tamar al-Islami, 26–28 Sha'ban 1403 A.H./8–9 June 1983), p. 5.
25 Al-Mahdi, 'Islam – Society and Change', p. 235. However, he is surely wrong in thinking that traditionalists are necessarily anti-*ijtihad*.
26 *Khitab jalala al-malik fahd*, p. 6.
27 Professor Sir Norman Anderson has done an excellent job of describing these changes in his *Islamic Law in the Modern World* (New York, New York University Press, 1959) and *Law Reform in the Muslim World* (London, Athlone Press, 1976). To give one example, the Tunisian government reasoned that although the Qur'an says that a man may take 'two, three or four wives', it virtually nullifies this in the next clause by requiring him to treat them 'equally' (4:3). Interpreting this to mean all aspects of their relationship, the government deemed equality to be a practical impossibility and thus outlawed polygamy in the Law of Personal Status of 1957 (Article 18). Others, however, argue that the only obligation on the man is to treat the wives equally in a financial sense, or, more simply, to treat them 'equitably' or 'justly'. (The Qur'anic term, *ta'udilu*, can convey the sense of either equality or fairness.)
28 Coulson, *A History of Islamic Law*, pp. 202–17. He also uses the term 'quasi-*ijtihad*'.
29 Punjab Government, *Report of the Court of Inquiry* (Lahore, Government Printing Office, 1954), pp. 215–18, quotation at p. 215.
30 The *hadith* is related by Muslim and can be found in the compilation of Imam Yahya ibn Sharaf

Notes

al-Din al-Nawawi, *Kitab al-arba'in*. See *Matn al-arba'in hadithan al-nawawiyya fi'l-ahadith al-sahiha al-nabawiyya* (Singapore, Maktabat wa Matba'at Sulayman Mara'i, n.d.), *hadith* 21, p. 65.
31 For example, see United Nations, Security Council Document No. S/16962, 'Prisoners of War in Iran and Iraq' (January 1985), pp. 19, 34.
32 Quoted in Tanzil-ur-Rahman, *Implementation of Shari'ah in Pakistan* (Islamabad, Council of Islamic Ideology, 1981), p. 13.
33 Even in Malaysia, which is not an 'Islamic state', it should be noted that every state has issued a *fatwa* saying that the Ahmadis, or Qadianis, are not Muslims, and that the federal government has accordingly said that Ahmadis will be deprived of their status as Malays under the constitution: *The Straits Times*, 25 October 1982.
34 Quoted in *Le Monde*, 9 December 1983.
35 Quoted in advertisement of the Libyan embassy in London, *The Guardian*, 15 April 1976.
36 Clifford Geertz, *Islam Observed: Religious Development in Morocco and Indonesia* (Chicago and London, University of Chicago Press, 1968), p. 1.
37 Bernard Lewis, 'Politics and War', in Joseph Schacht and C.E. Bosworth (eds), *The Legacy of Islam* (Oxford, Oxford University Press, 2nd edn, 1979), p. 156.
38 See, for example, Sayyid Qutb, *Ma'alim fi'l-tariq* (Cairo, Dar al-Shuruq, 1981), p. 36.
39 See, for example, Muhammad Salim al-'Awwa, *Fi'l-nizam al-siyasi li'l-dawla al-islamiyya* (Cairo, al-Maktab al-Misri al-Hadith, 4th edn, 1980), pp. 15–23; and W. Montgomery Watt, *What is Islam?* (London, Longman, 2nd edn, 1979), p. 3.
40 E.M. Forster, *A Passage to India* (Harmondsworth, Middlesex, Penguin Books, 1979; first printed, 1924), p. 41.
41 'Ali 'Abd al-Raziq, *al-Islam wa usul al-hukm* (Cairo, Matba'at Misr, 2nd edn, 1344 A.H./1925), pp. 102–3.
42 I have reviewed some of this literature in my introduction to J. Piscatori (ed.), *Islam in the Political Process* (Cambridge, Cambridge University Press, 1983), especially pp. 3–6.
43 Fazlur Rahman, *Islam and Modernity: Transformation of an Intellectual Tradition* (Chicago and London, University of Chicago Press, 1982), p. 140.
44 *Ibid.*, emphasis added.
45 Quoted in Ann K.S. Lambton, 'Quis custodiet custodes? Some Reflections on the Persian Theory of Government', *Studia Islamica*, 5 (1956), 130.
46 Rebellion was virtually out of the question, according to medieval legal theory, and 'sixty years of tyranny are better than one hour of civil strife' became the principle to follow: Hamilton Gibb, 'Constitutional Organization: the Muslim Community and the State' in Majid Khadduri and Herbert Liebesny (eds), *Law in the Middle East* (Washington, D.C., Middle East Institute, 1955), p. 15.
47 Edward Mortimer, *Faith and Power: The Politics of Islam* (London, Faber and Faber, 1982), p. 396. He goes far, however, towards my point by arguing that Islam is a political culture: p. 407.
48 Goethe, *Sämtliche Werke* (Stuttgart, Cotta, 1902–7), *West-östlicher Divan*, 'Buch der Sprüche', p. 59.
49 Khadduri, *War and Peace in the Law of Islam*, p. 16.
50 Ibn al-Humam [Muhammad ibn 'Abd al-Wahid], *al-Tahrir fi usul al-din* (Cairo, n.p., 1351 A.H./1932), pp. 399–401.
51 'Ali 'Abd al-Raziq, *al-Ijma' fi'l-shari'a al-islamiyya* (Cairo, Dar al-Fikr al-'Arabi, 1366 A.H./1947), pp. 73–90.
52 He said, 'I should not like it if they had not disagreed.' See Joseph Schacht, *The Origins of Muhammadan Jurisprudence* (Oxford, Clarendon Press, 1950), p. 96.
53 Muhammad Iqbal, *The Reconstruction of Religious Thought in Islam* (Lahore, Sh. Muhammad Ashraf, 1971), p. 174.
54 Kemal Faruki, *Islamic Jurisprudence* (Karachi, Pakistan Publishing House, 1962), p. 157.
55 Coulson, *A History of Islamic Law*, p. 77.
56 Nadwat *'ilmiyya hawla'l-shari'a al-islamiyya wa huquq al-insan fi'l-islam* (Beirut, Dar al-Kitab al-Lubnani, 1973), pp. 67–8. This is the record of colloquia between Saudi and European jurists in the early 1970s.
57 *Khitab jalala al-malik fahd*, p. 6.
58 Allahbukhsh K. Brohi, 'Islam: Its Political and Legal Principles' in Salem Azzam (ed.), *Islam and Contemporary Society* (London, Longman, 1982), p. 86. Not everyone, however, would agree with Brohi's general perspective. See, for example, Fateh M. Sandeela's review of this book in *International Affairs*, 59 (Spring, 1983), 283. But I believe the Brohi-type view of non-retrospective *ijma'* is now the general one.

59 Faruki, *Islamic Jurisprudence*, p. 163.

60 Iqbal, *The Reconstruction of Religious Thought in Islam*, p. 174.

61 See, for example, Shakir Mustafa, 'al-Ib'ad al-tarikhiyya: azma li-tatawwur al-haduri al-'arabi', *al-Adab*, 22 (May 1974), 13–24. Bourguiba said the *'ulama* had 'sick heads' and the Shah called them 'black reactionaries': *al-Alam*, 14 August 1963 (I am grateful to Sami A. Hanna, from whose unpublished paper on al-Tahir al-Haddad this reference came to my attention); Willem M. Floor, 'The Revolutionary Character of the Ulama: Wishful Thinking or Reality?', in Keddie (ed.), *Religion and Politics in Iran*, p. 88. The quotation is from A.M. Klein's 'Sophist', in *Collected Poems* (Toronto and London, McGraw Hill Ryerson Limited, 1974), p. 121.

62 See, for example, the comments of the six lay members of the Commission on Marriage and Family Laws, which was charged with reforming family law in Pakistan, in *The Gazette of Pakistan* (20 June 1956). Selections are reprinted in John J. Donohue and John L. Esposito (eds), *Islam in Transition: Muslim Perspectives* (New York and Oxford, Oxford University Press, 1982), pp. 201–4.

63 See, for example, Sa'id Ramadan, *al-Mushkilat al-kubra al-thalath fi'alamna al-islami al-mu'asir*, no. 1 (Geneva, Islamic Centre, n.d.), p. 20; and Syed Muhammad al-Naquib al-Attas, *Islam and Secularism* (Kuala Lumpur, ABIM, 1978), pp. 99–126.

64 *The Four Year Instructional Programme for L.L.B. Degree* [brochure of the Faculty of Shariah, Institute of Shariah and Law] (Islamabad, Islamic University, 1401 A.H./1981); *Handbook of International Islamic University, 1984/85* (Petaling, Jaya, International Islamic University, 1984), pp. 56–61. It should also be noted that in the Islamic tertiary schools in Indonesia, the IAINs (Institut Agama Islam Negeri), students in the faculty of law are trained in both non-religious and religious subjects: interview, Harun Nasution, Rector of Jakarta's IAIN, Jakarta, 21 November 1981.

65 Muljanto Sumardi, 'Islamic Education in Indonesia: Recent Developments and Prospects', *Studia Islamika* [Jakarta], 1 (September 1976), 43–52. Sumardi says that at first there was Islamic opposition to this radical change in 1974, but that by now Muslim leaders have largely accepted it as a *fait accompli*: interview, Jakarta, 18 November 1981. The Islamic component, however, is stronger in the *madrasas* of the southern Philippines, where educators are consciously working against the prevailing Westernized ethos. See Abdullah T. Madale, 'Educating the Muslim Child: The Philippine Case', in Nagasura T. Madale (ed.), *The Muslim Filipinos* (Quezon City, Alemar-Phoenix Publishing House, 1981), pp. 262–5.

66 Recommendation 2 of Committee 1 reproduced in Syed Muhammad al-Naquib al-Attas (ed.), *Aims and Objects of Islamic Education* (Jeddah, King Abdulaziz University and Hodder and Stoughton, 1979), p. 159.

67 For example, the Islamic University in Islamabad says, 'While preparation to enter the world of work cannot be excluded from the objectives of university education, an "Islamic" university must simultaneously, if not mainly, educate its students for providing large and liberal service to humanity, to Islamic civilization and to the Islamic community.' See *Islamic University: Principles and Purposes* (Islamabad, Islamic University, 1402 A.H./1982), p. 15.

68 Hassan Turabi, 'The Islamic State', in Esposito (ed.), *Voices of Resurgent Islam*, p. 245.

69 Kemal A. Faruki, *Stability and Change in the Islamic World* (London, World of Islam Festival, 1976), p. 10.

70 Khumayni has not always been consistent on whether the *'ulama* are directly to govern. In his 1944 book, *Kashf al-asrar*, he said that although 'we do not mean to say that the Shah, the ministers, the soldiers and the dustmen should all be *faqihs*', these religious people would choose the leaders and either make up the legislative assembly themselves or supervise it.' This is the basis of his famous doctrinal innovation, *velayat-i-faqih*, or 'governance of the jurisconsult', which is the duty of the *'ulama* in the absence of the Imam. See Azar Tabari, 'The Role of the Clergy in Modern Iranian Politics', in Keddie (ed.), *Religion and Politics in Iran*, p. 62. However, as late as September 1978 Khumayni reportedly denied that the *'ulama* would directly rule in Iran. See James A. Bill, 'Power and Religion in Revolutionary Iran', *The Middle East Journal*, 36 (Winter 1982), 31. And in a speech on 2 September 1984 he is reported as saying that he had explained many times that the clergy must guide and not rule the state. See text of speech, as reported by Tehran home service, 2 September 1984, in BBC, *Summary of World Broadcasts*, [hereafter, *SWB*], ME/7739/A/2 (4 September 1984).

71 In his *Intizar . . . madhab-i i'tiraz*, Shari'ati said: 'The *faqih* and the *mujtahad* have suppressed true knowledge of religion and hindered the true understanding of Shi'i beliefs.' See Mangol Bayat's translation in Donahue and Esposito (eds), *Islam in Transition: Muslim Perspectives*, p. 301.

72 This is what Mawlana Ihstishan ul-Haq, the sole member of the *'ulama* on the Pakistani Commission on Marriage and Family Laws, said in his scathing minority report. See Donahue and Esposito (eds), *Islam in Transition: Muslim Perspectives*, p. 205.

73 Martin Kramer makes these points in a well-argued review of Fuad Ajami's *The Arab Predicament* in *Commentary* (July 1982), pp. 86–8.

74 Edward W. Said, *Orientalism* (New York, Pantheon Books, 1978), *passim*.

75 Edward W. Said, 'Crossing the Barrier', *The New Statesman* (6 June 1980), p. 863.

2 The nature of the Islamic revival

1 Interview, Javed Iqbal, Lahore, 6 May 1982.

2 See his inaugural essay in *al-'Usur* 1 (September 1927), 1–14.

3 Qustantin Zurayq, *Ma'na al-nakba* (Beirut, Dar al-'Ilm li'l-Malayyin, 1948); *Ma'na al-nakba mujaddadan* (Beirut, Dar al-'Ilm li'l-Malayyin, 1967).

4 See note 61 of Chapter 1 and the reference to Shakir Mustafa as example.

5 Sayyid Qutb, *Nahwa mujtama' islami* (Amman, Maktabat al-Aqsa, 1969). The 'straight path' is from the Qur'an, 1:6.

6 The secularist Jalal Al-i Ahmad made the term famous, but others have taken up the general theme. For example, see Khumayni's speech to Pars News Agency, as reported by Tehran home service, 26 September 1979, in the *Foreign Broadcast Information Service* [hereafter, *FBIS*], MEA-79-189 (27 September 1979), p. R1.

7 *The Veil (Al-Khimar)*, 1 (1 February 1983), 1. This is a student journal of the Muslim Sisters, Bayero University, Kano. A Muslim student journal at Ahmadu Bello University is reported as saying that 'nationalism or patriotism means nothing to us compared with our religious ideals'. See Arthur A. Nwankwo, *Nigeria: My People, My Vision* (Enugu, Fourth Dimension Publishing Co., 1979), p. 72.

8 Gordon Waterfield (ed.), *Letters from Egypt, 1862–1867, by Lady Duff Gordon* (New York, Praeger, 1969), p. 182.

9 John O. Voll, *Islam: Continuity and Change in the Modern World* (Essex, Longman, 1982), pp. 349–54.

10 See, for example, *Le Monde Diplomatique*, January 1980.

11 Daniel Pipes, '"This World is Political!!" The Islamic revival of the Seventies', *Orbis*, 24 (Spring 1980), 9–41; also see his *In the Path of God; Islam and Political Power* (New York, Basic Books, 1983), chapter 10.

12 Raphael Israeli, 'The New Wave of Islam', *International Journal* 34 (Summer 1979), 370, 381.

13 See, for example, 'Ali Jirisha, *'Indama yakhuma al-tughah* (Cairo, Dar al-I'tisam, 1975), pp. 48–50.

14 Lewis W. Snider, 'Political Instability and Social Change in the Middle East', *Korea and World Affairs*, 8 (Summer, 1984), 288.

15 Şerif Mardin, 'Religion and Politics in Modern Turkey', in Piscatori (ed.), *Islam in the Political Process*, p. 154.

16 Fuad I. Khuri, 'Sectarian Loyalty Among Rural Migrants in Two Lebanese Suburbs: A Stage Between Family and National Allegiance', in Richard Antoun and Iliya Harik (eds), *Rural Politics and Social Change in the Middle East* (Bloomington and London, Indiana University Press, 1972), pp. 204–10.

17 Federal Republic of Nigeria, *Report of Tribunal of Inquiry on Kano Disturbances* (Lagos, Federal Government Press, 1981), p. 79.

18 Saad Eddin Ibrahim, 'Anatomy of Egypt's Militant Islamic Groups: Methodological Note and Preliminary Findings', *International Journal of Middle East Studies*, 12 (December 1980), 438–9; 'Militant Islam Joins and Mainstream', *Arabia: the Islamic World Review* (April 1984), p. 68.

19 In 1966, for example, 5.8 per cent of the students at Cairo University were *fallahin*, or of rural background, whereas 45.5 per cent of al-Azhar University's students were *fallahin*: Nazih Nasif al-Ayubi, *Siyasat al-ta'lim fi misr: dirasa siyasiyya wa idariyya* (Cairo, Markaz al-Dirasat al-Siyasiyya wa'l-Istratijiyya [al-Ahram], May 1978), p. 72. Also see his 'The Political Revival of Islam: The Case of Egypt', *International Journal of Middle East Studies*, 12 (December 1980), 493.

20 Study by Fu'ad al-Bahi al-Sayyid in L. K. Malika (ed.), *Qira' at fi 'ilm al-nafs al-ijtima'i fi'l-watan al-'arabi*, vol. 3 (Cairo, Al-Hay'a al-Misriyya al-'Amma li'l-Kitab, 1979).

21 Dale F. Eickelman shows how the Moroccan bourgeoisie benefited from French encouragement of non-Sherqawi brotherhoods and, later, the Sultan's encouragement of 'scripturalist' Muslim authorities. Accordingly, its religious attitudes were accommodating to those of the official

establishment: *Moroccan Islam: Tradition and Society in a Pilgrimage Center* (Austin and London, University of Texas Press, 1976), pp. 222–32.

22 Alifa Rifaat, *Distant View of a Minaret*, trans. by Denys Johnson-Davies (London, Quartet Books, 1983), p. 3.

23 Marxists make a distinction between the two. For example, the Iranian Bizhan Jazani speaks of the sub-proletariat as the shanty-town urban poor who are potential revolutionaries, whereas the *lumpenproletariat* are thieves, hooligans, and prostitutes who are inevitably 'depraved', 'classless', and reactionary: *Capitalism and Revolution in Iran* (London, Zed Press, 1980), pp. 141–3.

24 Quoted in Charles-André Julien, 'Crisis and Reform in French North Africa', *Foreign Affairs*, 29 (April 1951), 455.

25 In Qatar, by 1975, only 37 per cent of families living close to each other were related, and since then the trend towards the nuclear family as the primary social unit has continued: Levon H. Melikian and Juhaina S. El-Easa, 'Oil and Social Change in the Gulf', *Journal of Arab Affairs*, 1 (October 1981), 83.

26 V. S. Naipaul, *Among the Believers: An Islamic Journey*, (London, Deutsch, 1981), p. 285.

27 James Finn, 'Secular Discontents', *Worldview*, 24 (March 1981), 5–8.

28 Daniel Bell, *The Cultural Contradictions of Capitalism* (London, Heinemann, 2nd edn, 1979), p. 170.

29 Quoted in Albert Hourani, *Arabic Thought in the Liberal Age, 1798–1939* (London, Oxford University Press, 1970), p. 30.

30 In 1974 Shi'i authorities, particularly Musa al-Sadr, established Harakat al-Mahrumin (Movement of the Disinherited) in Lebanon in order to advance Shi'i rights. A military wing, Amal (an acronym meaning 'hope'), was set up the following year.

31 A. Vasilyev, 'Islam in the Present-Day World', *International Affairs* (Moscow), no. 11 (November 1981), p. 53.

32 Farhad Kazemi, *Poverty and Revolution in Iran; the Migrant Poor, Urban Marginality and Politics* (New York and London, New York University Press, 1980), pp. 82–4. Kazemi also reminds us that anomie may lead to alcoholism or anti-social behaviour as well as to a renewal of religious sentiment.

33 For good discussions of Islamic political movements in the Middle East, see Nazih N. M. Ayubi, 'The Politics of Militant Islamic Movements in the Middle East', *Journal of International Affairs*, 36 (Fall/Winter 1982/83), 271–83; and Edward Mortimer, *Faith and Power; the Politics of Islam*.

34 See Elie Kedourie, 'Islamic Revolution', *Salisbury Papers*, no. 6 (November 1979), unnumbered pp. 3–4 of 5 pp.

35 Nikki Keddie, 'Islamic Revival as Third Worldism', in Jean-Pierre Digard (ed.), *Le cuisinier et le philosophe; hommage à Maxime Rodinson* (Paris, G. P. Maisonneuve et Larose, 1982), pp. 275–81.

36 *The Times*, 4 July 1981. Also see interview with Ben Bella, 'L'Islam au Present', in *Peuples Méditerranéens*, no. 21 (October–December 1982), pp. 49–56. Here he makes the rather extraordinary statement, given his earlier secularism, that 'it is Islam that saved Algeria' (p. 54).

37 Kedourie, 'Islamic Revolution', unnumbered p. 5 of 5 pp.

38 Cf. C. H. Dodd, 'The Revival of Islam and the Modern Nation–State', *Hull Papers in Politics* (March 1981), p. 10.

39 Hamid Enayat, 'The Resurgence of Islam', *History Today*, 30 (February 1980), pp. 18–19.

40 Anthony F. C. Wallace, 'Revitalization Movements', *American Anthropoligist*, 58 (April 1956), 264–81.

41 This is the title of a famous book by Godfrey H. Jansen: (New York, Harper & Row, 1979).

42 Quotation from Palmerston's letter to Lord Aberdeen, 1 November 1853, reproduced in Evelyn Ashley, *The Life of Henry John Temple, Viscount Palmerston; 1846–1865, with Selections from His Speeches and Correspondence*, vol. 2 (London, Richard Bentley, 2nd edn, 1876), p. 47. An example of Palmerston's general attitude is found in his letter to Lord Cowley, 25 November 1859: 'We do not want Egypt or wish it for ourselves any more than any rational man with an estate in the north of England and a residence in the south, would have wished to possess the inns on the north road. All he could want would have been that the inns should be well kept, always accessible, and furnishing him, when he came, with mutton chops and post-horses': *Ibid.*, pp. 124–5.

43 Carlyle's comments on the occasion of the National Conference on the Eastern Question, 8 December 1877, in London, quoted in *The Political Life of the Right Hon. W. E. Gladstone*, vol. 2 (London, Bradbury Agnew & Co., n.d.), p. 12.

44 Norman Daniel, *Islam, Europe and Empire* (Edinburgh, University Press, 1966), p. 468. Not

everyone, however, shared this view. Meredith Townsend, editor of the *Spectator*, wrote, for example, in 1901 ('Asia and Europe', *Westminster Review*): 'All Musalmans in particular are assumed to have fanaticism, as if it were some separate mental peculiarity, belonging to the Mahomedan faith, which accounted for everything, and especially for any very marked impulse.' Quoted in *ibid*.

45 *Hansard: The Parliamentary Debates (Official Report)*, 5th Series, vol. 95 (1934–5), House of Lords, 13 December 1934, p. 336. A similar contemporary view was expressed by John Buchan in one of his novels: 'The Syria army is as fanatical as the hordes of the Mahdi . . . The Persian Muslims are threatening trouble. There is a dry wind blowing through the East, and the parched grasses wait the spart . . . It looks as if Islam had a bigger hand in the thing than we thought . . . There is a Jehad preparing.' See *Greenmantle* (London, Thomas Nelson & Sons, Ltd, 1922; first published, 1916), pp. 16–17.

46 Raymond Aron, 'L'Incendie', *L'Express* (1 December 1979), p. 71.

47 Cyrus Vance, *Hard Choices: Critical Years in America's Foreign Policy* (New York, Simon and Schuster, 1983), quotations (in order) at pp. 410, 408.

3 The theory and practice of territorial pluralism

1 Palmerston used 'nonconformists' to refer, primarily, to Christians and, secondarily, to Muslim dissenters within the Ottoman empire. See his letter of 14 May 1855 to Lord Clarendon, in Ashley, *The Life of Henry John Temple, Viscount Palmerston*, pp. 89–90.

2 There are many typologies based on the views of these subjects. For example, Fazlur Rahman distinguishes between pre-modernist revivalism, classical modernism, neo-revivalism, and neo-modernism: 'Islam: Challenges and Opportunities' in Alford T. Welch and Pierre Cachia (eds), *Islam: Past Influence and Present Challenge* (Edinburgh, University Press, 1979), pp. 315–30. Yvonne Haddad refers to normativists, acculturationists (which include modernists and romantics), neo-normativists, and secularists: *Contemporary Islam and the Challenge of History* (Albany, State University of New York Press, 1982), pp. 7–23. Malise Ruthven speaks of the archaic, modernist, reformist, and neo-traditionalist responses: *Islam in the World* (Harmondsworth, Penguin, 1984), pp. 294–5.

3 There are about forty references to obeying God and His Prophet: 3:132, 4:80–1, 5:95, 8:20, 24:51–2, 64:12, for example.

4 This point was made to me by J.P. Bannerman. Prince Muhammad al-Faysal has also stressed the idea of commitment: 'Islam invites man to commit himself exclusively to his Creator, to harmonize his will with the Will of God and to recreate the world with this noble commitment': Inaugural Address to the International Conference on 'Islam and the Challenge of Our Age' in April 1976, published in Altaf Gauhar (ed.), *The Challenge of Islam* (London, Islamic Council of Europe, 1978), p. xxx. T.B. Irving says that '*islam* itself is the verbal noun of the IV or causative measure, and it means [peace's] achievement or attainment': 'Terms and Concepts: Problems in Translating the Qur'an', in Khurshid Ahmad and Zafar Ishaq Ansari (eds), *Islamic Perspectives: Studies in Honour of Sayyid Abul A'la Mawdudi* (Leicester, The Islamic Foundation, 1979), p. 128.

5 The *hadith* is related by both Bukhari and Muslim and can be found in the compilation of Imam Yahya ibn Sharaf al-Din al-Nawawi, *Riyad al-salihin*, ed. by Muhammad Nasir al-Din al-Albani (Beirut, al-Maktab al-Islami, 1399 A.H./1979), chapter 80, *hadith* 667, p. 284.

6 June S. Katz and Ronald S. Katz, 'The New Indonesian Marriage Law: A Mirror of Indonesia's Political, Cultural, and Legal System', *The American Journal of Comparative Law*, 23 (Fall, 1975), 653–81.

7 There are, however, some Muslims who would question that Islam is democratic, for democracy is a Western concept, displacing rule by Allah with rule by the people, and who would see any argument equating Islam and democracy as an indication of the extent to which Muslims have become Westernized. This criticism is often heard in Pakistan. Others, particularly non-Muslims, might criticize the view that Islam is democratic as apologetic.

8 I am conscious of the debate over the proper terminology here and realize that 'state' and 'nation-state' have obvious limitations. The first can be confused when federal political systems are considered; the second, when the political systems are multinational. J.D.B. Miller uses 'sovereign state' to get around these problems: *The World of States: Connected Essays* (London, Croom Helm, 1981), chapter 2. I will use the terms 'state', 'territorial state', 'sovereign state', and 'nation-state' interchangeably.

9 Bernard Lewis, *The Middle East and the West* (New York, Harper Row, 1964), p. 115. Writing in

1932, Robert Montagone similarly concluded that the nation–state was to Muslims 'totally alien' and a 'heretical innovation': *Foreign Affairs*, 30 (July 1932), 580.

10 Quotations (in order) in Elie Kedourie (ed.), *Nationalism in Asia and Africa* (London, Weidenfeld and Nicolson, 1970), p. 29; and Kedourie, 'Islam and Nationalism: a Recipe for Tension', *The Times Higher Education Supplement*, 14 November 1980.

11 Quotations (in order) in Adda B. Bozeman, 'Iran: US Foreign Policy and the Tradition of Persian Statecraft', *Orbis*, 23 (Summer 1979), 389; and Bozeman, 'Decline of the West? Spengler Reconsidered', *The Virginia Quarterly Review*, 59 (Spring 1983), 192–3. Also see her *The Future of Law in a Multicultural World* (Princeton, Princeton University Press, 1971), pp. 50–85.

12 Lewis, *The Middle East and the West*, pp. 135–6.

13 Kedourie, 'Islam and Nationalism: A Recipe for Tension'.

14 Bozeman, 'Decline of the West? Spengler Reconsidered', p. 193.

15 Peters, *Islam and Colonialism: The Doctrine of Jihad in Modern History*, p. 140.

16 Lewis, *The Middle East and the West*, pp. 131–6.

17 Bozeman, 'Decline of the West? Spengler Reconsidered', p. 193; Bozeman, 'Iran: US Foreign Policy and the Tradition of Persian Statecraft', pp. 387–402.

18 J.B. Kelly, *Arabia, The Gulf and the West* (London, Weidenfeld and Nicolson, 1980), quotations (in order) at pp. 388, 218, 491, 423.

19 *Mukhtasar sunan abi da'ud*, ed. by Ahmad Muhammad Shakir and Muhammad Hamid al-Faqi, vol. 3 (Beirut, Dar al-Ma'rifa, 1980), *Kitab al-jihad*, *hadith* 2525, p. 424.

20 *Sahih al-bukhari*, ed. by Muhammad Tawfiq 'Uwayda, vol. 5 (Cairo, Lajna Ihya Kutub al-Sunna, 1390 A.H./1971), *Kitab al-jihad*, *hadith* 2518, p. 50; *hadith* 2505, p. 42.

21 Khadduri, *War and Peace in the Law of Islam*, pp. 185–6.

22 *Sahih al-bukhari*, vol. 1 (Cairo, Mustafa al-Babi al-Halabi, 1372 A.H./1953), *Kitab al-iman*, p. 13. Also see Qur'an, 4:74. Note that other compilations of the Qur'an designate the verse cited in the text as 3:163.

23 Ameer, Ali, *The Spirit of Islam* (London, Christophers, 5th edn, 1949), p. 290.

24 Abul A'la Mawdudi, *Political Theory of Islam*, ed. by Kurshid Ahmad (Lahore, Islamic Publications Ltd, 1960), p. 26.

25 T.S. Eliot, 'Little Gidding' in *Four Quartets* (New York, Harcourt, Brace and Company, 1943), p. 39.

26 The *hadith* is related by Muslim and can be found in al-Nawawi's compilation, *Kitab al-arba'in*. See *Matn al-arba'in hadithan al-nawawiyya*, *hadith* 22, p. 66.

27 Based on a *hadith*, related by Abu Da'ud. The Arabic text can be found in the compilation of Wali al-Din al-Tabrizi, *Mishkat al-masabih*, trans. and ed. by Abdul Hameed Siddiqui, vol. 1 (New Delhi, Kitab Bhavan, 1980), *Kitab al-iman*, *hadith* 59, p. 38. The *hadith* refers specifically to the false messiah or anti-Christ (*al-dajjal*).

28 *Sahih al-bukhari*, ed. by 'Uwayda, *Kitab al-jihad*, *hadith* 2710, p. 159.

29 See, for example, 'Ali ibn Ahmad (Ibn Hazm), *Kitab al-fisal fi'l-milal wa'l-ahwa wa'l-nihal*, Pt. 4 (Cairo, Matba'at al-Tamaddun, 1321 A.H./1903), pp. 4, 135.

30 *Sahih al-bukhari*, ed. by 'Uwayda, *Kitab al-jihad*, *hadith* 2729, pp. 174–5. The *hadith* reports the Caliph 'Umar's instructions, as he lay dying, to his successor.

31 See Khadduri's translation of Muhammad ibn al-Hasan al-Shaybani's *Siyar: The Islamic Law of Nations*, pp. 154–5.

32 This, according to a *hadith: Sahih al-bukhari*, ed. by 'Uwayda, *Kitab al-jihad*, *hadith* 2730, p. 172.

33 See, for example, '"Islam is superior . . ."', *The Jerusalem Quarterly*, no. 11 (Spring 1979), pp. 36–42.

34 *Sahih al-bukhari*, ed. by 'Uwayda, *Kitab al-jihad*, *hadith* 2729, p. 174.

35 Khadduri, *The Islamic Law of Nations*, pp. 108–9, 141, 158–60, 172, 191.

36 Ibn Abi Zayd al-Qayrawani, *al-Risala*, ed. by Leon Bercher (Algiers, Editions Populaires de l'Armée, 6th edn, 1975), pp. 134, 162, 164, quotation at p. 164. The first example of Maliki thinking stands in particular contrast to Hanifi thinking.

37 Muhammad ibn Idris al-Shafi'i, *Kitab al-umm*, vol. 4 (Cairo, al-Matba' al-Kubra al-Amiriyya, 1322 A.H./1904), pp. 4, 103–4.

38 See Leonard Binder, 'Al-Ghazzali's Theory of Islamic Government', *The Muslim World*, 45 (July 1955), 229–41; 'Ali ibn Muhammad al-Mawardi, *Ahkam al-sultaniyya*, in Maximilian Enger (ed.), *Maverdii Constitutiones Politicae* (Bonn, Adolphus Marcus, 1853), *passim*.

39 A.K.S. Lambton, 'Islamic Political Thought' in Joseph Schacht and C.E. Bosworth (eds), *The Legacy of Islam* (Oxford, The Clarendon Press, 2nd edn, 1974), p. 415.

40 See Franz Rosenthal's translation of Ibn Khaldun's *Muqaddimah*, abridged and ed. by H.J. Dawood (London, Routledge and Kegan Paul, 1967), chapter 3.

41 Bernard Lewis, *The Muslim Discovery of Europe* (London, Weidenfeld and Nicolson, 1982), pp. 71–88, 106–10, 149, 296; quotations (in order) at pp. 75–6, 296. For an informative account of the particular case of Shah Abbas and the Sherley brothers, see J.P. Bannerman, *The Establishment of Permanent Diplomatic Relations Between Iran and the UK* (London, Foreign and Commonwealth Office, 1977).

42 W.B. Yeats, 'The Gift of Harun al-Rashid', *The Collected Poems of W.B. Yeats* (London, Macmillan, 2nd edn, 1969), p. 513.

43 J.D. Gurney's review of Lewis's book in *The Times Literary Supplement*, 11 March 1983. The point about the travellers in Iran is also Gurney's.

44 Sir Hamilton Gibb definitively dispatched the argument that al-Walid did not seek Byzantine help: 'Arab–Byzantine Relations Under the Umayyad Caliphate', *Dumbarton Oaks Papers*, 12 (1958), 219–33.

45 The text of the treaty can be found in J.C. Hurewitz (ed.), *Middle East and North Africa in World Politics: a Documentary Record*, vol. 1 (New Haven and London, Yale University Press, 2nd edn, 1975), Preamble, Articles 1, 2, 6 and 15, pp. 2–5. For the jurists' view of the length of a treaty between Muslims and non-Muslims referred to in Article 1 of the treaty, see, for example, al-Mawardi, *al-Ahkam al-sultaniyya*, p. 84, and Yaqub ibn Ibrahim (Abu Yusuf), *Kitab al-kharaj* (Cairo, al-Matba'a al-Salafiyya, 2nd edn, 1352 A.H./1933), pp. 207–12.

46 The Turkish text of this agreement and a translation of it into English are found in A.H. De Groot, *The Ottoman Empire and the Dutch Republic; A History of the Earliest Diplomatic Relations, 1610–1630* (Leiden and Istanbul, Nederlands Historisch-Archaeologisch Instituut, 1978), pp. 233–60. The relevant articles from the English text are, in the order mentioned, Articles 35, 14, 11 (and 34), 51, and 16. Quotation is at p. 258 (Article 51).

47 Hurewitz (ed.), *Middle East and North Africa in World Politics*, p. 27.

48 It should be noted that there were distinct second thoughts on the exemption of foreigners from the traditional poll-tax, *jizya* (or in Ottoman convention, *kharaj*). In 1613 the *qadi* of Galata said that the tax would be imposed on all Christian foreigners more than one year resident in the empire, and in 1616 it was briefly levied (although mainly in order to raise cash for war with the Persians). The Grand Vizier Khalil Pasha soon invalidated these actions and reaffirmed the validity of the capitulations, but many influential people felt that, if all foreigners should not be subject to the tax, then at least those who married local women should.

49 Hurewitz (ed.), *Middle East and North Africa in World Politics*, Articles 7, 17(2) and 25, pp. 94, 97, 99.

50 Quoted in Roderic H. Davison, 'Turkish Attitudes Concerning Christian–Muslim Equality in the Nineteenth Century', *American Historical Review*, 59 (July 1954), 847.

51 Note of Serim Efendi to the British Ambassador in Istanbul, in Hurewitz (ed.), *Middle East and North Africa in World Politics*, p. 284.

52 Disraeli to Austen Layard, 22 November 1877, quoted in George Earle Buckle, *The Life of Benjamin Disraeli, Earl of Beaconsfield*, vol. 6 (London, John Murray, 1920), p. 252.

53 Hurewitz (ed.), *Middle East and North Africa in World Politics*, Articles 1 and 2 of Annex to the Cyprus Convention, p. 412, emphasis mine. Text of the Treaty of Berlin, in *ibid.*, Articles 58, 60 and 62, p. 414.

54 *Ibid.*, p. 16.

55 *Ibid.*, Article 15 of 1623 decree, p. 18; Capitulations to France, pp. 50–5.

56 *Ibid.*, Articles 3, 5 and 7, p. 198.

57 *Narrative of the Embassy of Ruy González de Clavijo to the Court of Timour, at Samarcand, A.D. 1403–6*, trans. by Clements R. Markham (London, Hakluyt Society, 1859), pp. ii–iii, quotation at p. 133.

58 Hurewitz (ed.), *Middle East and North Africa in World Politics*, Article 2, p. 20.

59 For the text of the treaty with France, see Henry de Castries (ed.), *Les sources inédites de l'histoire du Maroc*, 1st Series, *Archives et Bibliothéques de France*, vol. 3 (Paris, Ernest Leroux, 1911), pp. 413–6. For a discussion of the letter to Charles I and Arabic text of the letter, see D.S. Richards, 'A Letter to Charles I of England from the Sultan al-Walid of Morocco, *The Islamic Quarterly*, 17 (January–June, 1973), 26–35.

60 Hurewitz (ed.), *Middle East and North Africa in World Politics*, Articles 1 and 9, pp. 64–5.

61 *Ibid.*, pp. 218–9, quotation is of Article 8. For a discussion of slaves in Islamic history, see Bernard Lewis, *Race and Color in Islam* (New York and London, Harper & Row, 1971).

62 *Ibid.*, third clause, p. 363.

63 Quoted from Minhaj-us Siraj Jurjani's *Tabaqat-i-Nasiri*, in Khaliq Ahmad Nizami, *Some Aspects of Religion and Politics in India During the Thirteenth Century* (Aligarh, Muslim University, 1961), p. 333.
64 J. Kathirithamby-Wells, 'Ahmad Shah Ibn Iskander and the Late 17th Century "Holy War" in Indonesia', *Journal of the Malaysian Branch of the Royal Asiatic Society*, 43 (July 1970), 52. Perhaps it was only to be expected that this alliance would trigger a revolt, which Prince Trunajaya of Madura led.
65 Texts of the 1761, 1763, and 1764 agreements can be found in H. de la Costa, 'Muhammad Alimuddin I, Sultan of Sulu, 1735–1773', *Journal of the Malaysian Branch of the Royal Asiatic Society*, 38, Part 1 (1965), Appendices, A, B and D. Quotations, in order, at pp. 74 (Article 6 of 1763 treaty) and 68.
66 Russel Jones, 'Two Malay Letters Written by Sultan Muhammad Jiwa Muazzam Syah of Kedah to Captain Francis Light', *Journal of the Malaysian Branch of the Royal Asiatic Society*, 54 (December 1981), 27.
67 Lee Kam Hing, 'Foreigners in the Achehnese Court, 1760–1819', *Journal of the Malaysian Branch of the Royal Asiatic Society*, 43 (July 1970), Article 6 and 7, quoted at p. 65.
68 Refer to note 5. The Hanbali jurist, al-Hajjawi, however, argued that there could be a peace treaty longer than ten years if the Muslims were in a weak position: see Khadduri, *War and Peace in the Law of Islam*, fn. 39, p. 220.
69 *Ibid.*, p. 235.
70 See P. Chalmeta, 'Concessions Territoriales dans al-Andulus: données inédites et rectifications', in *Proceedings of the Ninth Congress of the Union Européenne des Arabisants et Islamisants*, ed. by Rudolph Peters (Leiden, Brill, 1981), pp. 48–56.
71 Hurewitz (ed.), *Middle East and North Africa in World Politics*, p. 27. For an excellent discussion of this period generally, see Ramazani, *The Foreign Policy of Iran: A Developing Nation in World Affairs, 1500–1941*, p. 18.
72 Hurewitz (ed.), *Middle East and North Africa in World Politics*, Article 2 and Appendix, pp. 79–80.
73 *Ibid.*, Stipulations and Article 1, pp. 219–20.
74 *Ibid.*, Article 5, p. 454.
75 *Ibid.*, Article 3, p. 94.
76 See, for example, Article 4 of the Austro–Hungarian treaty with the Ottoman Empire of 1909, in Richard W. Brant (ed.), *British and Foreign State Papers, 1908–1909*, vol. 52 (London, HMSO, 1913), p. 181; also, Article 2 of Annex 2 of the Italo–Ottoman treaty of 1912, in Edward C. Blech (ed.), *British and Foreign State Papers, 1913*, vol. 56 (London, HMSO, 1916), p. 1099.
77 Quoted in Ramesh Chandra Varma, *Foreign Policy of the Mughals (1526–1727 A.D.)* (Agra, Shiva Lal Agarwala, 1967), p. 57.
78 Quoted in Nizami, *Some Aspects of Religion and Politics in India During the Thirteenth Century*, p. 327.
79 Quoted in Yann Richard, 'Ayatollah Kashani: Precursor of the Islamic Republic?', in N. Keddie, (ed.), *Politics and Religion in Iran*, p. 106.
80 J.C. Hurewitz (ed.), *Diplomacy in the Near and Middle East; A Documentary Record: 1914–1956*, vol. 2 (Princeton and London, D. Van Nostrand, 1956), Article 1, p. 147.
81 The text of the treaty can be found in League of Nations, *Treaty Series*, 71 (1928), 133–52 (Arabic text), 153–8 (English). Articles referred to in this paragraph are, in order, Articles 1, 2 and 7, pp. 153–4. For an excellent discussion of this treaty, see Daniel Silverfarb, 'The Treaty of Jiddah of May 1927', *Middle Eastern Studies*, 18 (July 1982), 276–85.
82 Sir Andrew Ryan (British Ambassador to Saudi Arabia) to Sir John Simon (Foreign Secretary), Letter no. 17 (22 January 1935), India Office Records, L/P & S/12/2135, p. 190. The reference is to Article 6 of the treaty of 1927.
83 Preamble of 1936 treaty, in League of Nations, *Treaty Series*, 174 (1937), 132 (English), 136 (Arabic); preamble of 1938 treaty, in *Treaty Series*, 190 (1938), 256.
84 Preamble, Articles 2 and 8 of pact, the texts of which can be found in H. Hassouna, *The League of Arab States and Regional Disputes* (Dobbs Ferry, New York, Oceana Publications, 1975), pp. 403–4, 406.
85 Article 2(B) and Preamble (in order), the texts of which can be found in Nizar Obaid Madani, 'The Islamic Content of the Foreign Policy of Saudi Arabia; King Faisal's Call for Islamic Solidarity, 1965–1975' (unpublished Ph.D thesis, The American University, 1977), Appendix B, pp. 200, 198 (in order).

86 Manoucher Parvin and Maurie Sommer, 'Dar al-Islam: The Evolution of Muslim Territoriality and Its Implications for Conflict Resolution in the Middle East', *International Journal of Middle Eastern Studies*, 11 (February 1980), 7. The idea of 'territorial exclusivity' is J.P. Bannerman's.

87 Adeed Dawisha, 'Anti-Americanism in the Arab World: Memories of the Past in the Attitudes of the Present', in Alvin Z. Rubinstein and Donald E. Smith (eds), *Anti-Americanism in the Third World* (New York, Praeger, 1985), p. 67.

88 Earl of Cromer, *Modern Egypt*, vol. 1 (London, Macmillan, 1908), p. 149.

4 The modern intellectual consensus on the nation-state

1 From his *Mu'allim-i shafiq*, translated by Nikki R. Keddie in her *An Islamic Response to Imperialism; Political and Religious Writings and Sayyid Jamal al-Din 'al-Afghani'* (Berkeley and London, University of California Press, 1983), p. 56. It must be noted, though, that al-Afghani at other times argued that Muslims should move away from tribalism, or pluralism, to universalism.

2 Both quoted from Shan Mohammad (ed.), *Writings and Speeches of Sir Syed Ahmad Khan* (Bombay, Nachiketa Publications, 1972), pp. 266, 257 (in order), emphasis in original.

3 For example, Nadav Safran, *Egypt in Search of Political Community; An Analysis of the Intellectual and Political Evolution of Egypt, 1804–1952* (Cambridge, Mass., Harvard University Press, 1961), p. 82.

4 From *al-Manar*, 33 (1933), translated in Donahue and Esposito (eds), *Islam in Transition*, p. 59.

5 Ahmad Lufti al-Sayyid, *Ta'ammulat fi'l-falsafa wa'l-adab wa'l-siyasa wa'l-ijtima'* (Cairo, Dar al-Ma'arif, 1946), pp. 68–9.

6 Jamil M. Abun-Nasr, *The Tijaniyya: A Sufi Order in the Modern World* (London, Oxford University Press, 1965), pp. 62–70. Although General Bugeaud's subordinate claimed that he took the *fatwa* to Cairo and Mecca for endorsement, scholars have definitely rejected his Mecca trip as pure fabrication, while the visit to Al-Azhar remains unproven.

7 W.W. Hunter, *The Indian Musulmans: Are They Bound in Conscience to Rebel Against the Queen?* (London, Trübner and Company, 1871), p. 120; also see pp. 123–8.

8 *Ibid.*, for partial texts of the *fatwas*: Appendix I, pp. 213–15.

9 From his 'Lecture on Islam' in Donahue and Esposito (eds), *Islam in Transition*, p. 40; Mehr Afroz Murad, *Intellectual Modernism of Shibli Nu'mani* (Lahore, Institute of Islamic Culture, 1976), pp. 91–3.

10 This discussion is drawn from John L. Esposito, 'Muhammad Iqbal and the Islamic State', in Esposito (ed.), *Voices of Resurgent Islam*, pp. 182–4. Quotations from Shamloo (ed.), *Speeches and Statements of Iqbal* (Lahore, al-Manar Academy, 1948), p. 224; and Iqbal, 'Presidential Address' in Syed Abdul Vahid (ed.), *Thoughts and Reflections of Iqbal* (Lahore, Sh. Muhammad Ashraf, 1964), pp. 170–1.

11 Interview, Datuk Musa Hitam, Kuala Lumpur, 26 November 1981.

12 Interview, Qadeeruddin Ahmed, Karachi, 10 May 1982.

13 Interview, Faruq Jarar, Amman, 26 May 1982.

14 Interview, Muhammad Jbayr, Riyadh, 7 June 1975.

15 Interview, Samir Shamma, Jidda, 12 June 1975. Shamma was talking about the Shah's Iran but he doubtless would have thought it even more true of Khumayni's Iran.

16 Interview, Sulayman al-Sulaym, Riyadh, 25 May 1975.

17 Translated from Dutch text in C.A.O. van Nieuwenhuijze, *Aspects of Islam in Post-Colonial Indonesia* (The Hague, W. van Hoeve, 1958), p. 205.

18 Mohammed Fadhel Jamali, *Letters on Islam; Written By a Father in Prison to His Son* (Oxford, Oxford University Press, 1965), pp. 86–7, 90–1, 103.

19 Interview, Mahathir Muhammad, Kuala Lumpur, 24 November 1981. Dr Mahathir's Qur'anic reference is to 49:13.

20 'Abd al-Rahman al-'Azzam, *al-Risala al-khalida* (Beirut, Dar al-Shuruq, 4th edn, 1969), pp. 274–5, 283, 288.

21 'Allal al-Fasi, *al-Naqd al-dhati* (Tetuan, Dar al-Fakr al-Maghrib, 2nd edn, 1960 [?]), quotations (in order) at pp. 260, 239, 261.

22 Hamidullah, *Muslim Conduct of State*, pp. 3, 78, 80–4, quotation at p. 107.

23 Mohammed Talaat al-Ghunaimi, *The Muslim Conception of International Law and the Western Approach* (The Hague, Martinus Nijhoff, 1968), pp. 64, 194–5. Also, generally, see his *al-Ahkam al-'amma fi qanun al-umam; al-tanzim al-duwali* (Alexandria, Mansha'at al-Ma'arif, 1971).

24 Interviews, Ma'ruf al-Dawalibi, Riyadh, 18 March, 23 March, 17 May 1975.

25 Interview, 'Abdullah al-Munifi, Riyadh, 13 March 1975. Also generally see his 'The Islamic Constitutional Theory' (unpublished thesis for Doctor of Juridical Science, University of Virginia Law School, 1973) in which he elaborates a theory of constitutional checks and balances for the Islamic state.

26 Interview, Syed Zain Abedin, Jidda, 19 May 1982.

27 Interview, Abdul Rahman Wahid, Jakarta, 20 November 1981.

28 Hasan Hanafi, 'Religious Change and Cultural Domination', paper delivered at the International Congress of Human Sciences in Asia and North Africa', Mexico City, 1976; *Religious Dialogue and Revolution, Essays on Judaism, Christianity and Islam* (Cairo, The Anglo–Egyptian Bookshop, 1977), pp. 125–73, quotation at p. 181; 'Arab National Thought in the Balance', translated from article in *Qadaya 'Arabiyya, The Jerusalem Quarterly*, no. 25 (Fall 1982), pp. 54–67; 'Hal yajuz shar'an al-sulh ma' bani isra'il?', *al-Yasar al-islami*, 1 (Rabi' al-Awwal 1401 A.H./January 1981), 96–127.

29 Al-Sadiq al-Mahdi, *Ahadith al-ghurba* (Beirut, Dar al-Qadaya, 1976); 'Islam – Society and Change' in Esposito (ed.), *Voices of Resurgent Islam*, pp. 230–40; 'Islam and Revolution in the Middle East and North Africa', lecture to the Centre for Middle Eastern Studies and Centre for African Studies of the University of California, June 1982; 'Social Change and the Role of Islam', lecture to the Royal Institute of International Affairs, London, 13 March 1979.

30 Interview, Kamal al-Sharif, Amman, 27 May 1982.

31 Interview, Chandra Muzaffar, Penang, 28 November 1981; *The Universalism of Islam* (Penang, ALIRAN, 1979), pp. 1–11, quotation at p. 3.

32 Interview, Anwar Ibrahim, Kuala Lumpur, 30 November 1981.

33 Interview, Harun Nasution, Jakarta, 21 November 1981.

34 Martin Wight, *Power Politics* (Harmondsworth, Penguin, 1979; first published, 1946), p. 25.

35 From a telegram to the Prime Minister, quoted in Azar Tabari, 'The Role of the Clergy in Modern Iranian Politics', in Keddie (ed.), *Religion and Politics in Iran*, pp. 67–8.

36 Interview of Nawab Akhbar Bugti, former governor of Baluchistan, in *Nawa-i-Waft*, 3 March 1984, p. 3, translated from the Urdu in *Joint Publications Research Service*, ME-84-059 (5 April 1984), p. 12.

37 Nels Johnson, *Islam and the Politics of Meaning in Palestinian Nationalism* (London, Kegan Paul International, 1982), pp. 38–46.

38 *Ibid.*, p. 76. Not every Palestinian leader, however, is explicitly Islamic. The infamous Abu Nidal, in a published interview that some people deny could have taken place, is determinedly secular. He said, for example, 'that when one says "Jewish", it is a religious determination, like Muslim'; religion thus has nothing to do with national self-determination. The interview was in *France Pays Arabes* (Paris), no. 124 (February 1958), pp. 10–14, translated in *FBIS*, MEA-85-045 (7 March 1985), quotation at p. A4.

39 Quoted from *Filastin al-thawra*, 20 February 1979, in Johnson, *Islam and the Politics of Meaning in Palestinian Nationalism*, p. 88.

40 See Thomas P. Weaver, J. David Gillespie, and Ali al-Jarbawi, 'What Palestinians Believe: A Systematic Analysis of Belief Systems in the West Bank and Gaza', *Journal of Palestine Studies*, 14 (Spring 1985), 110–26.

41 Interview, Samir Namir (leader of Muslim student bloc at Bir Zeit University), Bir Zeit, 5 June 1982; *The Washington Post*, 13 February 1982; *The Times*, 19 February 1982; *Contemporary Mideast Backgrounder*, no. 208 (21 May 1985), p. 2. Some of the support for the Muslim groups may be a political reaction to the dominance of Fatah and the PLO.

42 Interview, Gambi Baramki (Vice-President of Bir Zeit University), Bir Zeit, 5 June 1982.

43 *Time Magazine* (24 May 1982), p. 15.

44 Report of Ihdin Radio of Free and Unified Lebanon in Arabic, 6 March 1985, in *FBIS*, MEA-85-044 (6 March 1985), p. G3.

45 Damascus Television Service in Arabic, 10 April 1985, in *FBIS*, MEA-85-070 (11 April 1985), p. H1.

46 *The Washington Post*, 12 May 1985.

47 J. Spencer Trimingham, *The Influence of Islam Upon Africa* (London, Longman, 2nd edn, 1980), p. 45.

48 Keith H. Basso, 'Semantic Aspects of Linguistic Acculturation', *American Anthropologist*, 69 (October 1967), 471–7.

49 W.B. Yeats, 'At Algeciras – A Meditation Upon Death', *Selected Poetry* (London, Pan Books, 1975), p. 152.

Notes

50 John Cheever, *The Wapshot Chronicle* (New York, Harper & Row, 1973), p. 72.
51 See generally, Edmund Leach, *Culture and Communication; The Logic By Which Symbols Are Connected* (Cambridge, Cambridge University Press, 1976), pp. 9–27; and Roman Jakobson and Morris Halle, *Fundamentals of Language*, Janua Linguarum Series (The Hague, Moulton & Co., 1956), pp. 72, 76–82. Note, however, that Jakobson and Halle concentrate on an analysis of aphasia.
52 Lawrence Durrell, *Clea* (New York, Pocket Books, 1961), p. 235.
53 See, for example, Mohammad O. Madani, 'The Relationship Between Saudi Arabia Domestic Law and International Law: A Study of the Oil Agreements with Foreign Companies' (unpublished doctoral thesis, The George Washington University Law School, 1970), pp. 46–9. In general, I have refrained from identifying each informant unless his comments have appeared in print. Interviews were conducted in various Saudi cities and in London between 1975 and 1983.
54 Abul-Hamid Abu Sulayman, 'The Islamic Theory of International Relations: Its Relevance, Past and Present' (unpublished Ph.D. Thesis, University of Pennsylvania, 1973), pp. 187–90.
55 Another example is seen in the way Saudis speak of the equality of sovereign governments in the international system. In effect, governmental equality is a symbol-*qua*-sign of Islam. A Western-trained scholar says that, because Muslims are to deal with outsiders on political, not racial or religious, grounds, Islam enshrines the value of equality in interstate relations. An '*alim* stresses that equality of treatment is assured between Muslims and non-Muslims, regardless of war and peace. In support of the idea, he cites the story of the army commander 'Amr Ibn al-'As who, avenging his son's loss in a race, punished the Christian victor. The Caliph, outraged by the implication that Muslims ought to be superior, in turn punished Ibn al-'As for fostering inequality and thus misusing his position. By extension the '*alim* thinks that Muslim governments today have an obligation to accept as equals, and to treat impartially, non-Muslim governments. Because the early ideas and example seem to speak as forcefully to current circumstances as they did to an earlier time, the two contexts do not seem different.
56 Peters, *Islam and Colonialism; The Doctrine of Jihad in Modern History*, p. 140.
57 For a nineteenth-century view that Islam was being 'nationalized', see A.L. Chatelier, *L'Islam au XIXe siècle* (Paris, Ernest Leroux, 1888), pp. 120–2.
58 W.H. Auden, 'Law Like Love', *Selected Poems* (New York, Vintage Books, 1979), p. 89.
59 Arthur Jeffrey, 'The Political Importance of Islam', *Journal of Near Eastern Studies*, 1 (October 1942), 386.
60 For a discussion of apologetics, see Wilfred Cantwell Smith, *Islam in Modern History* (Princeton, Princeton University Press, 1957), pp. 115–55; and H.A.R. Gibb, *Modern Trends in Islam* (Chicago, University of Chicago Press, 1947), pp. 106–29.
61 This allusion is Albert Hourani's. See his *Europe and the Middle East* (London, MacMillan, 1980), p. 5.
62 My own earlier thinking was as critical of apologetics: 'Human Rights in Islamic Political Culture', in Kenneth W. Thompson (ed.), *The Moral Imperatives of Human Rights: A World Survey* (Washington, D.C., University Press of America, 1980), pp. 152–62.

5 Nonconformist thinking on the nation-state

1 Sayyed Abulala Maudoodi, *Nationalism and India* (Pathankot, Maktabat-e-Jama'at-e Islami, 2nd edn, 1947), pp. 9–10.
2 Siyyid Abul A'la Maududi, *Unity of the Muslim World*, ed. by Khurshid Ahmad (Lahore, Islamic Publications, Ltd., 1967), pp. 11–14; also see Maudoodi, *Nationalism and India*, pp. 28–31.
3 Maudoodi, *Nationalism and India*, pp. 60–2, 28 (in order); quotation at p. 13. Also see *Unity of the Muslim World*, pp. 1–2.
4 Maudoodi, *Nationalism and India*, quotations (in order) at pp. 59, 7; also see pp. 37, 42–3. See *Unity in the Muslim World*, pp. 24–5.
5 Maududi, *Unity of the Muslim World*, pp. 7–15, quotation at p. 14.
6 *Ibid.*, pp. 17–24.
7 Iqbal, *The Reconstruction of Religious Thought in Islam*, p. 159. It should be noted that Iqbal was originally an enthusiast of nationalism.
8 Mawdudi, 'The Task Before the Muslim Summit', originally published in *Dawn*, the Karachi newspaper, and reproduced as Chapter 2 in *Unity of the Muslim World*, quotation at p. 45.
9 *Ibid.*, pp. 45, 48.

174

10 Sharif al-Mujahid, 'Muslim Nationalism: Iqbal's Synthesis of Pan-Islamism and Nationalism', *The American Journal of Islamic Social Sciences*, 2 (July 1985), 29–40.
11 Syed Abul 'Ala Maulana Maudoodi, *Khutabat* (Chicago, Kazi Publications, 2nd edn, 1977), p. 4.
12 *Ibid.*, p. 56.
13 Maududi, *Unity of the Muslim World*, pp. 31–9, quotation at p. 39. Regarding ritual, Mawdudi made the *hajj* a symbol of unity: as all distinctions of status, wealth, language, and colour are obscured in the utter and uniform simplicity of the white covering (*ihram*) worn by every *hajji*, Islam provides the basis for a community of universal quality. See his *Khutabat*, p. 230.
14 Mawdudi, 'The Task Before the Muslim Summit,' quotations at pp. 43, 52.
15 For Mawdudi's and Nadvi's influence on Qutb, see Yvonne Haddad, 'Sayyid Qutb: Ideologue of Islamic Revival', in Esposito (ed.), *Voices of Resurgent Islam*, pp. 70, 84–5; and Emmanuel Sivan, *Radical Islam: Medieval Theology and Modern Politics* (New Haven and London, Yale University Press, 1985), p. 23. Nadvi's work includes: *al-'Arab wa'l-islam* (Beirut, al-Maktab al-Islami, 1965).
16 Qutb, *Nahwa mujtama' islami*, p. 9; *Ma'alim fi'l tariq*, pp. 175–6.
17 On the sovereignty of man rather than of God, see *Ma'alim fi'l-tariq*, p. 10. On Islam's moderation and 'middle way', see *Nahwa mujtama' islami*, p. 32; *Ma'alim fi'l-tariq*, p. 7; and *Fi Zilal al-Qu'ran*, vol. 1 (Beirut, Dar al-Shuruq, 1394 A.H./1973), pp. 130–2. The Qur'anic reference to Islam as a 'middle community' is 2:143.
18 Qutb, *Ma'alim fi'l tariq*, pp. 151, 157–9, quotation at p. 159.
19 Muhammad al-Ghazzali, *Min huna na'lam* (Cairo, Dar al-Kutub al-Haditha, 5th edn, 1965; first printed, 1953), pp. 55–74, quotation at p. 68.
20 Saïd Ramadan, *L'Islam et le Nationalisme*, no. 8 (Geneva, Centre Islamique, Dhul Hijjah 1382 A.H./May 1963), pp. 1–2, 13–15.
21 Albert Hourani, *Syria and Lebanon: a Political Essay* (London, Oxford University Press, 1946), p. 114.
22 Abu Khaldun Sati' al-Husri, *Muhadarat fi nushu al-fikr al-qawmiyya* (Cairo, Matba'at al-Risala, 1951), p. 20; *Ara wa ahadith fi'l-qawmiyya al-'arabiyya* (Beirut, Dar al-'Ilm li'l-Malayyin, 3rd edn, 1959), p. 36–70.
23 Richard P. Mitchell, *The Society of the Muslim Brothers* (London, Oxford University Press, 1969), Chapter 3 generally, pp. 15–16, 267–9.
24 From an address delivered to Nadi al-Ba'th al-'Arabi in Baghdad, January 1952, translated by Sylvia G. Haim, in *Die Welt des Islams*, 3, no. 3 (1954), pp. 207–11, quotation at p. 207.
25 *Ibid.*, p. 215; *Hathihi qawmiyyatuna* (Cairo, Dar al-Qalam, 1963), pp. 132–9; quotation at p. 138.
26 Sayyid Qutb, 'Mabadi al-'alam al-hurr', *al-Risala* (17 Rabi' al-Akhir 1372 A.H./5 January 1953), pp. 14–16.
27 From an editorial written by Sa'ada in 1949, the year of his execution, in *Al-Nizam al-Jadid* (November 1950), cited by Hisham Sharabi, *Nationalism and Revolution in the Middle East* (Princeton and London, D. Van Nostrand Co., 1966), p. 112.
28 Mishil 'Aflaq, *Fi sabil al-ba'th* (Beirut, Dar al-Tali'a, 2nd edn, 1963), pp. 43 ff, 122–36. Albert Hourani says that any charges that 'Aflaq was insincere about Islam's central role are unjustified. In a lengthy discussion with Hourani in 1945, the relationship between Islam and Arab nationalism was uppermost in 'Aflaq's mind: private letter from Hourani to me, 1 September 1985.
29 See Muhammad al-Ghazzali, *Haqiqat al-qawmiyya al-'arabiyya wa ustura al-ba'th al-'arabi* (Kuwait, Dar al-Bayan, 2nd edn, 1389 A.H./1969), pp. 19–35.
30 Qutb, *Ma'alim fi'l-tariq*, pp. 27–8, quotation at p. 28.
31 Sami Jawhar, *al-Mawta yatakallamun* (Cairo, al-Maktabat al-Misri al-Hadith, 1977), p. 135.
32 'Abd al-'Aziz Ibn Baz, *Naqd al-qawmiyya al-'arabiyya 'ala daw al-islam wa'l-waqi'* (Beirut, al-Maktab al-Islami, 4th edn, 1400 A.H.). Faysal, for example, established the World Muslim League (Rabitat al-'Alam al-Islami) in 1962 in order to 'combat the serious plots by which the enemies of Islam are trying to destroy their unity and brotherhood' – i.e., as a foil to the Arab nationalists. See al-Jazairi, 'Saudi Arabia: a Diplomatic History, 1924–64' (unpublished Ph.D. thesis, University of Utah, 1971), p. 80.
33 For example, see interviews with King Khalid in *al-Mussawar* (16 Rajab 1395 A.H./25 July 1975), unnumbered sixth page of interview; and then Crown Prince Fahd in *Kul Shay* (2 Sha'ban 1395 A.H./9 August 1975), pp. 17–18. Also see Saudi Press Agency report of 25 July 1982 on Crown Prince 'Abdullah's visit to Iraq and Syria,' in *SWB*, ME/7088/A/3 (27 July 1982); and report on King Fahd's speech to Pilgrimage delegations, *al-Hawadith* (8 October 1982), p. 24.
34 Interview, Muhammad al-Milham, Riyadh, 26 May 1975.

35 *Arab News*, 2 April 1984/1 Rajab 1404. His statement, issued on 1 April 1984, is entitled, 'Warning Against Travelling to Countries of the Heretics and the Danger which Such Trips Constitute for Faith and Morals'.

36 Fateh M. Sandeela, 'Hajj as Witness to Allah's Sovereignty', paper delivered at Hajj Seminar, London, 4–7 August 1982, quotation at p. 10; interview, London, 16 August 1982.

37 Akhtaruddin Ahmad, *Nationalism or Islam; Indo-Pakistan Episode* (New York, Vantage Press, 1982), pp. 329, 331, quotation at p. 329.

38 Fazlur Rahman, *Islam* (Chicago and London, University of Chicago Press, 2nd edn, 1979), pp. 227–8, quotation at p. 228.

39 Kalim Siddiqui, *Beyond the Muslim Nation–States* (London, The Open Press, 1980); Siddiqui (ed.), *Issues in the Islamic Movement* (London, The Open Press, 1982), p. 241–3 (although this *Crescent International* article is not signed, it may be seen as representing his views); *Jang*, 5 August 1982. Here he suggests four possible regional groups. I am grateful to Nasim Ahmed for translating this article from the Urdu for me.

40 Khumayni's speech to pilgrims, as reported by Tehran home service, 12 September 1980, in *SWB*, ME/6523/A/2 (15 September 1980); also see *Islam and Revolution; Writings and Declarations of Imam Khomeini*, trans. by Hamid Algar (Berkeley, Mizan Press, 1981), p. 302.

41 Khumayni's speech to revolutionary guards, as reported by Tehran home service, 19 December 1982, in *SWB*, ME/7215/A/9 (22 December 1982).

42 Quoted in R.K. Ramazani, 'Khumayni's Islam in Iran's Foreign Policy' in Adeed Dawisha (ed.), *Islam in Foreign Policy* (Cambridge, Cambridge University Press, 1983), p. 18. Principle 11 of the Iranian constitution commits the government to promote Islamic unity.

43 Khumayni's speech to Bangladesh Muslim leaders, as reported by Tehran home service, 8 September 1982, in *SWB*, ME/7127/A/7 (10 September 1982).

44 Montazeri's speech to Hojatoleslam Yasrebi and airport officials, 22 July 1983, in Islamic Republic News Agency's *News Bulletin* (London), no. 211 (22–3 July 1983), p. 3.

45 'From Here and There' Programme, as reported by Ahvaz regional service in Arabic, 1 September 1980, in *SWB*, ME/6513/A/11 (3 September 1980).

46 Khumayni's message to parade in honour of the sixth anniversary of the revolution, as reported by Tehran home service, 11 February 1985, in *FBIS*, SAS-85-029 (12 February 1985), p.I1. Also see *Le Monde*, 5 February 1985, for discussion of a speech by Khumayni calling for combat against the great powers.

47 This refers to Khumayni's doctrine of *velayat -i faqih*. See, in addition to note 70 of Chapter 1, Hamid Enayat, 'Iran: Khumayni's Concept of the "Guardianship of the Jurisconsult"', in Piscatori (ed.), *Islam in the Political Process*, pp. 160–80.

48 Quotation from speech of Prime Minister Mir Hussayn Musavi opening a port at Bandar Abbas, as reported by Tehran home service, 11 February 1985, *FBIS*, SAS-85-029 (12 February 1985), p. 16. Khumayni has said that the 'rays' of Islam have spread from Iran: 'We should safeguard this source; we should protect the centre of these rays.' Khumayni's speech at the Guards' Day celebration, as reported by Tehran home service, 24 April 1985, in *FBIS*, SAS-85-080 (25 April 1985), p. 12.

49 Unattributed political commentary on a meeting of the Iranian, Syrian and Libyan Foreign Ministers in Tehran on 26 January 1985, as reported by Tehran home service, 27 January 1985, in *FBIS*, SAS-85-018 (28 January 1985), p. 18.

50 For his *Kashf asrar*, cited in Farhang Rajaee, *Islamic Values and World View; Khomeyni on Man, the State and International Politics* (Lanham and London, University Press of America, 1983), p. 77. also see R.K. Ramazani, 'Iran's Islamic Revolution and the Persian Gulf', *Current History*, 84 (January 1985), 5. For another very critical Iranian view of nationalism along these lines, see Ali Muhammad Nagavi, *Islam and Nationalism*, trans. by Alaedin Pazargadi (Tehran, Islamic Propagation Organization, 1405 A.H./1984), especially pp. 65–76.

51 Khumayni says that the war between Iran and Iraq is the war between Islam and unbelief (*kufr*). 'It is necessary and Islamically obligatory that we defend Islam': Khumayni's speech to the *'ulama* in Qum and members of the military on 3 April 1985, as reported by Islamic Republic News Agency in English, 4 April 1985, in *FBIS*, SAS-85-065 (4 April 1985), p. I1. He has also said, 'We shall defend the rights of Muslims as far as we are able to. By Muslims I do not mean Iranians, I mean all Muslims.' Khumayni's speech in Tehran to celebrate Armed Forces Day, as reported by Tehran home service, 18 April 1985, in *FBIS*, SAS-85-076 (19 April 1985), p.I1. Also see the comments of Ayatullah Montazeri, which follow Khumayni's views, to members of

the military on 18 January 1985, as reported by Tehran home service, 19 January 1985, in *FBIS*, SAS-85-014 (22 January 1985), pp. I1.

52 According to Khumayni, Iran has nothing to do with the terrorist acts with which it has been associated. If anything, these acts are a spontaneous and natural reponse to 'the source of terrorism centered in the White House': message on honour of the sixth anniversary of the Iranian revolution, 11 February 1985, p. I1–2.

53 Quotations (in order) from political commentary of 27 January 1985, p. 18 and Montazeri's comments on 18 January 1985, p. I2.

54 Khumayni's has commented on the differences between Sunnis and Shi'a over the Iran–Iraq war: 'Could certain beturbaned Sunni clerics and court officials deem Saddam and his ilk as loftier than the holy men of [Najran] where 'Ali fought some of his opponents, whose foreheads bore the calluses of frequent nightly prayers?' Khumayni's speech to the Friday *imams* of Qum, as reported by Tehran home service, 4 April 1985, in *FBIS*, SAS-85-066 (5 April 1985), p. I1. He also criticized the predominantly Sunni *'ulama* who gathered in Baghdad in April 1985 as 'mercenaries': speech at a Guards' Day celebration, 24 April 1985, p. I1.

55 Quotations from Khumayni's speech of 11 February 1985, p. 15. Khumayni was specifically addressing these words to government functionaries, but he often returns to the general theme: 'We can only walk the straight path and do this when we are all united. We should all work as one, just as Islam has ordered us to. We should all speak with one voice, like one voice which calls out.' Khumayni's speech celebrating the birthday of Imam Rida, as reported by Tehran home service, 30 July 1985, in *FBIS*, SAS-85-147 (31 July 1985), p. I2.

56 There have been several reports on the Iranian 'network'. See, for example, *The New York Times*, 2 January 1984, 3 January 1984; *The Washington Post*, 4 January 1984, 9 January 1984; *Le Monde*, 21 January 1984; *Jeune Afrique* (25 January 1984), pp. 40–51; *The Washington Post*, 1 February 1984, 3 February 1984. I will deal with this network in the companion volume to this book.

57 Amal was formed in 1975 as the militia of Musa al-Sadr's Harakat Mahrumin, Movement of the Disinherited. Amal is properly known as Harakat Amal and is now led by Nabih Berri. 'Amal' is an acronym of Afwaj al-Muqawama al-Lubnaniyya (the Lebanese Resistance Brigades) and means 'hope' in Arabic. Husayn al-Musawi broke away from Amal in 1982, when Berri joined Bashir Gemayal and Walid Jumblatt in the Committee of National Salvation.

58 Transcript of 'War and Power – The Rise of Syria', Show Number 122 (14 June 1984), *ABC News Closeup* (New York), p. 7.

59 *Al-Nahar*, 1 May 1985.

60 Fadlallah staunchly maintains that he is not the leader of Hizbullah and has not authorized violent action against Westerners in Lebanon. See, for example, *La Stampa*, 6 March 1985.

61 Interview given to *Middle East Insight* (June–July 1985), p. 17. Also see *The Wall Street Journal*, 22 December 1983.

62 See, for example, *al-'Amal al-Islami* (bimonthly newsletter published in Europe), 15 Rajab 1402 A.H./May 1982; and its pamphlet, '*Iraq al-yawm yabhath 'an husayn* (n.p., 1 Muharram 1401 A.H.).

63 See Chapter 4.

64 See text of letter by Hizbullah, *al-Safir*, 17 February 1985.

65 Comments by Muhammad Farid Mattar at a seminar at Columbia University, 6 March 1985.

66 *Al-Nahar al-'Arabi wa'l-Duwali* (10–16 June 1985), p. 22.

67 *Al-Ittihad*, 19 Ramadan 1405 A.H./7 June 1985; interview published in *al-Harakat al-islamiyya fi lubnan* (Beirut, 1984), excerpts of which are translated in *Islamic Currents in Lebanon* (Beirut, Centre for the Study of the Modern Arab World, 1985), p. 17.

68 *Al-Risala al-maftuha alati wajuhaha hizbullah ala al-mustad'afin fi lubnan wa'l-'alam* (n.p., 26 Jumad al-Awwal 1405 A.H./16 February 1985), pp. 24–5.

69 Dr Abu Ali, 'Misconceptions about Iraqi Muslims', *Islamic Revival* (October 1981), pp. 11–3, cited in Michael C. Hudson, 'The Islamic Factor in Syrian and Iraqi Politics', in Piscatori (ed.), *Islam in the Political Process*, p. 97.

70 See Muhammad ibn al-Haran al-Tusi, *al-Nihaya fi mujarrid al-fiqh wa'l fatawa* (Beirut, Dar al-Kitab al-'Arabi, 1970); Ayatullah Ahmad Jannati, 'Defence and Jihad in the Qur'an', *al-Tawhid*, 1 (April 1984), 39–54; and interview with Shaykh Muhammad Shams al-Din, Deputy Chairman of the Supreme Shi'a Council in Lebanon, *al-Nahar al-'Arabi wa'l-Duwali* (11–17 March 1985), p. 17.

71 See Khumayni's speech to the Friday *imams* of Qum, 4 April 1985, pp. 11–2 of the *FBIS*, SAS 85-066 version.

6 Development of the Muslim nation-state

1 Cromer, *Modern Egypt*, vol. 2, p. 184.
2 Durkheim did say that developed societies have need of the functional equivalent of religion, but in suggesting that social differentiation gives rise to secularism and that this is a form of religion, he left the impression that older religious are atavistic: *De La Division du Travail Social* (Paris, Librairie Félix Alcan, 1926), pp. 269–76; *The Elementary Forms of Religious Life* (New York, The Free Press, 1965; first published 1912), pp. 244–5, 474–8.
3 Manfred Halpern, *The Politics of Social Change in the Middle East and North Africa* (Princeton, Princeton University Press, 1963), generally Chapter 8; quotation at p. 114.
4 M.E. Yapp, 'Contemporary Islamic Revivalism', *Asian Affairs*, 11 (June 1980), 195.
5 The phrase is Daniel Lerner's: *The Passing of Traditional Society* (Glencoe, Illinois, The Free Press, 1958), p. 405. For examples of this kind of thinking, see Morroe Berger, *The Arab World Today* (Garden City, Doubleday, 1962), pp. 414–15; and his article 'Economic and Social Change' in P.M. Holt, Ann K.S. Lambton, and Bernard Lewis (eds), *The Cambridge History of Islam*, vol. 1 (Cambridge, Cambridge University Press, 1970), pp. 719–20, 724.
6 Speech by Khumayni in Qum to commanders of the Revolutionary Guards, as reported by Tehran home service, 24 September 1979, in *FBIS*, MEA-79-187 (25 September 1979), p. R1. In a speech to Qum seminary teachers on 30 June 1985, Khumayni said: 'We must not expect to perform our morning prayers and expect everything to have been done.' Reported by Tehran home service, in *FBIS*, SAS-85 (1 July 1985), p. 11.
7 *Mithaq al-jabha al-islamiyya fi suriyya* (Damascus, Al-Amana al-'Ama, 12 Rabi' al-Awwal 1401 A.H./17 January 1981), pp. 6–7 and *passim*.
8 Interview, Khurshid Ahmad, Islamabad, 3 May 1982; also see his 'Islam: A Total Vision of Man and Society', *International Development Review*, 1 (1980), 48. He used the word 'legitimate' in the interview.
9 Interview, Kamal al-Sharif, Amman, 27 May 1982.
10 Interview, Abdurrahman Wahid, Jakarta, 20 November 1981. Also see his 'Making Islamic Law Conducive to Development', *Prisma*, 1 (November 1975), 87–94. With regard to birth control and despite the modern controversy, B.F. Musallam shows how, with few exceptions, the *hadiths*, medieval juristic opinion, and medieval practice support contraception, particularly coitus interruptus: *Sexa and Society in Islam* (Cambridge, Cambridge University Press, 1983), pp. 14–26.
11 Abdurrahman Wahid, 'Religion, Ideology and Development', *Prisma*, no. 19 (December 1980), pp. 56–65.
12 Article 2, the Supplementary Fundamental Laws of 7 October 1907, in Helen Miller Davis, *Constitutions, Electoral Laws, Treaties of States in the Near and Middle East* (Durham, North Carolina, Duke University Press, 1953), p. 118.
13 Iqbal, *The Reconstruction of Religious Thought in Islam*, p. 168.
14 *Nadwat 'ilmiyya hawla'l-shari'a al-islamiyya wa huquq al-insan fi'l-islam*, p. 61.
15 For example, see the books by J.N.D. Anderson cited in Chapter 1, note 26. Also see Herbert J. Liebesny, *The Law of The Near & Middle East: Readings, Cases, & Materials* (Albany, State University of New York Press, 1975); Joseph Schacht, 'Islamic Law in Contemporary States; *American Journal of Comparative Law*, 8 (Spring 1959), 133–47; David Bonderman, 'Modernization and Changing Perception of Islamic Law', *Harvard Law Review*, 81 (April 1968), 1169–93.
16 Hafiz Wahba, *Jazirat al-'arab fi'l-qarn al-'ishrin* (Cairo, Maktabat al-Nahda al-Misriyya, 4th edn, 1961), pp. 324–31.
17 *Nizam al-ta'din*, issued under Royal Decree No. 40, 11 Ramadan 1384 A.H. [5 February 1963] (Mecca, Matba'at al-Hukuma, 1384 A.H./1964), Article 1, p. 5.
18 Shaykh Ahmad al-Yamani presents another example of this procedure when he argues that Saudi Arabia is opposed to outright nationalization of foreign mineral-exploiting companies. He is sensitive, on the one hand, to the Hanbali view that Muslims are honour-bound to uphold solemn obligations and, on the other, to the Hanafi and Maliki views that rights are revocable if they are used for purposes other than those originally sanctioned or if their exercise leads to undue harm. He argues that although resources in the ground belong to the state, the state can create a right of private exploitation, which, however, cannot be revoked unless for 'a well-specified public interest and for prompt and adequate compensation'. The mixing of juristic opinions leads to the

conclusion that the concept of political nationalization is alien to the principles of Islam. This was obviously designed to reassure the Arabian American Oil Company, and thus to serve Saudi economic interests. See his *Islamic Law and Contemporary Issues* (Jidda, The Saudi Publishing House, 1388 A.H.), pp. 23–31, quotation at p. 31.

19 *Nizam al-ta'minat al-ijtima'iyya*, issued under Royal Decree No. M/22 of 6 Ramadan 1389 A.H. (Mecca, Matba'at al-Hukuma, 1389 A.H./1970), Article 2(8), p. 10. The Regulation for Nationality of 1954 is another instance where, by executive action, Saudi Arabia has put itself in line with prevailing notions of nationality in international law. The most significant aspect is the fact that it does not link citizenship to religious status. Islamic law distinguishes between the believer, who is a full citizen of the community, and the *dhimmi*, who is tantamount to a protected alien. But the Saudi code makes no mention that Saudi nationality is reserved only for Muslims. As well, it provides that women do not automatically lose their Saudi nationality by marriage to a foreigner – as we might at least expect under traditional principles when the foreigner is a non-Muslim. See *Nizam al-jinsiyya al-'arabiyya al-sa'udiyya*, issued under Royal Decree No. 8/20/5604 of 22 Safar 1374 A.H. [20 October 1954] (Damman, Arabian American Oil Company, February 1955), Articles 15 and 17, pp. 1, 5–7.

20 For instance, a judicial reform of 1927 created a three-tiered court system: expeditious courts, *shari'a* courts, and a review commission. There were other reforms in 1931 and 1936, and in 1961 the prevailing law came into effect. See *Tanzim al-'amal al-idariyya fi'l-dawa'ir al-shari'iyya* (Mecca, Matba'at al-Hukuma, 1382 A.H./1962).

21 Samir Shamma, 'Diwan al-mazalim', *al-Idara al-'amma*, no. 5 (Riyadh, Ma'had al-Idara al-'Amma, Ramadan 1386 A.H./December 1967), p. 19; 'Law and Lawyers in Saudi Arabia', *International and Comparative Law Quarterly*, 14 (July 1965), 1037–8. The Foreign Capital Investments Regulation provides that a complainant should appeal to the Board of Grievances if he feels that the government has wrongly revoked his licence or wrongly ordered the liquidation of his business; in such cases, the Board's decision is final. See *Foreign Capital Investments Regulation* of 1383 A.H./1964 (Riyadh, Industrial Studies and Development Centre, mimeo, n.d.), Article 12, p. 4. In general, the Board has been a tremendous success because it fills a clear public need, it does not as a rule become involved with *shari'a* complaints, and the Saudis believe that in its own way it contributes to meeting the general duty of all Muslims – to encourage good and suppress evil.

22 There are no such requirements for the Supreme Commission, whose members need only come from several ministries.

23 *Nizam al-'amal wa'l-'ummal*, issued Royal Decree No. M/21 of 6 Ramadan 1389 A.H. (Mecca, Matba'at al-Hukuma, 1389 A.H./1970), pp. 47–8. The subsidiary criteria for judgement are listed in Article 185.

24 'Explanatory Note' to *Nizam al-ta'din*, p. 24. Another example of where this idea was important was in promulgating an income tax law, mainly to increase the revenues to be garnered from foreign companies and specifically from ARAMCO. There was an ill-conceived attempt at first to create an income-tax obligation across the board, for Saudi and non-Saudi alike, but this was amended so that income tax was to be collected only from foreign individuals and companies. The rationale for this tax was 'the need to increase the revenue of the State to enable it [to] accomplish the general development and promote the welfare of the country and raise the standard of living'. In the amended law, Saudis were to pay *zakat* in place of income tax, but even here there has been a revision of the classical view that *zakat*, or alms-giving, is a voluntary act of piety: now Saudis *had* to pay the state one-half of the normal *zakat* contributions, with the other half being voluntarily collected and distributed 'among poor relations or destitute persons in whose favour *zakat* was imposed by God'. In an explanatory note the Ministry of Finance stressed that God intended that *zakat* be spent on the 'common affairs and social welfare' of Muslims. The original Royal Decree was No. 17/2/28/3321 of 21 Muharram 1370 A.H. [2 November 1950]. The major revision was in Royal Decree No. 17/2/28/8799 of 8 Ramadan 1370 A.H. [12 June 1951]. These are found in *The Law of Income Tax and Zakat in the Kingdom of Saudi Arabia* (Beirut, Centre d'Etudes et de Documentations Economique, Financières et Sociales, 1967[?], quotations at pp. 1, 26 and 30. I have not been able to consult the Arabic versions.

25 This is point 10 of Faysal's 'Ministerial Statement' of 6 November 1962, reproduced in *The Middle East Journal*, 17 (Winter–Spring 1963), 162.

26 Tanzil al-Rahman, *Majlis al-fikr al-islami bi-pakistan* (Islamabad, Majma' al-Buhuth al-Islamiyya, n.d.); interview, Islamabad, 5 May 1982.

27 See excerpts of Khumayni's thinking translated by the US Joint Publications Reference Service

(JPRS 72663), published as *Islamic Government* (Washington, DC, International Learning Systems, 1978[?]), pp. 17, 22, quotation at p. 22. Quotation in Khumayni's speech to Qum seminary teachers, 30 June 1985, p. 12.

28 Principle 71 of the 1979 constitution says that 'the National Consultative Assembly is authorized to enact laws concerning all issues of a general nature, within the limits set down in the Constitution'. See Principle 72 for those limits: *Constitution of the Islamic Republic of Iran* (Iranian Embassy pamphlet), pp. 36–7. Text of the banking law is in *al-Tawhid*, 1 (Rabi al-Thani 1404 A.H./January 1984), 166–74.

29 See, for example, Sayyid Qutb, *al-Islam wa mushkilat al-hadara* (Cairo, 'Isa al-Babi al-Halabi, 1962), pp. 185–90.

30 Najib Mahfuz, *Miramar* (Cairo, Maktabat Misr, n.d.), p. 279.

31 El Syed Yassin, a prominent Egyptian political observer, argues that even secular leftists have come to accept that any political ideology must be 'authentic'– that is, grounded in Arab-Islamic civilization. *Asala* has become the universal catchword. Interview, Cairo, 31 May 1982. However, there is great disagreement as to what the idea specifically means. For approaching the general question from the perspective of literature, see *Fusul*, 1 (October 1980), entire issue.

32 Ashfaq Ahmad, 'The Muslim World Seen from Economic Angle', *Islamic Herald*, 5, nos. 1 and 2 (1981), p. 29. *Islamic Herald* is a PERKIM publication.

33 Interview, Abu Bakr Bagader, Jidda, 19 May 1982. For information on the training camps, see, for example, *Islamic Vision*, 1 (August 1981), 4–6. *Islamic Vision* is the news bulletin of WAMY's Asia–Pacific region.

34 *Constitution (Ka'idodi)* (n.p., Jama'atu Nasril Islam, n.d.), Article 3, p. 7. To the end of propagating the faith, the JNI has published a very simple guide for the would-be convert: Abubakar Imam, *Ten Questions: Ten Answers; the Path to Islam* (Zaria, Jama'atu Nasril Islam, 1973).

35 P.B. Clarke, 'The Religious Factor in the Development Process in Nigeria: A Socio-Historical Analysis', *Genève Afrique*, 17, no. 1 (1979), p. 58.

36 *Nigerian Herald* (Ilorin), 3 February 1983.

37 Interview, Abubakar Gummi, Kaduna, 17 December 1982.

38 Interview, Muhammad Natsir, Jakarta, 21 November 1981.

39 Interview, Dawam Rahardjo, Director of Lembaga Penelitian, Pendidikan dan Penerangan Ekonomi dan Sosial (LP3 ES), Jakarta, 19 November 1981.

40 See, for example, *Perspective*, 1 (December 1979), 2. *Perspective* is the monthly newsletter of ABIM's International Relations Committee. The Malaysian government has prohibited the publication of *Risalah*, ABIM's Malay-language monthly bulletin, on the grounds that it had been used to inspire inter-community difficulties.

41 Interview, Anwar Ibrahim, Kuala Lumpur, 30 November 1981. Despite what Ibrahim says, an ABIM pamphlet indicates that one of its main objectives is 'to progressively carry out the Islamic da'wah to all people': *Revival of Islam in Malaysia: the Role of ABIM* (Kuala Lumpur, ABIM, n.d.). Also see interview with Ibrahim in *Asiaweek* (24 August 1979), p. 30.

42 Interview, Fadlullah Wilmot, Director of Information of PERKIM and Regional Islamic Da'wah Council of Southeast Asia and the Pacific, Kuala Lumpur, 25 and 26 November 1981.

43 Interview, Natsir.

44 For example, Dawam Rahardjo says that people are not searching for an Islamic state, and it is even unclear what creating an 'Islamic order' means: interview, 19 November 1981.

45 For an account of the revolt, which sought to establish an Islamic state, see, for example, Hioko Horikoshi, 'The Dar'ul Islam Movement in West Java (1948–62): An Experience in Historical Process', *Indonesia*, no. 20 (October 1975), pp. 59–86.

46 Natsir's words.

47 Interview, Anwar Ibrahim [then president of ABIM]; interview, Chandra Muzaffer [president of ALIRAN], Penang, 28 November 1981; *ALIRAN: Basic Beliefs* (Penang, ALIRAN, 3rd edn, 1979), p. 13. Muzaffer has even criticized *da'wa* organizations within trade unions for catering to Malays and thus being divisive and self-absorbed: *Far Eastern Economic Review* (3 February 1982), p. 15.

48 *Arabia: The Islamic World Review* (November 1984), p. 9. But Islamic groups have come in for rough weather since the military coup of September 1980 and even during the present period of civilian rule: Necmettin Erbakan, founder of the Milli Selamat Partisi, has been sentenced to a long prison term (though he has appealed), and there are penalties of up to seven years for attempting to make Turkey an Islamic state where the *shari'a* would be fully applied.

49 In the 1985 election, two prominent Muslim activists, Khalid al-Sultan and 'Isa Majid al-Shahan, were defeated, while the 'Democratic Rally' and the 'Conservative Movement' took the bulk of the seats: Kuwait News Agency Report in Arabic, 21 February 1985, in *FBIS*, MEA-85-035 (21 February 1985), p. C2; *The New York Times*, 22 February 1985. The Kuwaiti newspaper, *al-Ra'y al-'Amm*, reports that a draft bill has been submitted to the Parliament that, if approved, would allow women the right to vote: 11 March 1985. The exact number of Muslim activists in the 1981–5 Parliament is difficult to specify. Three members belonged to the 'Islamic Tendency' (*al-ittijah al-islami*), and four were Shi'i: *al-Mujtama'* (17 Jumada'l-Awwal 1401 A.H./23 March 1981), p. 9.

50 *An Introduction to the Institute for Consultation and Legal Aid for Women and Families* (Jakarta, LKBHUWK, n.d.), p. 9.

51 For example: 'A condition leads to various problems of women and families which cannot be solved merely through traditional institutions': *ibid*, p. 4.

52 I must note that Nani Yasmin, the director, specifically denies that LKBHUWK has the intention, or the effect, of undermining the basis of the 'New Order': discussion, Washington, DC, 28 March 1984.

53 This was the way one young activist in the Kuwaiti parliament described his aim: *The Christian Science Monitor*, 2 March 1981.

54 Gilles Kepel, *Le Prophète et Pharaon; Les mouvements islamiques dans L'Egypte contemporaine* (Paris, Editions La Découverte, 1984), pp. 74–5.

55 The concept of *jihad* has gone through many permutations. Medieval jurisprudential writing gradually made it *fard al-kifaya*, or an obligation attendant upon every able-bodied, free male adult. The idea was intimately associated with the expansion of Islam, but defence of the Islamic realm was also considered a kind of *jihad*. The idea came into its own again in the nineteenth and early twentieth century, when it was used as a way to rally Muslims around the banner of anti-imperialist struggle. This history accounts for the negative image that the *jihad* has had in the West. In turn, the reaction to this negative image explains the defensiveness of contemporary Muslims with regard to the concept. As I showed in Chapter 4, they argue that if *jihad* occasionally involves the use of force, it is only in self-defence. Partly in response to this ostensible emasculation of the idea, radical Muslims, highly critical of what they view as secularized rulers and obsequious *'ulama*, argue that the *jihad* must be pre-eminently directed inward and aimed at the removal of unjust, un-Islamic rulers. However, what is constant throughout the history of the idea is ambiguity over who may legitimately proclaim a *jihad*. One view of the theory would be that the Caliph in Sunni Islam and the Imam in Shi'i Islam are the key authorities, but in practice the effective political rulers invoked the concept for their own political purposes. This means that it has been used for a variety of reasons and in a variety of circumstances that have had little to do with any theory on the subject.

56 Qutb, *Ma'alim fi'l-tariq*, p. 72.

57 Mohamad Abu Bakar, 'Islamic Revivalism and the Political Process in Malaysia', *Asian Survey*, 21 (October 1981), 1050; M.L. Lyon, 'The Dakwah Movement in Malaysia', *Review of Indonesian and Malaysian Affairs*, 13, no. 2 (1979), pp. 37–8.

58 For example, *al-Ahram*, 13 Shawwal 1403 A.H./23 July 1983.

59 For example, *al-Liwa al-islami*, 18 Muharram 1403 A.H./4 November 1982.

60 Two Thai informants, March–April 1984. At one such meeting in 1984, 100,000 were assembled.

61 *The Jordan Times*, 24 May 1982.

62 British embassy official, Kuwait, 12 May 1982.

63 For example, *al-Da'wa*, no. 38 (Sha'ban 1399 A.H./July 1979), pp. 4–5, and no. 40 (Shawwal 1399 A.H./September 1979), pp. 55–6. It is interesting to note that in the *fatwa* which the *shaykh* of al-Azhar issued to legitimate the peace treaty with Israel, the Prophet's compact with the Jews of Medina and the Hudaybiyya treaty were cited as evidence of the permissibility of concluding treaties with non-Muslims. But, consistent with the conformist consensus that I discussed in Chapter 4, most critics of the treaty with Israel did not base their objection on the fact that it was an agreement with a non-Muslim power. Rather, objection was made that the treaty was with this particular state which had been in consistent violation of the norms of international and Islamic law. They also objected to the treaty because they thought it put Egypt in violation of its treaty commitments to other Arab states, and because they did not accept, as the *fatwa* proclaimed, that Egypt was acting in 'the public interest' and represented a new Arab consensus which saw further warfare as futile. See *al-Ahram*, 14 June 1979.

64 Mahathir's attitude towards PAS has been clear for some time. In a pre-election interview in 1982, he said: 'PAS is a problem because it splits the Muslims, and it diverts their attention from the problems they face and wastes their energy on irrelevant political differences among the Muslims': *The Straits Times*, 31 August 1981.

65 The NU fell into line in December 1983 and the PPP in August 1984, but the Muhammidiyya has not done so yet.

66 See M. Th. Houtsma *et al.* (eds), *The Encyclopedia of Islam*, fasciculus K (London, Luzac & Co., 1929), p. 628; Hamid Enayat, *Modern Islamic Political Thought* (London, Macmillan, 1982), p. 175; and Mohammed E. Ahrari, 'Theological Insurgency: Iran in the Region', *The Washington Quarterly*, 8 (Spring 1985), 48.

67 *Far Eastern Economic Review* (5 January 1984), p. 13. Reportedly, Abdurrahman Wahid was mainly responsible for this intellectual defence.

68 It is very difficult to determine the social and economic position of the activists, although hints have appeared in the official press: for example, *al-Jumhuriyya*, 9 May 1982, on the al-Jihad group. Kepel estimates that roughly 45 per cent of the activists who attacked the Military Academy in Heliopolis in 1974 had studied in the engineering and medical faculties, whereas 31 per cent of al-Jihad had done so: *Le Prophète et Pharaon*, Table 5, p. 208. Also see Saad Eddine Ibrahim, 'Egypt's Islamic Militants', *MERIP Reports*, no. 103 (February 1982), p. 11. In the case of Nigeria, however, the followers of Maitatsine seemed to be mainly poorly educated rural migrants and illegal immigrants from other countries. Many of the followers were children under sixteen: *Report of Tribunal of Inquiry on Kano Disturbances*, pp. 79–81; *New Nigerian*, 18 December 1982; *The Guardian* (London), 7 June 1985. *The New York Times* reports that in Tunisia the young engineers and technicians are more receptive to the revival than students of the humanities because, although they are trying to learn scientific lessons from the West, they are unconcerned with the philosophical underpinnings of Western civilization and in this sense are less secularized. The humanities students, by contrast, are thoroughly disillusioned with Western morality and philosophy, and generally more secularized, so that they turn to Marxism and other leftist ideologies as the alternative to Western liberalism. The engineers and technicians are presumably less alienated and therefore more willing to accept the traditional value system of Islam: 29 December 1979.

69 *Al-Ahram*, 28 Shawwal 1397 A.H./11 October 1977.

70 *Arab News*, 1 Shawwal 1403 A.H./11 July 1983.

71 Naipaul, *Among the Believers: An Islamic Journey*, pp. 309, 315, 319–20.

72 Interviews with various individuals, Pondok Pabelan, Muntilan, Indonesia, November 1981. For other information on this *pesantren*, see Ken Thomas, 'Islam and Grass-Roots Development in Indonesia', *AIA Journal* (August 1980), pp. 10–11; and *Asian Action* (Newsletter of the Asian Cultural Forum on Development), no. 5 (July/August 1976). I am grateful to M. Habib Chirzin of Pondok Pabelan for sending me further information in a private letter, 1 January 1982; and to Sidney Jones, formerly of the Ford Foundation office in Jakarta, for letting me read her very useful paper, 'Islamic Education in Indonesia', and for her guidance in a general discussion, Jakarta, 20 November 1981. For an analysis of the development of the *pesantren* concept, see M. Dawam Rahardjo, 'The Kyai, the Pesantren and the Village: A Preliminary Sketch', *Prisma*, 1 (May 1975), 32–43.

73 See, for example, Naipaul, *Among the Believers: An Islamic Journey*, p. 158. Naipaul says Muslims are caught in the dilemma of emotionally rejecting the West but having 'great dependence' on its scientific and technological accomplishments: p. 353.

74 Manning Nash, 'Fundamentalist Islam; Reservoir for Turbulence', *Journal of Asian and African Studies*, 19 (January and April 1984), 77, quotation at 76.

75 *Ibid.*, p. 76.

7 Conclusion

1 Tawfic Farah reports on a study of university students from various Arab countries at Kuwait University between the ages of seventeen and twenty-four, 99 per cent of whom were Muslim. The study was done in October 1977, but repeated in 1979, 1980, and 1981 without significant variation. The study showed that most students, regardless of sex or country of citizenship, ranked Islam first in their list of loyalties, followed by family, citizenship, 'national origin' (i.e., Arabness), and political ideology. Farah concludes: 'Citizenship and political party were not gaining in importance at the expenses of religious affiliation.' See Tawfic E. Farah, 'Politics and Religion in Kuwait: Two Myths Examined', in Ali E. Hillal Dessouki (ed.), *Islamic Resurgence in*

the Arab World (New York, Praeger, 1982), p. 173. Stewart Reiser reports on a study of Arab undergraduate and post-graduate students from many Arab countries at Northwestern University and Boston University. The study was done in 1979, 1980, and 1981, and it showed that over half of the students (53.1 per cent) listed Arab nationalism as their primary loyalty; 38.7 per cent, religion; and 24.3 per cent, nationalism. See Stewart Reiser, 'Islam, Pan Arabism and Palestine: An Attitudinal Survey,' *Journal of Arab Affairs*, 3 (Fall 1984), 191–3.

2 Muhammad ibn Muhammad al-Ghazzali, *al-Munqidh min al-dalal* (Cairo, Maktabat al-Jandi, n.d.), p. 14.

3 R. Stephen Humphreys, 'Islam and Political Values in Saudi Arabia, Egypt and Syria', *The Middle East Journal*, 33 (Winter 1979), 9.

4 Quoted in Isaac Disraeli, *The Calamities and Quarrels of Authors* (London, Frederik Warne & Co., 1867), p. 187.

5 Georg Büchner, *Danton's Death*, trans. By James Maxwell (London, Eyre Methuen Ltd, rev. edn, 1979), Act 1, Scene 5, p. 34.

6 Welcoming Remarks by Shultz to the Conference on Religious Liberty, Washington, D.C., 15 April 1985, *Department of State Press Release*, no. 72 (15 April 1985), p. 3. The Egyptian Coptic community feels similarly: 'The present situation in modern Islamic States illustrates the absolute inappropriateness of allowing any religious code to assume the status of common law in any country today. A state administered by a particular religious code, (whatever the religion), is bound to be restrictive and repressive. Reactionary pressures will inevitably prevail': 'The Shadow of Islam: The Nature of Fundamentalist Islam', insert to *Copts Newsletter* (published by the Coptic Association in Australia; n.d.), p. 1 of insert.

7 See Kenneth N. Waltz, *Man, the State and War* (New York and London, Columbia University Press, 1954), p. 82.

8 See Daniel, *Islam, Europe and Empire*, p. 11.

9 Daniel Pipes, 'Fundamentalist Muslims and US Policy', *International Briefing* [The Heritage Foundation, Washington, D.C.], no. 13 (10 August 1984), p. 12.

10 Edward W. Said, 'Orientalism and the October War: The Shattered Myths', in Baha Abu Laban and Faith T. Zeadey (eds), *Arabs in America: Myths and Realities* (Wilmette, Illinois, The Medina University Press International, 1975), p. 90.

11 This line of argument is understandable, given that Muslims themselves promote it. Khumayni, for example, has said: 'A nation whose young men beg us to pray for their martyrdom cannot be intimidated and made despondent!' Report on Khumayni's speech on the occasion of Armed Forces Day, as reported by Tehran home service, 18 April 1985, in *FBIS*, SAS-85-075 (18 April 1985), p. I1: Compare with the text of the full speech in *FBIS*, SAS-85-076 (19 April 1985), p. I1.

12 Secret Note I.R.Q.3 from the Middle East Department of the Colonial Office to the Cabinet, Committee on Iraq, 11 December 1922, Doc. No. CAB 27/206, Public Records Office, London, p. 3 of document. However, it must be said that most people today would agree with Rudolph Peters when he says that *jihad* appeals are now made for support of wars 'based on national considerations': *Islam and Colonialism: The Doctrine of Jihad in Modern History*, p. 158.

13 Aron's 1979 view has had an echo in Khumayni's thinking. In 1985 he said: 'The cry that comes from the heart of the believer overcomes everything, even the White House . . . This wave has already spread throughout the world, and the world is now liberating itself from the oppression to which it had been subjected': Khumayni's address on the occasion of 'Id al-Fitr, as reported by Tehran home service, 20 June 1985, in *FBIS*, SAS-85-120 (21 June 1985), p. I2. Despite Khumayni's words, this general view must be seen as more a rhetorical flourish than a description of reality.

14 An example of the appeal to unity was made by Saudi Crown Prince 'Abdullah in an interview with the Turkish News Agency (date not given): '[Israel's] continued arrogance . . . is due foremost to the division of Muslims in word, rank, and objective . . . I am fully confident Israel will melt as an entity and vanish as a body as soon as the Muslims move from the unity of conviction toward the unity of will and on to the unity of action.' As reported by Riyadh home service, 11 September 1984, in *FBIS*, MEA-85-178 (13 September 1984), p. C1.

Index

Index

Ottoman Empire, 8, 26, 62, 77, 78; inter-Muslim relations, 63–6; Persia, 62, 63–4, 69; territorial imperialism: Asia, 56, 59; Egypt, 52; European countries, 38, 50–5, 69–70; Russia, 51, 52, 53, 54, 56; Uzbekhs, 68; *see also* Turkey

Özal, Turgut (b. 1927; r. 1983–), 157

Pakistan, 148; Ahmadis declared non-Muslims, 5, 9; Baghdad Pact and, 73; cultural change in, 92; development in, 119, 139; Islamization, 18, 41; Muslim defined in constitution, 10; nonconformist thinking in, 101, 103, 110

Palestinians, 27, 92–3, 94

Palmerston, Henry (Viscount), 38

pan-Arab Congress, 107

pan-Islam, 77–8, 83, 144

Papua New Guinea, 127

Paris, Treaty of (1856), 53

Partai Islam Sa Malaysia, 131, 136

Partai Negara Islam Malaysia, 136

Partai Persatuan Pembangunan (Indonesia), 136

Party of God (Lebanon), 114, 137

Parwez, Ghulam Ahmad, 4

PAS (Partai Islam Sa Malaysia), 131, 136

Passarowitz, Treaty of (1718), 51

passport restrictions, abolition advocated, 104

patriotism, 108; permitted, 111

PERKIM (Malaysia), 129

Persatuan Aliran Kesedaran Negara, *see* ALIRAN

Persia, 42; Britain and, 55–6; classical students in, 49; France and, 55; League of Nations and, 72; Ottomans and, 62, 63–4, 69; Prophet and, 49; territorial pluralism, 54–6, 59, 66, 67, 68; *see also* Iran

Pertubohan Kebajikan Islam Malaysia, 129

pesantren, 86, 128, 140–2

Peters, Rudolph, 42

pillars of faith, five, 9, 46

Pipes, Daniel, 148–9

Plato, 48

Poland, 33

politics: *da'wa* and, 130–8; growth and diversification *see* development; ideology of, 32–3; parties, 128–37; religion and, 11–15, 25, 147; *see also* territorial pluralism

polytheists, 44

Pompidou, President, 10

Pondok Pabelan *pesantren* (Java), 140–2

Portugal, 68

poverty, 29, 34

pre-Islamic period *see jahiliyya*

priests, absence of in Islam, 4–5

Prussia, 64

al-Qadhdhafi, Mu'ammar (b. 1942; r. 1969–), 10, 155

qadis, 18, 123

al-Qahhar, 'Ala al-Din Ri'yat Shah (r. 1537–68), 68

Qalwun, ruler of Egypt (r. 1280–90), 63

qanun (law), 123

al-Qassam, Shaykh 'Izz al-Din (1871–1935), 92

Qatar, 30, 70, 72

qawmiyya, 77, 108–9

qiyas, 6

quasi-metaphoric association, 95, 98

Qur'an, 14; conformists and, 40–1; on fighting, 44–5; interpretation of, 3–5, 10; legal system and, 125, 126–7, 143; on national divisions, 46, 103, 144; nationalism contravenes, 103, 111; nonconformists and, 41; recitation of, 140; on slaves, 58, 124

Qutb, Sayyid (1906–66), 23, 105–6, 108, 109, 116, 125, 129, 155

racism: Christianity and, 102; nationalism as, 115

Raffles, Sir Stamford, 61

rahbar (supreme political leader), 5

Rahman, Fazlur (b. 1919), 12–13, 110–11

Ramadan, 46

Ramadan, Sa'id, 106

al-Rashid, Caliph Harun (ca. 766–809; r. 786–809), 49

raushanfikran (lay intellectuals), 19

Reagan, Ronald, 95

Règlement Organique (1861), 53

Regulation on Commerce (Saudi Arabia), 123

renewers (*mujaddids*), 24

repressive regimes, Islamic opposition in, 33–4

revival, Islamic, nature of, 22–39; Muslim view of decline, 22–4; background to, 24–6; reasons for, 26–34; interpreting, 34–7; *see also* nation-state, nonconformist

revolutionary activity, 35–6, 148; oil wealth and, 25–6; sermons on cassettes, 30; *thawra*, 92, 94

Reza Khan (Pahlavi) (1878–1944; r. 1921–41), 70, 154

riba, 119

Richard I of England, 49, 152

Rida, Muhammad Rashid (1865–1935), 24, 78–9, 81, 121, 153

Rifaat, Alifa, 29

rural–urban migration, 27–9, 34

Russia, 55, 64, 70; Ottomans and, 38, 51, 52, 53, 54; *see also* Soviet Union

al-Sabah, Shaykh Jabr Ahmad (b. 1928; r. 1978–), 158

Index

tadamun (solidarity), 83
tadhkir (reminding), 127
tajdid, 36
tajwid (recitation of Qur'an), 140
takallum (speaking about Islam), 127
takhayyur, 121, 122
takhsis al-qada, 121, 123
Tanzimat period, 51–2
taqiyya, 136
taqlid, 7–8, 87, 121
tariqas, 28
tawhid, 11, 105
Tennyson, Alfred Lord, 88
territorial pluralism, theory and practice of, 40–75, 144–5; classical and medieval theory, 45–8; consensus of action, 48–74; inter-Muslim relations 62–74; non-Muslim states, relations with 49–62; historical experience, lessons of, 74–5
Thailand, 135
thawra (revolution), 92, 94
'theology of human growth', 120
Timur (Tamerlane) (1336–1405; r. 1360–1405), 56–7, 59, 65
tradition, 7; return to, for comfort, 27, 29
Trans-Jordan, 70, 71
tribalism, 115
Trucial States, 56, 58, 60, 69
Tunisia, 33, 35, 60, 63, 138, 182
al-Turabi, Hasan (b. 1930), 19
Turkey, 12, 42; cultural change in, 90; development in, 131; France and, 72; inter-Muslim relations, 73; Islamic education in, 18; League of nations and, 72; migration in, 28; Soviet Union and, 70; *see also* Ottoman Empire
Turkmanchay, Treaty of (1828), 55
Twelfth Imam, awaited, 113

'*ulama*, 76; control of, 90; criticized, 8; development and, 121, 122, 133, 137, 139; disputes among, 5, 9; *ijtihad* and, 5, 6, 17–18, 19; *ijma*' and, 15, 19; of Indonesia, 41; of Iraq, 70; *jihad* and, 96; nation-state consensus and, 77, 79, 83, 89, 91–2, 96, 98–9, 113, 146; Ottoman, 66; respect for, 30; *shari'a* and, 97; *see also* Shi'a; Sunni
'Umar ibn al-Khattab, Caliph (ca. 586–644; r. 634–44), 16, 41
umma, 8, 31, 42, 60, 62–3, 66, 72; nation-state consensus and, 77, 83–4, 86, 103–16 *passim*, 139, 144, 146
unbelievers, 44
United Development Party (Indonesia), 136
United Malays' National Organization (UMNO), 32
United Nations Resolution on Permanent Sovereignty over Natural Resources, 124
United States, 56, 60; hostages in Iran, 39;

Muslim attitudes to, 35, 105, 112; symbolic language in, 95
unity, 46–8, 110; language of, 78; pacts, 73, 103–5; *see also* consensus; Muslim Brotherhood; nation-state; pan-Islam; religion and politics
urban areas, migration to, 27–9, 34
Uris, Leon, 2
'Usuli' school, 7
al-'Utaybi, Juhayman, 157
Uthman, Caliph (r. 644–55), 41, 151
Uzbekhs, 63, 68–9

Vance, Cyrus, 39, 149
Victoria, Queen, 80, 81
Voll, John, 24–5

Wahid, Abdurrahman (b. 1940), 86, 120, 126
Wali Allah, Shah (1702–62), 7–8
al-Walid, Caliph (r. 705–15), 49
al-Walid, Sultan (r. 1631–6), 58
waliy-yi amr (guardian of affairs), 5
Wallace, Anthony, 36
WAMY (World Assembly of Muslim Youth), 127–8, 129
waqfs, 90
watan (nation), 77, 79, 93
wataniyya (nationalism), 77, 79, 107–8, 109
welfare, social, 123–4, 127–8
West: corrupt, 23–4, 43–4, 101, 105–7, 112, 115, 120, 133; fears of 'fanaticism', 38–9, 107, 148; fights against, 80–1, 92, *see also* revolution; legal system, 18, 109; Muslim revival, attitude to, 38–9; nationalism and, 77–8, 87, 101–2, 109–11, 115; technical and military superiority, 76, 121
West Bank, 93
West Germany, 33
Westernization, 88, 139–43
'Westoxification', 23; *see also* West
Westphalia, Treaty of (1648), 50
women, 131, 132, 135
World Assembly of Muslim Youth, 127–8, 129
World Conference on Muslim Education (1977), 18–19

Yahya (al-Mutawakkil), Imam (1867–1948; r. 1904–48), 70
al-Yamani, Ahmad Zaki (b. 1930), 178
Yapp, Malcolm, 118
Yayasan Dakwah Islamiah Malaysia, 135
Yemen, 27, 63, 70, 72, 109
Young Turk revolution (1908), 69, 153
Young Women Muslim Association (Jordan), 135